D1445774

ENGLISH MEDIAEVAL ARCHITECTURE

A mason of Westminster at work in his lodge

ENGLISH MEDIAEVAL ARCHITECTURE

Hugh Braun
F.S.A., F.R.I.B.A.

Bracken Books
LONDON

First published 1951
by Faber and Faber Limited
as *An Introduction to English Mediaeval Architecture*

This edition published 1985 by Bracken Books
a division of Bestseller Publications Limited,
Brent House, 24 Friern Park, North Finchley,
London N12 9DA

ISBN 0 946495 42 4

Printed and bound by R. J. Acford,
Chichester, England.

Preface to Second Edition

In 1951, when this book was first published, the professional archaeologist had almost lost interest in the study of mediaeval buildings and was becoming more and more involved in Romano-British and prehistoric sites. The archaeological 'dig' had become a popular way of spending a summer holiday.

The excavation of mediaeval sites was being left for the most part to the Minister of Works in whose care so many great memorials of the Middle Ages are now vested. More recently, however, archaeological departments of universities have begun to transfer their interest away from the prehistoric towards the mediaeval. But although one's knowledge of individual buildings such as Cirencester Abbey or Ludgershall Castle has been expanded, few important fresh discoveries of general significance have been added. Exceptions are Mr. Philip Rahtz's work on the Saxon palace at Cheddar and Mr. Martin Biddle's exploration of the badly-robbed foundations of the Old Minster at Winchester.

Literature has benefited by the publication of Margaret Wood's monumental work on *The English Mediaeval House* (1965) and documentation has been elaborately dealt with in Salzmann's *Building in England* (1952) and in their contribution to the *History of the King's Works* by R. A. Brown, H. M. Colvin, and A. J. Taylor. Two valuable papers on mediaeval priests' houses by W. A. Pantin appeared in Volumes I and III of the Journal of the Society for Mediaeval Archaeology, founded in 1957.

With the aid of these and other published sources, and by the continuation of his own researches, the author has revised the text of his book and added an appendix in extension of this. In doing so he has been assisted by the comments of Mr. John Harvey.

All superior numbers in the text refer to the numbered notes in the Appendix beginning on page 286.

Contents

Illustrations

Illustrations

Illustrations

Illustrations

Line Drawings in Text

Line Drawings in Text

Foreword

Of all our national treasures, the mediaeval cathedrals of England are undoubtedly the most universally prized. The stateliness of Lincoln, the daintiness of Salisbury, the grandeur of Durham's nave, the piled glories of Ely—it is impossible not to approach such as these without a sensation of wonder, if not of awe. To what powerful presence may we ascribe the intense emotional appeal of these great buildings. Even by modern standards, of course, their scale is enormous, their height overpowering. The least impressionable amongst their visitors must be instinctively aware that the winds of many centuries have sighed around their walls and towers, while suns in their tens of thousands have risen to warm the ancient stones and filter through the tracery to cast a glow upon pillar and paving within. Yet this is only half-way to the truth. It is not only the centuries which cling to these glorious buildings, but the living souls of a host of devoted human beings —their creators.

They were humble men, those builders of the Middle Ages. They could cut and lay stone, trim and fix timber; such were the twin pillars upon which the architrave of their craft was borne. They were uneducated men. Ignorant of Arabic numerals, they lacked the most elementary knowledge of mathematics; multiplication was beyond their powers, addition and subtraction could only be effected with the aid of an exchequer board. Their astonishing feats of engineering were inspired by the breath of genius alone and tempered by—often bitter—experiences.

They were uncultured men. You may exhaust your eloquence in dilating upon the exquisite proportions displayed in their creations; they would be delighted—could they understand what you were talking about —to hear your praise of their humble efforts to achieve space and scale. Should you wax enthusiastic concerning the entrancing details of their architecture they would introduce you to a host of helpers—those carvers whom they gladly permitted to embellish their masonry with a wealth of ornament, each artist to his fancy. But perhaps they would be offended should you display a keener interest in this idle decoration than in the details of the mighty canvas to which it has been applied.

This is a book about buildings. Architecture is doubtless an art, yet buildings are practical things, to be studied primarily in the light of their

Foreword

success as solutions of planning and structural problems. Applied sculpture may convert, for example, a corbel to an *objet d'art*; to the architect it remains a corbel, with a function to perform—let the connoisseurs of art deal with the rest.

To serious students of English mediaeval architecture it must have long been obvious that the existing nomenclature familiarly attached to the various styles and periods is overdue for revision.

The term Gothic, though both incorrect and inapt, is not only long-established but indeed far too well-beloved for any alternative designation to be conceivable. The three subdivisions of the style, also too firmly founded not to be perpetuated, are nevertheless still distinguished by terms—Early English, Decorated, and Perpendicular—which besides being unsuitable have nowadays become slightly ridiculous. It is suggested that the expressions Early Gothic, Mid-Gothic, and Late Gothic, might with propriety be substituted for these outworn labels.

It is less easy to suggest an alternative name for the pre-Gothic styles. The term Romanesque should now be reconsidered as palpably misleading: for the architecture of western Europe is entirely an offshoot of Byzantine culture and owes little or nothing to Classical Rome. As recent research has now made it clear that our western architecture emerged from the Dark Ages under the aegis of the Carolingians it would not sound amiss if it should be termed Frankish.

The pre-Gothic styles are not easily subdivided into periods. It is suggested that the earliest definite period, that which includes the centralised churches introduced into this country by Alfred the Great during the second quarter of the ninth century, should be called Carolingian. The spectacular building renaissance inaugurated by Dunstan a century later produced a series of great churches which have now almost entirely disappeared; it represented however the absorption of this country within the scope of Ottonian culture and thus may be so designated.

It is most unfortunate that the buildings of the half century following the Norman Conquest should to-day be entirely attributed to those piratical invaders of our countryside. The masons who built Durham, Peterborough, Ely, or St. Albans—in their day the finest buildings in the world—were Anglo-Saxons with a long tradition behind them; it is exceedingly unjust as well as misleading to call the architecture they created 'Norman'. It may be with accuracy termed Post-Conquest; better still the eastern art may be described as Anglian and the slightly later style which produced Gloucester, Hereford, and other great western churches Mercian or even Saxon. But 'Norman', like Romanesque, is a term which should be dropped forthwith.

The period covering the second half of the twelfth century and known to-day as the Transitional is in fact that during which western

18

Foreword

Byzantine architecture was acquiring a measure of refinement through being brought into contact with the more advanced craftsmanship of the Armenians, Syrians, and other eastern Byzantines. As this fusion occurred at the time of the Crusades it might be as well to refer to the period of transition from Frankish to Gothic which produced such a wealth of magnificent buildings in this country as the Crusader era.

Let there be no doubt concerning the strength of English tradition in English architecture. Various primitive and abortive efforts due to early missionary expeditions notwithstanding, English ecclesiastical architecture first achieves a firm foundation as an offshoot from Carolingian building in the Rhineland. Thereafter our English masons develop a magnificent style, entirely along their own lines and but superficially affected by minor innovations introduced during that period of cultural upheaval which occupied the twelfth century. It is a very great mistake to treat English architecture, whether 'Norman' or Gothic, as if it were but a poor relation to that of France. We probably taught the continental masons just as much as we learned from them; certainly the churches of Normandy are very inferior copies of our glorious minsters. The masons who built Durham or the great Anglian churches march in the forefront of those who follow their wonderful trade.

CHAPTER I

Historical Architecture

Much of the attraction which mediaeval English buildings have for many of us to-day is undoubtedly due to the evident artlessness of the inspiration which underlies their designs.

In those days, men built as best they could. Their limited scientific knowledge enabled them to raise roofs high above the ground upon structures often exceedingly clumsy. They had to provide certain accommodation; in monumental architecture they strove to accentuate the luxury factor of height. Their greater buildings often took generations to complete; such, therefore, could hardly be considered as entities to be designed as a whole. Tastes changed as the walls rose. Symmetry was hardly considered and readily sacrificed to utility or a change of fashion. The mediaeval engineers were intent on raising a building; such art as might later appear would be fortuitous. Scale might be impressive, or there might be the excitement of a daring achievement; art would be left to the taste of individual masons, or, in its highest form, to the carvers.

It was before the days of those stern men, equipped with efficient instruments, whose minds—thoroughly instructed in the rules which govern the science of architecture—began to direct along orderly courses the creative impulses of the Renaissance. Before that sophisticated era each designer had been influenced, for the most part, by the requirements of his client; having then to draw on his own experience and those of his immediate predecessors and neighbours in order to discover how these requirements could best be satisfied. Schools devoted to such subjects as masonry and its adornment were probably in existence throughout the Middle Ages. But there were no schools of architecture.

Some men undoubtedly possessed a certain inherent genius for the design of buildings; it was a genius derived, however, from centuries of experience. Let us therefore begin to examine the progress of the building experiments of men throughout the long centuries preceding the dawn of the mediaeval period in England.

The first structures were, presumably, those provided for the simple purpose of sheltering their occupants from the weather. As races developed from pastoral nomads to settled agriculturists, such shelters would naturally become larger and more permanent, until at last they could become sufficiently considerable to attain to the dignity of buildings.

The primary essential in all ordinary domestic architecture is a roof; for it is this which performs the actual function of shelter. Thus walls are in reality only a device for increasing the height of a building, and are not really necessary except when required to support a flat roof which has in itself no height. The simplest form of house, therefore, is merely a small enclosure covered by a single roof.

The size of the space enclosed will vary with the importance of the owner and the capabilities of the individuals actually designing and constructing the building. Thus an aristocratic building proprietor might require a multiplicity of apartments in order to house his followers or to serve as common rooms for, for example, purposes of debate. More particularly, a man possessed of many goods would need accommodation in which to store them.

At the summit of the architectural scale we find public buildings, of which those devoted to religious purposes will probably be of monumental character. This factor of the monumental is generally attained by increasing the height of a structure. Enlargement of the area covered by the building would probably be dictated by the practical requirements of accommodation; height, however, being actually unnecessary, is thus essentially a luxury, to be employed as the monumental factor in the design. Indeed, it will generally be found that really monumental architecture is employed in buildings which appear to have been erected less for practical reasons than for a desire to display them as propaganda.

By reason of its lack of durability, timber is the most despised material employed in building. Yet it must not be forgotten that, for a great many centuries, it formed the only material in use, not only in this country, but throughout the greater part of the continent of Europe.

The early shelters employed by primitive families, even after these had been combined in some sort of tribal organisation, were frameworks of sticks covered with foliage. At first the hut would be merely a lean-to closing the mouth of a cave, or acting as a wall before a shelter provided by an overhanging rock. The first free-standing hut was probably a ring of inclined sticks meeting in the middle; the height of this tent-like structure could be augmented by digging out its interior, or, if the soil did not permit of this, to pile up low walls of rubble stone and bed the feet of the sticks in this. The rectangular hut, however, would have had to be provided with a ridge-pole against which the two framed sides could lean. This produced a rectangular type of plan, fundamentally in opposition to the circular form produced by the hut described above. It is these two plans, the circular and the axial, which govern the designs of most buildings, no matter what their scale or magnificence.

The timber architecture which we are for the moment considering

Historical Architecture

was generally developed on a rectangular plan, as its primary factors were the two planes of the roof meeting at the 'ridge' or central spine of the building. The span of such a building is governed by the length and strength of the rafters obtainable, unless intermediate support in the form of posts can be provided. Such posts suggest the aisled type of plan met with in both the Classical temples and the early Christian churches of Rome. Improvement in the design of the supporting pillars is apt to become an important factor in the development of timber architecture. Forms of strutting and bracing are devised, and the science of joinery is employed in order to improve the rigidity of the structure.

If greater height should be needed in a building in order to emphasise its monumental function, it then becomes necessary to raise the feet of the rafters from the ground by interpolating walls. Such might be built of logs laid horizontally in imitation of stone courses, or a framed wall could be constructed by slotting vertical boards into timber baulks at the head and foot.

At some period in the history of the timber architecture of northwestern Europe the foundation of buildings supported by timber posts was greatly improved by providing large baulks laid on the ground to support the feet of the posts. It is this 'sleeper' construction which rendered possible the erection of the multi-storied timber houses of the early Middle Ages, the tall timber churches of Essex, and the even finer masted structures which may still be found in the valleys of southern Norway. During the tenth and eleventh centuries, timber building had attained such a degree of excellence that towers of a considerable height could be erected, not only on the ground, but also high-perched above the roofs of the great churches. It was the development of braced construction which rendered this possible.

It is unfortunate that practically the whole of the timber buildings of the early Middle Ages in Western Europe have disappeared. Contemporary writers have described their glories, not the least of which must have been the porticoes by which the thin wooden walling was surrounded in order to provide additional protection from the elements.

Timber towers may have been invented at a very early stage in the history of this vanished style, as a form of square plan based on four supporting pillars is met with throughout the history of architecture in Europe, and it seems most probable that these four supports represent the angle posts of a timber tower.

In this country, however, we are most familiar with timber architecture as displayed in the magnificent roofs of our churches. Up to the seventeenth century, when it became customary to conceal roof timbers behind a plaster ceiling, English carpenters were able to continue to display their skill in the design and construction of cunningly braced and ornamented roofs. As far as England is concerned, it seems probable that it was an early emphasis on the design of timber roof-trusses which caused English builders to set out their plans on a system of 'bays'; each 'bay' being punctuated by the transverse line which would finally be represented by a timber 'truss'.

As timber architecture developed and building in this material expanded, the consequent denudation of the forests supplying the wood made it necessary for the carpenters to devise methods of economising in timber; this, too, all helped to improve the design of the structural components of the building.

It has already been mentioned that practically the whole of the timber architecture of Europe has disappeared. It must not be forgotten, however, that throughout the Middle Ages a host of good timber buildings always existed alongside the masonry structures which for the most part form the subject of this book.

In order to study the beginnings of the architecture of organised communities, such as those which occupied the cities built at the dawn of civilisation, it is necessary to leave the forests of north-western Europe and pass thence to the timberless plains through which flow the Nile and the twin rivers of Mesopotamia. In these districts it was from the first impossible to erect anything in the nature of a timber hut. The most primitive structure, therefore, was bound to have walls in order to support its flat roof of mud, precariously stiffened with a few poles made from the trunks of palm trees. These first walls were probably built some six thousand years ago out of rubble found in the foothills of the mountains of Kurdistan and southern Persia. In order to give stability to the structure, the rough materials were laid, each course inclined to oppose its neighbours, in what is known as 'herringbone' fashion. Later, as the peoples settling in the fertile plains below began to use the same form of construction, they made up for the lack of rubble stone by using rough pats of sun-dried brick strengthened with chopped straw. The whole primitive structure was plastered inside and out by covering the wall faces with the same material, applied wet and allowed to dry on the wall. The flat roof was of wattling supported on widely-spaced tree trunks; covered with many layers of the reinforced mud, left to dry *in situ*. Such were the first houses to be erected when civilisation began six thousand years ago. The simple hovel of one room would expand into a chain of these until the rooms eventually met round an open courtyard left in the middle. Access to this was only through one of the rooms, and from it all the other rooms were entered. This courtyard plan forms the basis of all oriental architecture; also the domestic architecture of classical Greece and Rome, as well as that of Egypt.

The temples of the Sumerians were merely large houses enclosed by very thick walls to give dignity to the exterior; their palaces were a multiplicity of such features. The city-states were surrounded, for protection against their neighbours, by immensely thick walls of mud brick; this was the first appearance of military architecture. The climax of this Mesopotamian architecture came in the eighth century B.C. with the foundation of the Assyrian Empire. By this time some of the mud-brick building had given place to walling constructed of burnt bricks such as were later used in vast quantities both by the Persians and by their western neighbours the Byzantines.

One important feature which emerged from this early mud-brick architecture was the arch. The early Sumerians could seldom find enough timber with which to bridge over the tops of their doorways. One day, however, it was discovered that the bricks could be arranged to lie along a man's forearm, held inclined with the hand pressing against one of the jambs of the opening to form a primitive centering; the heat of the sun quickly drying the mud mortar, the bricks stayed in position and a very crude and shapeless arch had been created to span the opening. The Assyrians developed the arch, turning it on properly constructed timber centerings over wide spans. In particular they employed it to cover the entrance tunnels through their immensely thick city walls, which gave entirely adequate abutment to the 'barrel-vault' they had thus created.

At the same time as the Babylonian civilisation was developing in Mesopotamia, a similar style of mud-brick architecture was being employed in the valley of the Nile. In Egypt, however, monumental architecture developed along entirely different lines, for the reason that the narrow Nile valley was bordered by hills providing an easily accessible source of stone from which lintels could be made to solve the problem of bridging over the openings of doorways. There was thus no need to use for this purpose the valuable wood of the palm trees needed for roofing beams.

Soon after 3000 B.C., Egypt was launching out into a full-blooded stone architecture. In its monumental buildings, palm-tree props were replaced by towering pillars of hewn stone, set very closely together in order that they could be joined at their summits by the stone lintels already discovered. In place of the rubble walling of the Sumerians, the early Egyptians discovered how to make walls of wrought stone, laid in orderly courses and presenting a fair face to the outside world. If they wished to present an equally fair face to the occupants of the structure, without wasting material by using it in such masses that each stone passed through the wall from side to side, it was necessary to construct the wall in two skins. Thus, five thousand years ago, was born the science of masonry.

Egyptian monumental buildings seem to have been masonry copies of timber structures in which the roof was supported over a wide span by means of systems of palm-tree props. One of the most striking features of Egyptian architecture is its use of great courtyards as purely monumental features; endowing the space enclosed with the dignity of isolation, and giving, also—what was so very much desired in the torrid Nile valley—the blessing of shade. The lining of the walls of these courtyards with rows of ornamental columns added to the shadiness of the courtyard and also introduced the form of portico which was eventually to be such a feature of classical architecture. Where a courtyard preceded a building, the rows of columns shading its entrance were often multiplied.

Soon after the middle of the second millenium B.C., the beginnings of a European architectural style were appearing in Anatolia, where the Hittite nation was adopting a settled existence and building stone copies of timber structures which were innovations in that they were two stories in height and were covered by 'pitched' roofs. Hittite buildings were far simpler in form than the mighty creations of the Egyptians but were surrounded with elaborate systems of masonry fortifications. These beginnings of military architecture were subsequently copied by the Assyrians and, still later, by the Byzantines.

The great scale of Egyptian architecture was probably due to the vast amount of labour, mostly enslaved, which the people of the Nile valley had, for centuries, at their command. The same, however, could not be said for another civilisation which was progressing at the same time in the tiny island of Crete. One of the reasons for the success of the Mesopotamian and Egyptian civilisations was the existence of water transport. Crete also had the same facilities for trade provided by the surrounding waters of the Mediterranean. The islanders, however, were an entirely different race from their two great neighbours. Although living in a country possessing an excellent building stone, which they were at an early period using to great effect, their tradition seems to have been one of building in timber. They constructed no large temples, but the palaces of their kings were magnificent multi-storied structures designed in a style far in advance of anything to be seen in the world of their day.

About the time when the people of Crete were ruling the waters of the Mediterranean, a strange stone architecture was appearing among its islands and around its shores. The countryside was a barren one, rocky and with little soil, so that from earliest times agriculturalists had been forced to terrace the hillsides in order to obtain a sufficient depth of earth to hold an adequate water supply for their crops. This enforced excavation of rock, and the erection of sturdy retaining walls of masses of rubble stone, appears to have given the primitive farmers the idea of employing some of the larger stones in the construction of strange temples, in honour of the sun which ripened their crops. This 'megalithic' architecture, as it is called, simply consisted in making lines and enclosures of great stones propped up, one against the other, in the same fashion as a child makes a house of cards. While this queer aberrant architecture had very little effect on the history of building, it must have encouraged many people to think in terms of building in stone.

At the middle of the first millennium B.C. the people of the peninsula of Greece embarked on the first of the great cultural civilisations of Europe. A humble race, still in the Bronze Age and with no access to slave labour, they nevertheless built fine monumental structures in carefully wrought stone. In their method of construction, the Greek temples showed little or no advance on those of the Egyptians; they were, moreover, on a very much smaller scale. Being, however, keenly interested in the higher forms of mathematics, the ancient Greeks introduced into their buildings a number of refinements, in the way of optical corrections, which have ever since impressed their successors to a degree exceeding, perhaps, the actual value of their contribution to the history of building.

The Greeks also invented variations of architectural design within their national building style. These sub-styles, which are known as 'Orders', have been followed by their successors up to the present day. Chief of these Orders are the most primitive, known as the Doric (Plate 191), which is based on a sturdy column having a very simple form of capital, and the most refined, known as the Corinthian (Plate 195), which has a tall capital embellished with leaves of fern. These Orders were mainly employed in the ornamentation of the stone verandahs which the Greeks erected round the external walls of their temples in order to keep the interiors of the buildings cool. At the ends of the structures these colonnades were often deepened to form porticoes reminiscent of those protecting the entrances to Egyptian temples.

As befitted a highly cultured civilisation, the Greeks built fine public buildings, chief of which were the theatres, excavated in the sides of their hills and lined with rising semicircles of tiered seating. The life of Greek communities centred round the market places, paved spaces surrounded by pleasant colonnades and porticoes.

Away to the east their great rivals, the Persians, were also developing a civilisation and beginning to employ an architecture of stone. Although using the same structural forms of columns and lintels as had the Egyptians, the more barbaric Persians seem to have based their plans, not on the timber hall of the settled agriculturalist, but rather on the many-poled tent of the pastoral nomad. Thus the interior of the great hall of a palace erected by one of the early Persian kings appears as a forest of great pillars, closely spaced, and supporting a flat roof.

It will be noted that in classical Greek architecture there appears, for the first time in a masonry style, the 'pitched' roof with a central ridge.

Such roofs are the normal form of covering a building in a region which produces winter snow, an accumulation of which upon a flimsy flat roof would cause this to collapse. The early Greek roofs undoubtedly derive from the coverings of timber prototypes in Asia Minor.

The amazing civilisation of these Early-Iron Age Greeks, subsequently carried eastwards by Alexander the Great in his wars against the Persians, took root along the shores of the eastern Mediterranean. Developing still further as a result of contact with other races, the Hellenists developed a magnificent style of architecture, possibly never equalled, for sheer beauty, by any successor. Contact with Mesopotamia introduced them to the arch; a still more important discovery, however, was their development of the use of lime mortar as a matrix in which to bed the stones of which their masonry was constituted.

In the Middle East, a mortar of mud had been in use for a great many centuries. The Assyrians and Babylonians had used natural bitumen for the purpose of bedding their burnt brickwork; this had greatly assisted them in the construction of their arches. The district now being colonised by the Hellenists, however, was fortunate in possessing a remarkable substance known as bituminous limestone. This is inflammable, and, when burnt, forms quicklime which, when slaked with water, forms the principal ingredient of lime mortar in which all properly-constructed masonry is set. It may have been the discovery of this substance which enabled the brick arches of the Assyrians to be translated into the arcuated masonry style of Hellenistic Syria and the neighbouring regions.

The enormous monumental structures of Imperial Rome derived most of their aesthetic excellence from Hellenistic sources. The art of the Roman architect, however, resulted in a very different style from that which had graced the lovely creations of his mentors. The material which enabled the Romans to construct their huge public edifices was concrete. The discovery of this material probably came about as a result of the custom of placing a mixture of mortar and chips hewn from the stone when it was being dressed, into the space left between the two skins of stone forming the faces of a masonry wall. If, subsequently, these faces should have been for any reason removed, it would have been revealed that the 'core' of the wall had become a homogeneous conglomerate which was, in fact, concrete.

The Romans discovered that by erecting something to take the place of the wall-faces and filling in with the mixture of mortar and stone chippings, removal of the temporary 'shuttering' would disclose the fact that a complete wall had been cast out of concrete. This form of construction was eminently suited to the Romans, who had plenty of unskilled labour, and were always in need of very large public buildings which had to be erected without too much expenditure of time and skill. The technicians who calculated the mechanics of the structure, and the craftsmen who provided such embellishment as might be considered desirable, were generally Greeks.

At first, the Roman designers copied the colonnaded style of Hellenistic Greece; they also made great use of its monumental planning schemes, which arranged buildings in groups to show them off one against the other. About the beginning of the Christian era, however, the development of a concrete style was producing buildings of a type never before seen. The Romans, who were beginning to replace the timber roof with a concrete 'vault' which could cover vast spans, succeeded in discovering the cross-vault, which was a vault set at right-angles to the main one. The tunnel-like barrel-vault, set across a wide building, seemed a ponderous and unsightly affair; cut by cross-vaults, however, its vastness became true grandeur. The huge halls of the public baths of Rome generally had three cross-vaults, so that the building was laid out in three large vault-bays.

The invention of the cross-vault revolutionised architectural planning in that buildings covered with it now had no need for strong walls with which to support the great roof as this now rose from the points at which the 'groins' of the vault met. At these points, huge masses of masonry, called 'piers', were constructed to take the load and the thrust. Thus structures had now to be planned with a view to the provision of *points*— not *lines*—of support; thus lengths of walling gave place to groups of piers.

Colonnades, still greatly esteemed in connection with the design of streets and market-places, ceased to be employed in actual buildings save as applied decoration. Thus the Orders which had been the pride of Classical Greece became—except in such traditional buildings as temples—of decorative value only. But from the colonnaded streets was eventually developed what was to become the principal civic feature of the Roman town, the 'basilica'. At first this was an open space of rectangular form— the *exaeron*—surrounded by colonnades providing shade and shelter, but in cooler climates the *exaeron* was often covered with a timber roof; the whole basilica thus became a true building and in this form was copied by the builders of the first great Christian churches. Eventually the civic basilica became a great cross-vaulted structure, supported on a few widely-spaced masses of masonry in the form of piers, and ornamented with a modified version of the Corinthian Order, magnified to a giant scale.

Opinions vary considerably as to the aesthetic value of the contribution of the Romans to the art of architecture. It is certain, however, that the imperialist energy displayed by the Roman colonists was the direct cause of the cultural development of the backward lands of western Europe, including England, which would otherwise never have begun to build in masonry, for example, until perhaps a thousand years later than it did.

It was into this world of Roman might, leavened with so much Greek culture, that Christianity was born.

For several centuries, as was to be expected, the new religion had no effect at all upon architecture. When, at last, Christian churches began to be built, they were on a very humble scale compared with the mighty public buildings of the Augustan Age. Nor did the ecclesiastical architecture of Rome ever succeed in becoming a notable style, for the religion was unable to take sufficient hold of the community before the time when the Roman world itself collapsed under the shock of barbarian invasions

CHURCH PLANS
BYZANTINE AND ROMAN

Tinted areas are
external to the main spans

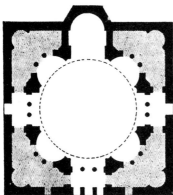

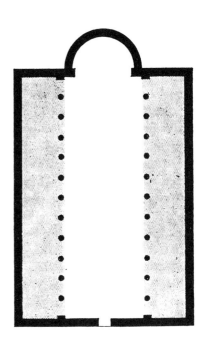

Fig. 1

out of central Europe. The first Christian buildings in the Roman empire were the octagonal structures raised over the holy sites by Constantine during the first half of the fourth century. The pagan temple had been a sanctuary, public worship having been conducted in the open air; the problem of accommodating the vast congregations attending the Mass of the Christians had to be met by constructing huge barn-like naves attached to the original circular *nuclei*. These colonnaded structures bearing some resemblance to the ancient Hellenistic basilicas it became customary to describe as basilicas large congregational churches as such. As the church-plan became standardised, the elaborate memorial chapel which had formed its original termination became replaced by a single apse recalling that of the early civic basilicas (Fig. 1).

The original 'basilican' church was therefore a plain rectangular building, having its main walls carried upon colonnades in order to provide communication between the central portion and the lean-to 'aisles' by which this was usually flanked. The main roof was set rather higher than those of the aisles, in order to provide a 'clerestory' of small windows to assist in the lighting of the central 'nave'. Primitively-designed structures of this description were all that the early church-builders of Rome could achieve. Even the largest churches were on this simple plan, of which the only feature was the apse which, marking the position of the altar, became the essential characteristic of all churches, great and small, for centuries to come (Plate 3).

But away to the east a new empire was arising. Greek culture, carried by the commerce of Rome, was spreading through the mountains of Thessaly to the shores of the Euxine Sea. Christianity was the spirit of the new civilisation which, inspired by Constantine the Great, swept across the wild country of Asia Minor to join the Hellenistic outpost already established in the Holy Land.

The first churches to be erected in the Syrian regions during the fourth century were three remarkable structures erected by Constantine above the Holy Sites in Palestine. These buildings, each an octagonal chapel entirely surrounded by an aisle, were of a type never before seen in architectural history. Meanwhile, however, the architectural development of the Middle East had been progressing considerably, by reason of the strides which had been made in the direction of adapting the structural device of the arch in order to enable it to be used as a roof to cover a circular or square building.

It was almost certainly in Persia that domes—probably of brick—were first experimented with to any considerable extent; migrant Hellenistic engineers may also have assisted in the work. By the beginning of the Christian era, the Sassanid kings of Persia had so far progressed in engineering knowledge that they were building rectangular halls, covered with a barrel-vault, abutment to which was provided by a series of apses covered with semi-domes. The true purpose of a domed style, however, is to roof a circular space; primitive circular huts, roofed with tall beehive domes, such as can be seen to-day scattered thickly over the plains of southern Anatolia, have probably existed from very early times.

The Graeco-Roman engineers, coming under the oriental spell of the soaring dome, abandoned their primitive plans and developed what is perhaps the most perfect of all architectural styles—the Byzantine. Under the aegis of the Christian rulers of the Empire of the East, Greek engineers were encouraged to calculate how they could perch the wide-flung domes upon piers of masonry which, although indeed massive, were nevertheless cunningly designed in order to withstand the thrust without unnecessary waste of material. The heirs of Graeco-Roman contractors converted the designs into glorious structures which were the pride of Byzantium and the whole Christian world.

As Roman architecture was the most commercialised, so was Byzantine the most sophisticated; for the latter was created by engineers of great erudition, who knew exactly what they were doing and left nothing to chance. None of the haphazard vagaries which enliven mediaeval cathedrals may be seen in the great Byzantine churches. There is nothing whimsical to relieve the effect of awful grandeur within the cathedral of the Holy Wisdom—generally known as St. Sophia—in Byzantium itself.

The Byzantine architects, like the Romans, planned their buildings upon a series of great masses of masonry supporting arches of a wide span; columned Orders were only used as secondary features, such as beneath galleries or in decorative screens (Plate 1). This combination of massive pier and subordinated column afterwards played an important part in the development of the architecture of western Europe, including England itself.

But the most important characteristic of Byzantine architecture is the constructional principle employed in the design of monumental buildings. The Roman use of the groined vault enabled the engineer to carry this on a few points of support instead of having to utilise the whole of the main walls of the building for this purpose. Accepting the new principle that walls had now been relieved of their supporting function, the Byzantines concentrated their efforts on the arrangement of a series of piers, which they afterwards surrounded with a comparatively light screen wall playing no primarily structural part (Fig. 1).

The culminating glory of every Byzantine church was its dome. Although the plan of this was necessarily circular, this shape is too awkward for use as a floor plan, especially if the main walls of the building have to be carried upon arches. By employing the triangular device known as the 'pendentive', however, it was found possible to set the dome upon an octagon, so that the arches could be straight, instead of curved, on plan (Fig. 1).

In the case of great churches, the spaces between the principal, or 'cardinal' faces of the octagon and the surrounding screen wall were covered with barrel-vaults set high up near the springing of the dome; in this way there originated the cruciform plan which was to revolutionise church architecture. The portions of the building next the 'ordinal' faces of the octagon provided the main abutment to the dome and were constructed in two stories, with galleries on the first floor which were usually carried across the four arms of the 'cross' (Plate 1). Galleries came to be

1. Erected by Justinian in 527, the church of Sts. Sergius and Bacchus in Constantinople is the earliest surviving ancestor of the churches of western Europe

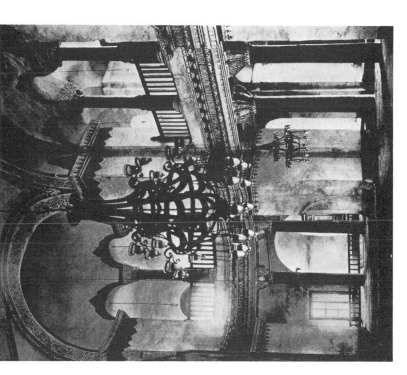

2. Beneath the central lantern of a great Benedictine church of the early twelfth century at St. Albans in Hertfordshire

3. A 'Romanesque' church of Ravenna, begun in 534 by Justinian

4. A West of England attempt at Gloucester Abbey, later the cathedral, to imitate the 'Romanesque' nave

universal features of a great church; most of the English cathedrals of the eleventh and twelfth centuries possess them.

While the cruciform plan continued to be developed—even in churches far more humbly constructed than the great Byzantine cathedrals—as the standard arrangement for churches, the builders of the larger churches of the era were fascinated by the great octagons, continuing to employ them in quite simple forms, with two-storied aisles entirely surrounding the building. During the second quarter of the sixth century—the era of Justinian—a number of magnificent churches were rising throughout the Byzantine realm. Besides those in the capital itself—such as Sts. Sergius and Bacchus (Plate 1)—the new style spread to St. Vitale in the important colony of Ravenna, and thence, across Lombardy, to St. Lorenzo in distant Milan. By the end of the eighth century Charlemagne had brought the Byzantine octagon to his capital at Aachen; by the twelfth century, the Templars had reintroduced it, in a circular form, to this country.

The Byzantine architects—who were building, without doubt, to demonstrate their skill—encountered two obstacles which, in the end, brought their style to decline. The first was a practical difficulty: there is a limit to the span of a dome, after which it is impossible to expand a building the plan of which is based on a central circular space. The second was the dislike of the Roman church for centralised buildings, the traditional taste being for an axial structure orientated east and west. It is interesting to note how this struggle between Orthodox and Catholic is displayed throughout the centuries in the changing design of churches as impoverished but fanatical Rome gradually ousts brilliant but indolent Byzantium. Even in the fifteenth century, when the Pope inaugurated the competition for the design of the new St. Peter's, practically all the architects based their designs on the centralised Byzantine plan. But St. Peter's was built with a long nave all the same.

The cathedral at Byzantium, begun in 532, was built upon an axial plan. Its lay-out reflects the later type of Roman basilica or *tepidarium*; it is roofed, however, with a huge central dome over the central portion, supported by what are, in fact, the two halves of a normal Byzantine great church, placed over the end bays of the building. The church has thus a large apse at either end; a feature which is reflected in the plans of twelfth-century Rhineland cathedrals and in our own little church of Langford in Essex.

The Byzantine architects were not allowed to continue with their towering creations piling up from all sides towards a central dome. The insistence upon an axial plan forced them to extend their churches westwards; we have seen their successors throughout the centuries faced with the same demand. This combination of Byzantine and Roman plan-forms appears at an early date in Syria: a country which, by reason of the richness of its Hellenistic legacy, produced some of the finest Byzantine buildings in the world. The fifth-century attempts to combine a long-columned nave with a terminal feature in the form of three-quarters of a normal domed church were not, however, always productive of the best results; such experiments continued, however, until the obliteration of Byzantine culture in these regions in 636.

By the middle of the eighth century, the large Byzantine church had settled down to a standardised plan consisting of two portions. The square area covered by the high dome formed the eastern half; west of this was a slightly lower 'west nave'. The fine church of St. Irene in Byzantium is perhaps the best example of this type of building, copies of which spread all over the districts coming immediately under the influence of the capital. The influence of Rome, however, prevented its acceptance in, for example, Lombardy.

As Christianity spread throughout pagan and half-civilised central and western Europe, it brought with it the centralised style in church planning; the spiritual appeal of the high-piled structures was irresistible.

The great octagons of the Byzantines became, in provincial hands, humbler squares supported on four piers instead of eight. In small churches the piers became columns; these taken, perhaps, from some ruined Roman building. Where there were no masons, timber posts took the place of columns. Sometimes there was no one capable of designing an isolated support of this nature; the church then became either a simple square of walls or a cruciform structure of four arms, with the central feature rising from the angles formed by their intersections. Such were the Visigothic churches of Spain before Roman influence converted their architects to the axial plan.

It will readily be appreciated that the domed construction employed by the Byzantines was essentially oriental, of stone origin, and quite foreign to those timber-using regions of western Europe into which the Byzantine style of church-building continued to spread. In those districts, therefore, the central portion of the church became a tall tower-like structure, finished, not with a dome, but with a pointed wooden roof, similar to that which is required to cover any other class of building having to be provided with some means of shedding winter snows unknown to the designers of the saucer domes of Byzantium.

Despite the fundamental influence which the Byzantines had on the church architecture of this country, subsequent Roman modifications have all but swept away the remnants of their principles. But there is one feature—due entirely to them which, perhaps, makes up for the loss of cohesion brought into church design by Rome-inspired mediaeval designers. This is the central tower, which, relic of the soaring domes of sixth-century Byzantium, even to-day pulls the whole design together and provides this country with a feature unsurpassed in any other land or style.

It was not only in the matter of religious architecture that Byzantium set new fashions. The oriental custom of building flat-topped houses, upon the roofs of which people could walk and live, was improved upon by the Byzantine builders, who began to specialise in houses of more than one storey covered, after the fashion of their Hittite and subsequent mentors, with pitched roofs to suit the Byzantine climate. The best rooms soon came to be sited on an upper floor, away from the bustle and traffic below; this is the origin of the *piano nobile* principle in the planning of private houses which was introduced into this country during the eleventh century.

The rich city of Byzantium, situated in a position much exposed to the attacks of Central European barbarians, was provided in the early part of the fifth century with a system of immense towered fortifications on a scale which set the fashion for mediaeval military architecture.

Upon this august civilisation burst, in the seventh century, the sudden onslaught of the Moslem Arabs, who, spreading out of the desert, began founding their capitals in Damascus, Baghdad, and, later, Cairo. The principal building in Moslem architecture was the mosque, in the design of which—as the keynote of their religion was a form of reaction from any suggestion of idolatry—they eschewed any form of building resembling a temple or church. To provide themselves with a place of worship they adopted the plan of the large colonnaded temple forecourt; omitting the building itself they aligned the most monumental side of the court, which would previously have given access to this, on Mecca. As time went on, they enlarged still further the portico upon this side, giving it domical roofs and, eventually, enclosing it within walls to form the mosque with which we are familiar in the later periods of Moslem architecture.

Perhaps the principal feature of all oriental architecture is the richness of its ornament. The Arabs, who were not permitted to employ representations of anything living in their ornament, utilised their skill in devising intricate patterns based on the figures of geometry with which their scholars were so familiar; repetitive wall-decoration of the diaper type was a popular feature of Moslem ornament. Following upon the Arab conquest of the Middle East their empire spread at an amazing speed across North Africa and into Spain, upon whose architecture it had a notable effect for many centuries. Southern and central France, also, were not immune from the influence of Moslem art.

The new eastern empire of Byzantium had founded in the old land of Italy a colony which subsequently became the important town of Ravenna. This place began to develop a fine building style of its own, assimilating to the sophisticated architecture of Byzantium some of the humbler features which were at the time being employed in the churches of Rome.

The principle Roman contribution was the axial plan, upon which its church-builders were absolutely insistent. Architecturally speaking, this class of building is far more primitive than the monumental forms created by the Byzantine engineers. As, however, the simple 'basilica' plan was more convenient when it came to the problem of accommodating large congregations, the plans of 'Lombardic' churches are Roman rather than Byzantine. The ordinance of the design, nevertheless, is more advanced than in the early churches of Rome; the buildings have come to be planned in architectural 'bays' and properly 'punctuated' with vertical features which indicate, on the exterior of the building, the arrangement of its interior.

The art of Ravenna began to spread rapidly throughout the plain of Lombardy up to the foothills of the mountains which separated this from the dark land of Central Europe. So fertile was this growing architecture of Lombardy that schools began to be formed of masons skilled in the art of building churches; it was these Lombardic schools—the chief being the Comacine—which, crossing the Alpine passes, laid the foundations of the so-called 'Romanesque' architecture of the west.

Passing up the long trade routes which led to the ports of the Flemish coast, however, the Lombardic culture encountered the national timber building style which already existed there. That this was of some consequence is indicated in the existing description, by a sixth-century Italian traveller, of the timber houses of the Rhineland at this period; he considered them in no way inferior to the stone-built houses of his own country.

It is unlikely that at this early date there could have been much influence from outside sources; the style was thus probably entirely indigenous. On the other hand, the Early Teutonic Church may well have copied—as did much of Europe at this time—the design of its buildings from Byzantine prototypes. The structural methods of the Byzantine architects were, as will be shown later, eminently suitable for translation into a timber style of sturdy posts and light screen-walls, such as is met with in later centuries in western Europe. And that there was an elaborate and efficient timber style is indisputable; it is greatly to be deplored that no traces of it remain. It is interesting to note that the plan of Charlemagne's little church at Aachen—which caused much stir at the time of its erection about the year 800—has its angles planned as if they were of timber construction, instead of as properly-designed stone piers.

At the time of the Western European renaissance which began during the reign of Charlemagne—a contemporary, by the way, of Harun ar Raschid, the cultured Caliph of Baghdad—the architecture of the coun-

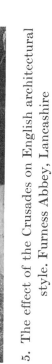

5. The effect of the Crusades on English architectural style. Furness Abbey, Lancashire

6. An Armenian church of the year 623 at Zromi

7. The nearest of these sixteenth-century houses at Weobley in Herefordshire is built on 'crucks'

8. Fifteenth-century timber-framed house at Lavenham in Suffolk having the upper storey 'jettied out'

try was a medley of ideas derived from all sources. Basically, there was the indigenous timber style—whatever that was—upon which was forever being imposed the mutually antagonistic influences of the Byzantines and the Romanesque Lombard schools.

In the distance would be two other dim sources of culture. One was Scandinavia, with its tradition of wooden architecture and elaborate carved ornament. The other was the Celtic world, which was slowly but relentlessly being colonised by the Roman Church.

Further south, where the lonely ruins of mysterious brick and stone buildings remained as memorials of a vanished civilisation, the architecture of the early Christian churches of Rome was now steadily filtering, to find an eventual home, under the aegis of Benedictine monks, where the great monasteries were rising about the middle reaches of the Loire, in the very heart of the country of the Franks.

Well caught up within the sphere of all this turmoil of styles was England: always potentially rich, and now being developed on a scale probably exceeding that of the days of that old Empire which had been wrecked by the very races who were now engaged in restoring its prosperity and its culture.

Contact with the mainland was primarily with Flanders; thence, through the Rhineland, to Lombardy and Byzantium. Despite this important material connection, however, the principal cultural influence was probably that of Rome, instilled through the medium of Benedictine monasticism. Whatever the native tastes in such subjects as architecture may have been, there can be no doubt that it was the Roman monks who inspired the great churches of the land. Doubtless their task was no easy one, for requirements—especially that stubborn insistence of the ignorant upon what they believe to be the thing they want—come before the architectural taste of the cultured sophist who endeavours to introduce something new.

In order best to appreciate the detailed development of the architecture of mediaeval buildings, it is necessary first to consider the primary factors governing their design. First and foremost comes the matter of the actual accommodation required. The plan produced to meet these requirements will be affected by such factors as the materials at hand, the skill of the designers, the labour available, the money with which to pay such labour, and the various checks and disturbances which may hinder the builders during the carrying out of the work.

The natural growth of an architectural style is probably due to individual research and discovery; for example, by visits abroad to copy the work of others. It was thus probably rarely in the history of architecture that experts were specially imported to introduce new ideas, or that there was any deliberate international interchange of views, except where such semi-cultural organisations as the Benedictine Order existed. It is strange, but probably true, to suggest that the manner in which an architectural style spread was probably due, more than anything, to the deliberate purloining of designs—especially masons' 'templates' or patterns—by rival builders. Such an important centre of learning as a great monastery would doubtless have eventually become something of the nature of a school of design; nevertheless it is very doubtful whether, in this country, anything approaching a mediaeval School of Architecture was ever deliberately founded for this purpose.

It is a popular fallacy that great political changes affect architectural design. It is doubtful, however, whether even such a revolution as an invasion by foreigners—as, for example, in the case of the Norman Conquest—would have produced much change in the national craftsmanship of a country. For it should always be kept in mind that, throughout the Middle Ages, only the plan and general form of a structure was set out by the 'engineer'—as the designers of buildings were called in those days—who might, it is true, be a foreigner. The actual erection of the building and its ornamentation was the job of the masons, whose craft was hereditary, and not to be changed in an instant at the bidding of an alien instructor.

Where records are not available for the purpose, the dating of a building by its appearance is always a source of difficulty. When considering the architecture of this country as a whole, therefore, it has to be borne in mind that, at various periods, some regions, for different reasons, were more advanced economically or culturally than others. In considering, therefore, the comparative dates of buildings in relation to their design, the important factor of 'time-lag' has always to be taken into account.

CHAPTER II

England in the Middle Ages

From an early period, England has been naturally divided, both geographically and economically, into two zones. The hilly regions of the west and north form one of these; the other is represented by the interior of the country, flanked by those eastern and southern coastlines which most nearly approach the mainland. From one or the other of these coasts various cultural influences have invaded the country; in the west and north, backward elements have been slow to accept innovations.

In a primitive economy having no vehicular transport, the numerous rivers of the east and south would have proved valuable arteries of communication. They were found to be exceedingly useful for shifting building stone—from the belt of this which passes between the two zones—to sites in the more progressive portion of the country. Thus there are strong geographical reasons why the east and south of England have always been in advance of the rest of the country, despite the fact that, for the very same reasons, it was just these areas which suffered most from the successive invasions of the early period and the various anarchical phases of later mediaeval times.

Very little indeed remains of Roman building in this country. Although the destruction perpetrated by the Anglo-Saxons must have been considerable, it seems scarcely reasonable to suppose that they deliberately overthrew every Roman building they found; one is therefore forced to the conclusion that the architectural achievements of the Romans in this country were probably of a much humbler character than those of their continental contemporaries.[1] The greater part of the Romano-British buildings were probably of half-timber construction— the country certainly produced at this time an inexhaustible source of material for the purpose—with framed walling set upon a foundation of brick or stone. There were no native masons and no indigenous masonry style to encourage any to colonise the misty outpost of the Empire. Any carved work would have to be imported; hence the absence of classical architectural ornament in this country and the slowness with which its forms penetrated into the vigorous style afterwards developed by the Anglo-Saxons.

England in the Middle Ages

It was in all probability the generally flimsy nature of the Romano-British buildings which caused these to vanish so swiftly and utterly at the time of the invasions of the fifth century. Be this as it may, this assumption that the Romano-Britons, as well as their successors, employed a timber building technique, coupled with the fact that the examples of both have vanished equally without trace, makes it impossible to tell just what effect the architecture of Roman Britain had upon that of Anglo-Saxon England.

Despite the uncertainty which still exists as to the manner in which the Anglo-Saxon invasions, and the subsequent settlement of the countryside, may have taken place, it seems clear that, broadly speaking, the eastern littoral was colonised by the Angles and the southern by the Saxons. The former, possibly by reason of the shorter sea communication with the continent, seem to have been the most progressive, and were not long in penetrating into the heart of the country, where they eventually founded the important kingdom of Mercia. The Saxons, passing westwards and up the marches of Celtic Britain, seem to have remained a backward race; which had, however, one burst of glory after a great king of Wessex had successfully defied the Scandinavian invaders who had all but destroyed the Anglian civilisation. It was, nevertheless, the Angles who gave their name to the country which has retained it to this day.

It is generally accepted that the Romano-British civilisation was practically wiped out by the invaders. One thing, however, is certain; a great cultural factor survived the general disaster. The Romano-British Church, driven into the mountainous regions of the north and west, survived there, nourished from time to time by the Celtic churches of Scotland and Ireland which, in their turn, were being carefully nursed by Gaulish missionaries despatched by Rome for the purpose. At either end of the no-man's-land between British Christianity and Saxon paganism, the former maintained an outpost. In Northumbria, the Christian stronghold was the island of Lindisfarne; in the south-west, the marshes protected mysterious Glastonbury.

At the end of the sixth century, the Roman monk St. Augustine landed on a missionary venture in the heart of pagan Kent. He made converts, and built churches (Plate 12); yet the gain was but temporary, and most of the converts soon lapsed again. Canterbury, however, was thereafter established as the headquarters of Christianity in England.

Throughout the seventh century the Christian faith spread slowly; bishops were introduced from Gaul and colonies of monks established in the interior of England. Dioceses were organised to correspond with the more important Anglo-Saxon tribal areas. At the end of the century St. Benedict Biscop and St. Wilfred between them expanded the Northumbrian outposts; whilst at the opposite end of the frontier St. Aldhelm began a church-building campaign in Somerset.

Meanwhile the steady infiltration of monks was continuing. The habitation of the ordinary man in the England of those days was a primitive hut of a minuteness and squalor quite inconceivable. The early monasteries in England were simply a collection of such huts, endowed with sanctity merely by virtue of the profession of their occupants.

The early Anglo-Saxon colonist in England was a family man; many families subsisted on an all-absorbing scale and amounted in effect to a tribal organisation. In all probability the settlements occupied by each such tribe—the occupants of which would be housed in the most primitive of hovels—would be dignified by some kind of large building, perhaps serving as barn, byre and, on occasion, as a meeting place for the community. It is certainly a well-known fact that the 'hall' formed the headquarters of the settlement, the nucleus of the subsequent manor-house, and—above all—the embodiment of the Feudal System. Every building —whether church, hall or peasant's hut—would have been constructed entirely of wood. The Anglo-Saxon vocabulary included no verb 'to build'; the term employed being 'to timber'. The village carpenter or 'wright'—the most important tradesman in the Anglo-Saxon economy— performed all building work (Plate 9).

As the seventh century wore on, Christianity took firm root in English soil, watched and encouraged by distant but ever-helpful Rome. The country began to be divided up into dioceses. Each of these was an area supervised by a bishop who moved among his flock but had no proper see as did his mediaeval successors. The Anglo-Saxon bishop was of a tribe, and not of a town; it is thus probably profitless to search for the site of a seventh-century English cathedral.

During the eighth century the efforts of the bishops resulted in the appearance of an organised priesthood. Many villages had now a church of some sort, and priests were found to serve these. The sphere of jurisdiction of each became firmly established; thus the parish with its boundaries becomes an integral feature of the English topography.

The latter part of the eighth century saw the rise of Teutonic power in western Europe. In Aachen, Charlemagne, ruling over his wide-flung empire, corresponded profusely with Offa the Great, King of Mercia and ruler of that empire which was the Anglo-Saxon Heptarchy. Although this country never formed a political part of the Holy Roman Empire, economically they were separated by a very narrow sea-lane which but served to aid mercantile communication with their respective coasts. Away to the east lay the two respected but already ageing civilisations of Rome and Byzantium; the latter, focal point between east and west, sending out its mercantile emissaries towards this country via the great trade route across Lombardy, over the Alpine passes, and down the Rhine to Flanders. Aachen was the western focal point of this great trade route; the eastern littoral of England was its ultimate limit.

There is no doubt that Anglo-Saxon England, ever growing wealthier, was engaged in considerable trade with Flanders from an early period. With the interchange of goods and wealth there must have reached this country much of the culture of Byzantium. But if the great eastern city was the origin of wealth and culture, it was nevertheless Rome, with its persistent missionary efforts, which had the chief influence on this country in so far as ecclesiastical matters were concerned. France came early under the influence of Rome; centres of Benedictine monasticism growing up throughout the country, thence sending small but important missions to England where they founded similar monasteries. It may have been these early monastic houses, and the small towns which grew up round them, which provided the first centres of culture in this country, as opposed to the purely mercantile centres, chief of which were probably the river ports of the eastern littoral.

Into this expanding civilisation of Anglo-Saxon England were thrust the devastating attacks of the Scandinavian pirates. Even on the less-exposed continent the ninth century was known as the *Siècle de Fer*; the Carolingian empire itself almost collapsed beneath the assaults of the barbarians upon its already softening civilisation. England suffered very badly indeed. Enormous numbers of its timber buildings of all descriptions must have perished in the savage holocausts which followed Danish victories. The Anglian kingdoms were swept away, never to recover their lost supremacy.

It was then the turn of Saxon England—further removed from the brunt of the attack—to take over the leadership of the stricken country. The king of Wessex, Alfred the Great, and his kindred, were indefatigable in their efforts to fortify and hold their towns; these *burhs*—the prototypes of the walled cities of the later Middle Ages—formed fortresses around which the countryside just managed to hold its own. The genius and devotion of Alfred set the seal on the Anglo-Saxon settlement of England. From his day the culture of the country, and the economic stability through which this could be supported, became assured. The wealth of England—acquired, despite the continual Danish wars, through trade with the Continent—enabled the English to collect ample funds with which to buy off the invading armies again and again.

One important result of the Danish attacks and the resultant eclipse of the Anglian kingdoms was that cultural England became temporarily severed from the Continent, in particular from those Teutonic regions with which Anglo-Saxon economy had been so closely associated since its inauguration four centuries earlier. There is evidence that the Saxon England which Alfred was leading to victory was more in contact with the Latin countries and, through them, with Byzantium, the cultural leader of all Europe.

With Alfred's death was ushered in the Golden Age of Anglo-Saxon England: the tenth century. At this time, western Europe was entering into a Frankish renaissance: a revival of Carolingian supremacy known as the Ottonian Empire. England itself, soon linked once more with Flanders, shared in the cultural expansion; a grand-daughter of Alfred the Great married the Emperor Otto. Architecture in particular, under the aegis of the Benedictines, flourished exceedingly. Even when the line of Alfred was failing in a succession of weak kings, the great ecclesiastic, Archbishop Dunstan, ruled the land in the name of the ever-vigilant Church of Rome. The hold of the Benedictine monks upon the country was tightened to a very marked extent; with the wealth they began to acquire from pious beneficiaries, fine churches, on a scale never before seen, began to rise throughout the land.

It was in two districts of Mercia that this monastic colonisation began to develop. The most important was the eastern, in the rich agricultural land bordering the Fens; here, around the great twin houses of Ramsey and Peterborough, the fine masonry style which may be called the 'Anglian' came to be born. At the other end of the building-stone belt the orchards and sheep-pastures of the west began to be developed by Benedictines based on Winchcombe, around which great house a series of important abbeys were eventually founded; whence there emanated, at a later period, another, somewhat different, architectural style.

At this stage in the history of English mediaeval building design, therefore, we already find the nuclei of two schools of masonry appearing: one at either end of the belt of building stone crossing the country along the line of the Fosse Way which passes from Somerset to Lincolnshire.

The south-western region, removed as it was from Continental encouragement, remained backward until the expansion of Mediterranean trade during the thirteenth century enabled it eventually to assume and hold the initiative. It was the Anglian settlement, however, with its access to the excellent building-stone of the Barnack region, which became the birthplace of English architectural style. By the Norman Conquest the Anglian masons, closely related racially and culturally with Flanders and the Rhineland, had developed a style of architecture as fine as anywhere in western Europe; by the end of the eleventh century, they were rapidly outpacing their Continental colleagues.

The English rulers stubbornly maintained their political insularity until the very end of the Anglo-Saxon era, even when Edward the Confessor began to establish connections with those Normans who, closely related to the Danish colonists already established in the Anglian districts like them had derived most of their building knowledge from Ottonian sources. When the actual Norman Conquest took place it seems to have had very little effect on the architecture of this country. It is true that some of the great churches built in England after the Conquest show a French influence in their planning; many more, however, retain the plan which was common to the Rhineland, Flanders and Anglo-Saxon England. In practically all cases the actual execution belongs to this north-western European style, and shows few traces of French influence in its detail until some years after the Conquest. All this, however, is not in the least surprising when we realise that the net result of the Norman Conquest on the population of England was to add about one per cent of Normans, to a native population of some two millions from which the whole of the craftsmen, equipped with their hereditary skill, would have been drawn.

The principal architectural contribution of the Normans was in military architecture. The Anglo-Saxons had practically none; the initial efforts of the Normans in this respect were restricted to curious earthworks crowned with barbarous-looking stockades which only at a later period became stone walls. In some districts, notably Yorkshire, the Norman contribution was in fact one of destruction—rivalling, even, that brought upon the country by their ancestors the Danes.

The chief influence which followed in the train of the colonists was that emanating from the ubiquitous Benedictines. Wealthy monasteries, still further enriched with the spoils of vanquished England, grew more and more powerful. Once again the fine monastic churches were rebuilt, even vaster and more magnificent than before. New monasteries, also, were being founded all over the countryside. The mediaeval church was taking a firm hold on England.

All this monastic development, however, having been instituted for the benefit of the Benedictine Order, was contributing little to the ecclesiastical organisation of the country as a whole. A very important step was taken, however, by the Conqueror in 1075, when he ordered the abolition of the vague rural dioceses of Saxon England and founded in their place proper episcopal sees in the cities which were now being firmly established throughout the country. For example, the bishopric of the East Anglian region of Elmham, after setting up a see first in the seaport of Dunwich and then in the small inland town of Thetford, found itself at last firmly and permanently established in the great river port of Norwich, economic capital of East Anglia. From this period the secular church and its bishops began to be established on a footing which enabled them to compete with the well-founded Benedictine monastic centres. At last a cathedral church could be endowed and built in a fashion to rival those of the great churches of the monks.

44

9. The rough 'bratticed' walls of a timber church at Greensted in Essex

10. Rubble stonework

11. East Anglian 'flushwork'

12. A church built by St. Augustine at Bradwell in Essex

13. A church at Bradford-on-avon in Wiltshire probably built by St. Aldhelm

England in the Middle Ages

One very important feature resulting from the expansion of the monastic colonisation in England was the development of the hitherto backward western side of England. From Carlisle down the Marches of Wales to Exeter in the far west, cathedrals as well as great monasteries began to arise to inspire architectural achievement in these regions. In this connection it is important to note that the eleventh-century and later architecture of the west differs considerably from the style created by the Anglian masons and shows clear affinity with French sources.

In addition to its nearby continental connections, England always maintained relations with Byzantium. Many fugitives from Hastings found service with the Emperor of the East. At the close of the eleventh century a still closer contact was formed as a result of the Crusades; at this stage several features taken direct from the Byzantines appear in English architecture, having been copied from buildings met with in Syria. The architecture of the Holy Land had taken a different course from that established in the Frankish regions, owing to the emergence of an Eastern Byzantine style of building devised by the brilliant architects of Armenia, a province which from its bleak mountains had so far managed to hold out against the onslaught of Islam. The eastern Christian style had by the sixth century become much lighter in construction than the metropolitan Byzantine and was already employing the pointed arch (Plate 6).

The reaction from the Norman settlement of England took place early in the following century when firm government dissolved into the anarchy following Stephen's usurpation. It is interesting to note, in parenthesis, that the rightful queen, Matilda, was the Empress of that old Empire of which Anglo-Saxon England had formed an economic, if not a political, part; Stephen being a representative of the new French influence which was beginning to take a hold on England.

Perhaps the principal feature of the Anarchy was the impetus it gave to the building of castles. Although these were still of the primitive type described above, many were subsequently consolidated as masonry structures of considerable architectural importance.

It is unfortunate that the term 'Norman Architecture' is now too well-established for it to be easily abandoned. Up to little more than a century ago, this style was known, far more correctly, as 'Saxon Architecture'. The facts are these: although it is true that the Norman barons set out the plans of their castles, and the Norman abbots, in many cases, those of their great churches, it was Anglo-Saxon masons who were actually responsible for the building of these in that style which they, and they alone, had conceived and developed throughout many generations. True, it was the wave of building following the Conquest which enabled the art of masoncraft to expand itself enormously; so that, by the end of the building boom—which corresponds roughly with the Anarchy—the Anglo-Saxons were able at last to turn to the task of rebuilding their wooden parish churches in a fine masonry style such as they had not hitherto been able to employ for their own buildings.

The twelfth century—the era of the Crusades—is perhaps the most important period in the history of the development of English architecture. Not only were the English masons introduced to their Eastern Byzantine colleagues, but also to the cultural achievements of Islam, at this period vastly superior in such matters to Christendom. In this connection it is well to remember that when Charlemagne wrote from his humble palace at Aachen to Harun ar Raschid the latter received the missive in one of several residences each of which covered several acres of ground.

Early in the twelfth century a new monastic Order was founded in that district, Burgundy, which formed the link between the spheres of French and Teutonic influence. This Order, known as the Cistercian, was founded as an ascetic revolt against the magnificence of the Benedictines, who were settling in the cities and surrounding themselves with great power and wealth. The Cistercians founded their monasteries in the thinly-populated pastoral regions of Yorkshire and the western Cotswolds, where they lived humbly and supported themselves with flocks of sheep. It is to these Cistercian monks that we owe two things in particular. Firstly, they were the pioneers of mediaeval civilisation in the backward lands of the north, as the Benedictines had been in the west. Above all, they were the founders of the woollen industry which brought such wealth and power to mediaeval England that the woolsack to-day is still the emblem of the Lord Chancellor.

Political changes had little immediate effect upon a mediaeval community, and the sporadic fighting which took place during the Anarchy was mostly limited to the movement of small bodies of mercenaries and operations connected with the sieges and reliefs of castles. The campaigns were mostly taking place in the south and east of England, from the ports of which both sides obtained their troops. The Cistercians of the north and west were therefore able to pursue their peaceful avocations more or less unhampered by political struggles.

While the poor peasants of the agricultural regions groaned under the yoke of the warring nobles and their ruffians, the cities of England continued to flourish and expand their trade. The national connection was still with Teutonic Flanders and the Rhineland with its trade routes into central Europe. The expansion of the Angevin Empire, however, was bringing powerful new political influences to bear upon cultural education.

It will be found that twelfth-century architecture may be divided into two broad styles. The first and most important is the native product of the Anglian school which, based on the Fenland abbeys and the great cities of Lincoln and Norwich, later spread to London and Winchester—the two Anglo-Saxon capitals—and the south-east of England generally. The second is the same style considerably modified by the influence of French monks; the two sources of this being Canterbury and the western abbeys of the Cotswold area.

The later part of the twelfth century saw much expansion of learning. University life at Oxford was already in full swing: contact with the Moslem world during the Crusades probably also assisted matters, for the Arab philosophers led the world in the more abstruse sciences. Practical science was also being developed. The mechanics of the primitive engines of the period was being studied. Military architectural design was being revolutionised through the invention of a powerful new siege-engine; the windmill was invented. The larger sizes of stones which came to be employed by masons indicate that improved hoisting methods for these had been developed.

The first real settlement of the post-Conquest era was due to the personality of Henry II and his determination to make the central authority supreme over turbulent feudal lordlings. Permanent stone castles began to be built by the Crown. In order to supervise the construction of these and at the same time to provide himself with an organisation which would enable him to conduct his military campaigns, Henry provided himself with skilled engineers, officially attached to his court.

As castles were by now becoming more suited for permanent residence, it was not long before these military engineers began to acquire enough knowledge of building design for them to be employed on the royal palaces which Henry was founding throughout the country. The domestic designer being thus placed on an official footing with the man who created great churches, it is not surprising that an era of stone houses appears in the latter half of the twelfth century. Nobles built them within the walls of their castles and even upon their rural estates. Wealthy and intelligent merchants—always in touch with the latest developments in such matters—built rows of stone houses along the alleys of their towns. The rebuilding of the closely-packed town houses in permanent form necessitated the provision of laws governing urban planning, drainage, and so forth; the Crown gave attention to these matters and produced suitable bye-laws.

The political changes brought about by the loss of Normandy probably had no effect whatever upon English architecture. What was of more consequence was the ever-increasing volume of trade; this became very noticeable after the hard-won peace of Henry II had set Anglo-Norman England at long last upon its administrative feet. The Hanseatic League, with its offices in many English ports, provides an illustration of the mercantile importance of the country in the eyes of thirteenth-century Europe.

The countryside, too, was prospering. The spate of military and monastic building, which had for close on a century been absorbing most of the building potential, was at last released so that the parish churches—hitherto either wooden buildings or humble constructions in rubble masonry—could now be rebuilt, in decent fashion, and to a scale commensurate with the populations they served.

What Henry II had inaugurated in the sphere of architectural organisation, his grandson Henry III—a king with a passion for building—made full use of in carrying out his projects. Teuton and Frenchman, carpenter and mason, had contributed each his share in the creation of that lovely architectural style which we have come to call Gothic. English masons were probably as skilled as could have been found anywhere in the world. What was needed, however, was the introduction of new ideas in respect of the architectural ordinance of buildings. Henry III imported these—as was very right and proper—from the far wider resources of the Continent. That his experiment met with small success was not his fault; the English engineers and masons, aided by the carvers, developed their beautiful architecture along their own unrivalled lines.

The notable success of English builders in creating magnificent churches encouraged the higher ecclesiastics to enlarge the choirs of their buildings for the greater glory of their office. Cathedral churches, in particular, began to forge ahead of those of the great abbeys which had been supreme a century earlier. In this, the loveliest period of English mediaeval architecture, the parish churches, also, began to enlarge their primitive chancels to conform with the new idea as to the importance of the eastern arm.

An important factor in the development of thirteenth-century ecclesiastical life is the appearance of the Orders of Friars, professed priests of better education and with broader international experience than their predecessors the monks; enthusiastic preachers, they raised churches with spacious naves to serve as auditoria and thus helped to balance a church-plan which was tending to become overweighted towards the east.

English insularity notwithstanding, the political effects of the Norman conquest of a century earlier were at last becoming apparent; the wide areas of France which the Angevin kings of England had included within their dominions were by this time bound to be influencing the culture of this country. During the Anglo-Saxon era, Flanders had been the point of contact with the Continent, to the advancement of the eastern littoral and its ports. But now it was south-eastern England which was taking premier place in the cultural leadership of the country. Thus the new 'Gothic' style was late in developing among the long-established

14. Masonry of the
time of the Conquest

15. Early Gothic
masonry

16. Late mediaeval
masonry

17. Pre-Gothic axed stonework

18. Stonework showing early use of the bolster

19. Late mediaeval diagonal tooling

masons of the east. Instead, it by-passed them, in the north, and up the western Marches, towards the new Cistercian colonies in Yorkshire. It is believed that new western schools of masons were established about this time in the building-stone areas of the western Cotswolds.

Many consider—probably with justification—that the cultural zenith of 'Gothic' England came to pass during the reign of Henry III. This is certainly true in so far as the close of his reign brought to an end the romance, as well as the struggles, of the Early Mediaeval Period and witnessed the transition towards the mercantile era represented by the Late Mediaeval Period which opens with the reigns of the first three Edwards. The year 1265 which saw the Battle of Evesham may be taken as an arbitrary date for the commencement of the new era.

During the 'Edwardian' period, the boundaries of England towards Wales and Scotland were being enlarged and consolidated, and communications with these being improved. Great castles, the like of which had never before been seen, were rising throughout these border regions. Wealthy market towns were surrounding themselves with proud walls in emulation of their Continental rivals. The palaces of the nobles, lay and ecclesiastic, fortified and unfortified, were being rebuilt in greater magnificence than before. Even the rural manor-houses were now on the way to becoming established as stone buildings built upon a standard plan.

Mediaeval England was in full swing. . . .

In 1349 came a devastating blow.

In these so far distant days, it is difficult to realise the appalling disaster which the 'Black Death' proved to our country.

One half of the total population of some four millions died.

Manors were left ungoverned, monasteries were depopulated. Merchants fled the country. Peasants died like flies, so that there was no more labour. The race of English craftsmen almost perished; as did the leaders, lay and ecclesiastical, of the organisations which had sponsored them. Thus, in the space of a few months, leaders, wealth, labour and craftsmanship were all swept away, and a pall of anarchy, social and economic, settled upon the stricken land. Peasants—their power enhanced through the labour shortage—revolted. The loss of leadership hastened the breakdown of the old feudal organisations which had been the backbone of mediaeval England.

No more great churches were built in the land. The custodians of those buildings which were in need of rehabilitation performed this not, as of old, by sweeping away and rebuilding. The cathedrals of Gloucester, Winchester and Norwich illustrate the new method of encasing an older structure within a new skin in an endeavour to make it look as if it had been rebuilt.

It was the merchants who saved the country—aided by the now

firmly-established sheep-farming industry, which had not been so badly hit as labour-employing agriculture. As soon as the country could recover from the shock of the great pestilence, a great wool boom spread throughout the land. The remaining feudal lords began to rear flocks of sheep. What was of more importance to the economic life of the country, however, was that now the poor man could graze his animals on rough hillside pastures, to his financial advantage. Thus even humble peasants could become sheep-farmers and join in the boom which was making all rich.

In this fashion, England began for the first time in her mediaeval history to develop a social class of 'yeomen', midway between the squires and the poverty-stricken peasantry who had hitherto formed the bulk of the population. These yeomen needed houses of a better sort than the wretched hovels which still housed the mediaeval peasantry: merely wattled huts, often with their squalid floors below the surface of the ground.

The improvement in the financial status of the middle-class villager resulted in benefactions to his parish place of worship. The fifteenth century is the era of fine rural churches; the rich mercantile towns, also, built huge churches from the profits of wool.

But for the building of ordinary homes there were far too few masons to meet the demand for stone houses. The village wrights, therefore, were summoned to try their hand at house-building on a greater scale than ever before. In the pastoral west, especially, the wrights distinguished themselves, their unsurpassed creations in old black oak striking curious patterns across the white lime plaster.

The men of the eastern regions had used up much of their oak forests in the wasteful architecture of early mediaeval days. Yet East Anglia was becoming the richest part of England—pouring wool into Flanders and along the old trade route. The ships came back in ballast. That ballast was Flemish brick: an ideal material for building fine houses cheaply and quickly without assembling all the paraphernalia attached to the mason and his team of assistants.

The East-Anglian brick style is, of course, practically entirely of Flemish inspiration. Very probably the first bricklayers were Flemings; it must have taken several generations for the craft to spread even through East Anglia. By the fifteenth century, however, the style had become completely established in those parts; soon, throughout most of south-eastern England, brick was becoming a recognised material even for great houses. By Tudor days the bricklayer had almost abolished the mason; most of the magnificent palaces of that wealthy era were constructed, not of traditional masonry, but in upstart brick.

Two centuries after the disaster of 1349, the newly arisen middle-class of England had pulled the country together and even succeeded in re-placing the whole of the lost population, in readiness for the spacious era of Tudor rule. Meanwhile, however, the remnant of the feudal aristocracy, ensnared and enriched by the wool boom, had been taking advantage of disputes in connection with the succession to the Crown and were en-gaging once more in senseless faction fights. Squandering their wealth in surrounding themselves with hordes of mercenaries, this backwash of the old mediaeval nobility began to fortify its manor houses, garrisoning them with soldiery collected by means of the principle of 'livery and maintenance'. To this twilight of feudal England can be ascribed many of the charming later castles of England.

The last of the mediaeval rulers of the country were wiped out when the Crown began to strike at the now too-powerful church which, as well as having acquired far too large a proportion of the country's wealth, was becoming disconcertingly influential in such matters as international politics. Starting with the dissolution of those monastic houses which were colonies of Continental houses, the Crown at last decided upon dis-solving the whole elaborately organised complex of the monastic system in England.

Both socially and economically the step was one much overdue; cul-turally, however, the disaster was cataclysmic. In a few months, rough hands were being laid on the finest creations of mediaeval designers and craftsmen to be found anywhere in Europe. The valuable lead, stripped from the roofs of the great churches, was melted into pigs over fires built in the monastic choirs from the stallwork which had so recently dis-tinguished those glorious structures. Mines, hitherto employed for the destruction of hostile fortifications, were sunk beneath the pillars sup-porting soaring towers which had for centuries been the glory of the En-lish countryside; the resulting heap of stones was used as a quarry to build hovels in the surrounding district.

In some cases the monastic buildings were used as homes and farm buildings for the new lay owners; in others, houses were built of stones from the vanished monastery. Secondhand freestone, however, if re-dressed, soon weathers away;[2] such stones, therefore, were generally used as rubble, producing buildings of inferior appearance.

But the Dissolution of the Monasteries, and the universal redistribu-tion of their lands, replaced the spiritual aristocracy of the country with a *nouveau-riche* upper middle class; this, by producing leaders for the yeoman society which was the backbone of Tudor England, played a very great part in the life of that era. The New Rich were needing fine houses in which to display their state. But mediaeval England was practically extinct and its architectural achievements far too old-fashioned to suit these Tudor magnates.

England in the Middle Ages

Henry VIII—anxious to replace, in so far as possible, the more desirable features of the lost monastic regime—founded, in addition to palaces, schools and colleges in which education could be continued; his example was followed by men of all classes who in city and country town began to build humble school-houses for the furtherance of the newly-aroused interest in education. The popularity of education with the upper and middle classes—a factor unknown in mediaeval times—began to draw Tudor England into the sphere of that remarkable cultural movement known as the Italian Renaissance, the architectural achievements of which were being keenly studied by the successors of the mediaeval designers.

The sudden entry into the market of a great deal of extremely valuable property, which included a vast amount of building, meant that persons had to be found to survey all this property and report upon its accommodation and value. Thus was created a new profession—that of surveyor.

These Tudor surveyors learnt a great deal about the buildings which they were measuring and the methods employed in their construction. Being for the most part keen and intelligent men, they turned their taste for improving their knowledge towards studying the Renaissance architecture which had by now spread from Italy across France and was approaching the shores of England.

Thus it was the Tudor surveyors who turned their backs for ever on mediaeval architecture and brought to this country the new style—so stern and sophisticated when compared with the whimsical architecture which had breathed romance upon the England of the Middle Ages.

CHAPTER III

Mediaeval Builders

Throughout the early mediaeval period, the humble peasant probably built his own miserable hovel without any assistance save that of his own hands. In Anglo-Saxon days, for example, even such an important tradesman as a weaver might live and work in nothing more imposing than a circular hut of poles.

But the rectangular hut with a ridge-pole was probably the most general form of peasants' home until, perhaps, the Edwardian period. The simple framework of sticks could be roofed either with a wattling of willow-withes daubed with mud; or—on higher land perhaps—roughly thatched with heather. A thatch of reed—only possible where such plants grow—would be a type of roof for the most part unprocurable by the primitive peasant; it is, of course, only in comparatively recent times that wheaten straw has been grown long enough to be of any use as a thatching material.

In very barren lands, where hardly any timber at all might be available, a rough walling of rubble stones would have to be employed. The stones would have to be laid in a mortar of mud; skilled amateur builders might set them 'herring-bone' fashion, like the Cornish hedges of the present day.

A form of hut which existed in the rocky western parts of England during and immediately after the Roman era was constructed by building a very thick wall of two skins of rubble filled with earth, into which the feet of the poles supporting the hut were stuck. This type of habitation actually exists to this day in the Hebrides. Such huts might be thatched with the sturdy moorland turf.

It is perhaps not generally realised what an important part in rustic architecture has always been played by common mud. A mortar of lime would be much too expensive for use except in the best mason-built structures; mud, therefore, was the universal mortar with which the poor man formed his hovel. In many parts of England the rustic builders followed the example of their great predecessors, the Romans, and made a sort of concrete of mud and gravel with a leavening of the dung dropped by their animals as they passed along the village tracks. This primitive concrete was rammed into a temporary 'shuttering', which could be raised, a foot or two at a time, until a complete wall, afterwards plastered with mud and dung, had been erected. In many parts of England it was actually the practice to imitate masonry by casting imitation stones in this reinforced mud which has played such an important part in primitive architecture for six thousand years.

But the real builders of mediaeval village homes were the 'wrights', whom we should call to-day carpenters. Every village had its wright, who was needed to make ploughs, sledges, and even carts (hence his later designation). Along the coast he would make ships; everywhere he built houses.

In craftsmanship with his own particular material he was eventually superseded by his rival the joiner, who, by specialising in devices for joining timbers together, was able at last to construct such luxuries as furniture (in mediaeval days only to be found in the most magnificent houses) or to complicate the design of the lofty roofs and churches with various cunning tricks of his fascinating trade. Aided by the carvers, the joiners were able to set the seal of mediaeval craftsmanship upon the great cathedrals by furnishing these with all the glories of screens and stallwork.

But it was the wrights who were the backbone of ordinary mediaeval building in England. Together with the peasant fighting-men they were impressed into the armies of Anglo-Norman kings to prepare military engines. During one of Henry II's campaigns against a troublesome East Anglian noble, the king was able to summon no less than five hundred wrights to meet him at a single village for the purpose of constructing the engines necessary for the assault of the rebel castle. It was the 'wall-wrights' who constructed the stockades crowning the earthen ramparts of the early castles and, when these were replaced by stone walls, followed the miners into the siege galleries, shoring these up preparatory to the springing of the mine and the destruction of the masonry above.

When stone walls first came into use they were merely roughly piled up by unskilled hands in rubble of assorted sizes (Plate 10), either roughly-coursed or utilising the principle of herring-bone masonry. Another method of laying rubble stone is to fit the pieces carefully together in what is known as 'rag-stone' technique; this was common throughout the Middle Ages in Kent and is also met with in the districts where flint is used. Rubble walling is raised evenly and has no core as in a true masonry wall.

The difficulty of constructing the angles of the walling in rubble was probably originally countered by utilising stones from ruined Roman buildings; possibly in many cases such valuable material would have been transported from some distance if necessary. The huge, roughly-hewn quoins of the old tower-naves of Old Shoreham church in Sussex and Broughton church in Lincolnshire were probably from this source. In many cases bricks from ruined Roman buildings were used.

By the end of the first millenium English builders were turning out very creditable examples of true masonry, in roughly-squared coursed rubble presenting quite an orderly appearance. The north wall of the nave of the old cathedral at Dorchester in Oxfordshire, and the remains of the cathedral at North Elmham in Norfolk show work of this description.

The advent of the first true mason, with his mysterious knowledge of how to construct walls of hewn 'freestone', must have proved a fascinating experience to many a primitive village community of Anglo-Saxon days.

Let us consider the significance of the craft of the mason and the all-important part it played in mediaeval architecture. The first principle of masonry is to extract from the earth stones of such a nature that, after certain operations have been performed upon them they can be, as it were, rebuilt to form the walls of a building. (To illustrate one of the factors governing the laying of stone, for example, it is a rule that it should be 'bedded' exactly as it lay in the quarry.) As has already been explained the actual method used in building a wall is to construct its two faces separately, filling in the space between with a rough concrete made of mortar (or possibly, in low-grade work, merely earth) mixed with the 'spalls' hewn from the stones when they were squared up.

The term 'mason' is apt to be somewhat loosely applied to any trades-man connected with the erection of masonry constructions. Masons, how-ever, were of varying grades, performed entirely different operations, and worked independently of each other during the course of their various tasks. Obviously there had to be someone who could organise and direct the operations connected with the erection of a building. This individual, in whom practically the whole responsibility for designing and construct-ing the building rested, was known as the 'master-mason'.

In order to get the stones prepared for him, each master-mason has to employ a team of perhaps up to a dozen stone-cutters or 'hewers'. These may be of varying grades of skill, from the axe-men who cut plain blocks of walling-stone to the experienced dressers who can, under the master-mason's direction, prepare stones of any shape required. Great accuracy is needed, or the result will be a clumsily-built wall. Unusually-shaped stones for special positions must be within the capabilities of the hewers; ordinary Gothic mouldings, also, were prepared by them. From the 'lodges' occupied by the stone-cutters, gangs of labourers carried the dressed stone to the position in which it was to be laid; here would be found other masons, known as 'setters', who would carefully place the stones on their new beds and set them in their matrix of mortar.

So it will be seen that the master-mason was not, as is sometimes supposed, a man whose work is of the same nature as that of a bricklayer; he was in fact the director of the labours of a considerable number of men. He may be said to represent the mediaeval equivalent of a building contractor. One master-mason alone might construct a parish church. When the wright was needed to erect the roof timbers, the plumber to cover these with lead, or the smith to hang the doors on the 'hooks and bands' which were the mediaeval equivalent of hinges—all these tradesmen would come under the direction of the mason.

Most of the great monastic houses would have a master-mason permanently attached to them for repairs and the continual expansion which these places were always undergoing. An extensive building operation, such as the construction of a new nave, would mean that other master-masons with their teams would have to be imported to take over various sections of the project.

In the architectural world of his day the mason was by far the most important tradesman in the mediaeval economy. The master-mason in charge of the construction of a building such as a great church would be represented nowadays by an architect of the first rank. The architectural ordinance of the building would have been entirely co-ordinated, not by its original designer—who would, in all probability, have been an amateur —but by the master-mason in consultation with his various colleagues.

In 1306, Richard of Stow—a local man—contracted to build the great tower of Lincoln Minster for the bishop. One has only to glance at the result to be able to assess the ability of Richard of Stow, master-mason. In 1334, Richard of Farleigh contracted to build one of the principal glories of English mediaeval architecture, the tower and spire of Salisbury Cathedral. East Anglia can boast John Meppershall; Somerset, William Winford. William Ramsey—another East Anglian—worked for the Crown throughout much of the Edwardian era until the Black Death brought his brilliant career to a close. Such were the men who, at the instigation of priests and princes, created our mediaeval buildings.

Let us endeavour to reconstruct a picture of the scene of operations connected with the building site of the Middle Ages. One can imagine the walls and pillars at all stages of erection, with scaffolds rising to the higher portions. In sheltered angles the lean-to 'lodges' (see Frontispiece) of the masons, each surrounded by scattered heaps of newly-delivered stone, indicate where the hewers are cutting on their 'bankers' the stones which are being called for, from time to time, by the mason directing operations from the actual course which is now being laid. Pairs of labourers carry the dressed stones, suspended from a pole resting on the shoulders, from the lodges to the working site. Other labourers are carrying cauldrons of lime mortar to the men who are setting the stones in place.

Behind the scenes are many other humble contributors. Most important are those who quarry the stones from the earth; in parenthesis, it is interesting to note that it was these men who were impressed when it became necessary to assault a castle by means of mining operations.

Another important tradesman of whom little is heard is the man who burns limestone for making the lime used in mixing mortar. This operation probably took place for the most part beside the quarry, but there is evidence that, during the erection of very large buildings, the lime was actually burnt in kilns constructed on the building site.

From quarry and kiln—year in, year out—the endless stream of transport of all descriptions flowed towards the building site. If—as was seldom—the sources of materials were close at hand, pack-ponies or even horse-drawn sledges would be used for the whole journey. More often, however, the stone would be brought from a distant quarry by water, unloaded at the nearest staithe and taken thence overland. Thus it will be seen that, behind the actual building workers, there was in addition a host of drovers, shipmen and labourers supplying materials to the works.

Let us consider how all this building organisation became, when the need arose, set into motion. The individual who would have inaugurated the scheme—that is to say, the man who inspired the original design—would almost invariably have been an amateur with a taste for building. The largest mediaeval buildings—the great churches—were probably designed either by a high ecclesiastic or by one of his monks or canons with an aptitude for planning. We shall later see how, in actual fact, the plans of buildings in common use were, at any particular period, roughly standardised. There was thus little to do except to determine the accommodation required and the scale of the structure relative to the building resources available.

When it came to what we now call the 'elevation' of the building, however, the problem of the mechanics of the construction had to be considered. At this stage, it must be realised that the most skilful mediaeval designer was in all probability almost entirely uneducated in scientific matters, having nothing of the knowledge of, for example, an architect of the Byzantine world. His conception of the probable stability of his design would therefore be based, partly upon a study of other buildings which had succeeded in defying gravity and the elements, and partly upon a combination of instinct and commonsense. This is not an over-statement of the ignorance of mediaeval designers. One of the mightiest of the French cathedrals was designed, at an enormous expense of labour, materials, and wealth, in this fashion . . . it fell down.

Mediaeval Builders

There is no doubt, however, that the professional masons were able to assist designers very considerably with their projects. Indeed, if the facts were known, it would probably be found that in most cases great deference was paid, even by the proudest archbishop, to the wisdom, experience and skill of his master-mason.

But as the Middle Ages expanded, it became obvious that the size of structures had increased to such an extent that it was becoming necessary for individuals to be trained in their design. It seems that the pioneer in this line of thought may have been that vigorous and efficient king, Henry II. In his campaigns for the pacification of the country, and its release from the depredations of his turbulent nobles, the king was for ever engaged in military schemes; these necessitating, in some cases, the assault and reduction of rebel castles, and, in others, the erection of his own castles from which to police the country.

For the first purpose he appointed an individual called Ailnoth to be his royal engineer. It was Ailnoth who organised the construction of siege-engines; also the operations, which included mining, against such castles as the king was endeavouring to reduce. As time went on, Ailnoth began to design new castles for the king, who had, of course, none of the advantages possessed by the ecclesiastical organisations, which could generally produce individuals of some slight education, experience, or cultural achievement to try their skill at design.

Ailnoth was perhaps the first professional designer of buildings—excepting, of course, the early masons themselves—which this country produced. Before long he was helping the king with improvements to the royal palaces. His name indicates that he was apparently not a Norman or Frenchman, but a native Anglo-Saxon. It is interesting to recall that Vitruvius, the Roman who published a treatise on architecture some twenty-five years before the birth of Christ, was the military engineer in charge of the imperial artillery park.

The example of Henry II was followed by a king who is far better known than his grandfather as a lover of buildings. Henry III—creator of palaces and, above all, of the existing church of Westminster Abbey—established a complete royal building organisation with which to carry out his projects. Thus at the Palace of Westminster he had, besides his engineer—later to be known as the 'clerk of works'—a 'comptroller' to supervise the building accounts, and a 'purveyor' to find the labour and materials. There was, of course, a master-mason and a master-carpenter on the permanent staff; upon which were subsequently incorporated a smith, a plumber and a glazier. These lesser tradesmen were later given the title of 'sergeant'.

This royal recognition of the importance of organising the national building style and methods indicates the height to which the architecture of England had attained during the thirteenth century, at which time it was, in point of fact, at its aesthetic zenith.

The records of this period often refer to matters connected with building design. Thus we hear of drawings being prepared; not on paper, however, but on deal boards which were probably carried about in all weathers on the job. We sometimes hear of 'models' of certain features being constructed; it is probable, however, that these were not three-dimensional, in the present sense of the term, but in the nature of detailed drawings. Above all, we hear of 'forms'—which we should call to-day 'templates'—being prepared by the designers and passed to the masons. It was probably the interchange—doubtless often by pilfering—of these templates, which helped to spread architectural style through the country.

By the end of the twelfth century a building boom had spread through the land. There must have been a considerable expansion of masonic strength to cope with this. Probably this was done by an apprentice system of lads passing through the stages of labourer, carrier, hewer, and setter, until if they passed each grade they might themselves achieve the dignity of becoming fully-fledged master-masons.

Some modern architects believe that actual 'schools' of masonry were set up in various parts of England. It is more probable, however, that indications of a regional style are merely due to the working of the 'guild' system common to all members of mediaeval trades, which carried on their crafts from generation to generation through the medium of apprentices. During the thirteenth century a number of master-masons were beginning to acquire such fame that they were often summoned to all parts of the country to give advice in the design of buildings. These persons were, in fact, beginning to set themselves up as amateur architects—though the term was not used in mediaeval days—and making the *design* of structures, rather than their erection, their profession.

Having discussed the men to whose skill and devotion we owe our mediaeval buildings, let us consider for a while something of the technique of the various tradesmen. First, chronologically, come the wrights, whose quarries were the primaeval oak forests of England. English timber-building differs from much Continental work in the same material in that the hardwood employed in this country necessitates much harder work—for the material, as well as being much tougher than coniferous timber, is apt to be very irregular in shape—and a more finished technique in order to make use of the wood available and counteract its awkward propensity to bow and warp. The English mediaeval wrights used only the heart of the tree for building, rejecting the less durable sapwood. Their principal tool—also employed by the mason—was the axe; held in both hands, it was employed, hatchet-fashion, in short chops.

Mediaeval Builders

Timber architecture in this country derives from two sources. The first of these to be considered is the very primitive style which has always obtained in the north of the country and in the Midlands.

It has earlier been explained that the simplest form of a rectangular hut is that which, having no walls, is simply a tent-like structure like an inverted 'V', having two opposed roof-planes constructed and covered in various ways. If the hut is sufficiently large for it to be necessary to employ rafters to carry the roofing material, the easiest way to support these is to lean them against a 'ridge' timber which passes from end to end of the building. The primitive method of carrying the ridge is to provide, at either end of the hut, a pair of heavy timbers, inclined towards each other like rafters, but of sturdy enough form to carry the whole weight of the roof. These pairs of heavy timbers were called 'crucks' (Plate 7). In mediaeval days the difficulty of the lack of lateral headroom, due to the fact that the roofs rose direct from the ground, was met by selecting curved timbers for the crucks; this is without doubt one of the origins of the change of arch form which differentiates earlier mediaeval architecture from the fully-developed 'Gothic'.

Cruck construction—which was always the easiest method of building a peasant's hut—continued in use throughout central and northern England; even as late as the seventeenth century, hundreds of houses showing the queer massive crucks in their gable ends, were still being erected in the northern and midland counties.

In its most primitive form the cruck is composed of a pair of straight timbers inclined towards each other. The Gothic form, in which the timbers are arched, provides better headroom at the sides of the building. The final arrangement is to select timbers which can be worked into angled beams; each of these has two straight portions representing the rise of the wall and the slope of one side of the roof.

By the thirteenth century the principle of the cruck had been accepted by the designers of roofs of good stone buildings. The pairs of curved timbers, modified and expanded by means of additional members, became, as 'trusses', the most notable features of the mediaeval roof. In the mid-Gothic period especially, the arched roof-truss became a magnificent architectural achievement, especially in the western parts of England. Whether crucks were ever employed in the more sophisticated south and east is not certain, as no examples are now discoverable in those regions (which have, however, always been very much advanced architecturally over the districts more removed from Continental influences).

The method of roof-construction employed in western Europe—which never used cruck construction to any great extent—consisted in assembling the rafters in pairs, known as 'couples', each pair pegged together at what was to become the apex of the roof. The roof timbering being thus formed of a series of closely-spaced couples, there was no ridge-piece. It seems probable that the Anglo-Saxon builders employed this form of roof; it certainly appears in the Scandinavian churches of the eleventh century, is frequently mentioned in twelfth-century English building documents, and remains a common form of roof construction throughout the mediaeval period, continuing in use even as late as the Elizabethan era. Various devices for stiffening the couples (Plate 27), to prevent the roof from spreading, engaged the attention of the wrights, until the cruck system—with the crucks themselves replaced by proper trusses built up from tie-beams—became introduced into large buildings to enable a ridge-piece to be introduced which obviated the necessity for coupling the rafters.

It seems clear from the descriptions extant of the fine timber buildings of the Rhineland and Flanders, that contemporary English timber construction, if it did not actually derive from Continental sources, must have developed along parallel lines. The first principle involved was that of the post, mounted as if it were the mast of a ship—upon a foundation or keel formed by a horizontal baulk or 'sleeper' laid along the ground (Plate 74).[3] These posts, which in the remaining English examples are rather less than two feet square in section, were well and truly hewn from heart of oak. They were buttressed into position by raking struts morticed into them; further stiffening was provided by various forms of diagonal bracing.

At a later date these timbers must have been squared with the saw, as the construction includes partitions formed of vertical boards, curved from the tree externally, and morticed at either end into heads and sills (Plate 9). The tool with which this was done was probably a frame saw, consisting of a blade held in a horizontal frame, having two end members by which the two operators pulled the saw to and fro. The ends of these members were joined to each other by the side pieces of the frame. Such saws could be used either in connection with trestles, or, in sawing large trees, with a pit. The boarded partitions referred to above were known as 'bratticing'. In addition to being employed for the walls of houses and churches, bratticing was also used as stockading around the summits of castle ramparts.

It is impossible to lay too much emphasis upon the importance of giving due attention to the vanished timber constructions of the Middle Ages. What we see to-day is the masonry skeleton of a building from which its timber partitions have been removed. Only external and weight-carrying walls were in masonry. The stone arcades of a hall are not for ornament, but to carry the roof; the interior of the building could then be planned as desired by the insertion of timber partitions. The chambers of early houses are to-day but stone rectangles; they must have originally been divided into rooms.

As the Middle Ages developed, and timber external walling began to give place to masonry, the wrights turned their skill to the devising and embellishment of fine roofs with which to crown the achievements of the tradesmen who had supplanted them.

One feature, so well-known to us to-day, was not in common use until well into the Middle Ages. This was the timber floor. To a primitive people, a floor is simply the earth upon which a building has been erected. The domestic customs and manners of the majority of our mediaeval forefathers were such that a wooden floor would have been next to an impossibility, except in the chambers of the aristocracy. Moreover, it was some time before a plank which was flat on both sides came to be generally employed.

The construction of a timber house of the Middle Ages must have been a much more sociable operation than the building of homes is to-day. Each dwelling would be pieced together, section by section, in the yard of the village wright, and every joint carefully marked before the framework was taken down again and transported to the actual building site. There it was reassembled, and hauled upright, section by section, with the aid of the neighbours. If the owner offended the community, his house might be literally 'pulled down' again.

It is a pity that so few of the tools which were used by the village wrights have survived to this day. Besides the axe and the saw, it is known that they used the 'celt' or chisel—a specially strong form of which was known as the 'groping iron' and was used for cutting mortices —and a 'wimble' or auger for drilling the holes through which were driven the wooden pegs holding the joints in position.

The Anglo-Saxon wrights were undoubtedly skilled in turnery: that they, or their colleagues the early masons, were able also to turn freestone is illustrated by the early stone 'balusters' which yet remain in many ancient churches (Plate 2).

By the fifteenth century, the wrights, their more skilled colleagues the joiners, and the wood-carvers, were not only achieving magnificent examples of timber construction in the roofs of great buildings but also developing an impressing artistic style in the screens and stallwork with which they were furnished.

The eleventh-century change of fashion which converted the designers of important buildings from timber to masonry construction made little difference in the progress of village architecture. Timber was to remain the poor man's building material; the village 'wrights' continued to improve upon their hereditary skill in using it. Economy resulted in refinement as the massive sleepers, posts and beams went out of fashion in favour of more cunningly framed systems of horizontal 'sills' and vertical 'studs'. At first used for partitions within stone buildings, these studded walls later were employed for the main structural features of houses. An examination of the timbering system of an early wooden farmhouse gives the clue to that close-panelled effect which forms such a notable factor in fifteenth-century masonry architecture (Plate 8).

The master-carpenters of the Middle Ages run very close to their colleagues, the masons, when it comes to assessing the chief responsibility for our lovely Gothic buildings. Thus, although it is said to have been Prior Alan of Walsingham who conceived the idea of the glorious octagon at Ely (Plate 152), it was nevertheless William of Hurley, master-carpenter to the Crown, who was called in as consultant when it came to the matter of the actual construction.

But nearly all the great buildings of the Middle Ages which remain to this day are of stone construction. This country is fortunately well supplied with good freestone, a belt of which runs across the country from the Severn to the Wash. It was probably the north-eastern end of this, as the portion nearest to the Continent, which was first developed; the monastic invasion of the tenth century was presumably taking into consideration the other termination of the belt when planning its colonising schemes in the West Country.

At the beginning of the eighth century, St. Aldhelm was building a series of churches in Somersetshire. He probably made use of the stone of Doulting (at which place, as a matter of fact, he is known to have been at his death). It seems reasonable to suppose that the exquisite little church at Bradford-on-Avon (Plate 13) was built by him. Its masonry is of exceptional quality; we shall see nothing like it until the twelfth century. Probably he brought over from Rome a Lombardic mason to teach the local people his craft; the tiny building bears some slight resemblance to St. Apollinare in Classe by Ravenna. Perhaps this was the first masonry effort of English hewers; it does not appear, however, to have founded a style, or even introduced the craft of masonry into the country. It was probably not until the Benedictine expansion at the end of the eleventh century that full use began to be made of the western building-stones.

After the Conquest, the whole of the south of England began to take advantage of the excellent water-transport facilities available with Normandy to make use of its quarries in the neighbourhood of Caen. Quarry areas invariably breed masons; doubtless the French masons of the Caen region helped to a large extent with the introduction of French ideas into English architecture. Even as late as the fourteenth century the masons of the south of England were ordering ready-made features, such as window-tracery, from Caen to fit into the openings which had been made to receive them.

Mediaeval Builders

Methods of quarrying freestone vary little with the district. The principle followed is to cut the stone into sections, subsequently levering each portion off its bed with wedges. Sandstone, which is not so easily quarried, was probably not used until well into the Middle Ages; and then only in the Midland areas having no limestone quarries easily accessible by water.

It may be taken as a general rule that the sizes of stones employed in English masonry increase as time goes on. Probably this is due to the improvement of the devices employed for hoisting up to scaffolds. Thus, until the middle of the twelfth century, courses are low and the stones themselves small (Plate 14); often they are very little longer than they are high. By the fourteenth century, however, the courses have become higher and the stones two or three times their depth in length (Plate 16).

Once the mason has selected his quarry, its stones are transported, as roughly-squared chunks, by pony, sledge or barge to the building site. They then come under the care of the stone-cutter or 'hewer'. The stones are cut in a temporary shack with a lean-to roof, known as a 'lodge', erected against some part of the walling of the building which has risen high enough for the purpose.

First, each stone is trimmed more nearly square with an axe. Until the middle of the twelfth century, the whole of the 'dressing' was completed with this tool (Plate 17). It must have taken a very steady eye and hand to chop away the stone until the lines of face, beds and joints, already marked out by means of the square, were exactly reached, and each plane trued up.

The dressing of stone is done on a massive bench known as a 'banker' (see Frontispiece). Many hewers, a particular stone completed, accepted responsibility for its accuracy by incising upon it a personal sign-manual. Each man was assigned, by his guild of masons, a mark which would last him throughout his career; his sons, or, perhaps, apprentices, would take the same sign with a line or tick added. By means of these chiselled 'banker marks' a great deal can be learned about the history of our great buildings; there are many hundreds to be found in one cathedral—such as, for example, Ripon—alone.

In the early days of English mason-craft, everything was done with the axe. Even circular work such as shafts or mouldings was executed with it. At the time of the Conquest, however, a wide chisel called a 'bolster' came into use for this purpose; a century later it was being employed for all purposes connected with the dressing of freestone. With the aid of his wooden mallet or 'mell' the mason drove his tool across the face of the stone (see Frontispiece); each blow marking a line upon it. Throughout the thirteenth century these bolster marks—or 'toolings', as they are called—can be seen running vertically across the face of the

20. The nave of the Ottonian church of Gernrode Abbey in Saxony

21. The nave of 'a pseudo-cruciform' church at Worth, Sussex, showing the lateral arches leading into its 'wings'

23. This system is yet more clearly seen at Durham

22. An Anglian nave showing vestiges of the 'duplex' bay system, Ely Abbey, later cathedral

stones as a series of parallel grooves (Plate 18) which have sometimes been so neatly aligned as to make the stone look as if it had been machined.

As knowledge of masoncraft improved during the twelfth century another discovery was the 'claw-tool', a bolster with a serrated edge which during the next century became employed to remove the worst of the irregularities of the stone before tooling proper was commenced. The use of the claw produces a spotty appearance very noticeable in Late Mediaeval masonry.

After the thirteenth century the masons took less pains with their work and held the bolster in a lazier fashion so that the lines of tooling run diagonally across the face of the stone (Plate 19).

It was the hewers in their lodges who cut the deep mouldings which so delighted the Gothic masons. Beginning with deftly-aimed blows of their heavy axes the craftsmen continued with the claw and bolster, chipped away the deep hollows and undercuttings with chisels of various sections, and then finished off with the comb or 'drag', a scraper held in the hand and used to remove the marks of tooling. Towards the end of the Gothic era the drag was even used on ordinary masonry—particularly in connection with features such as chantry chapels or tombs, so as to give the work as smooth an appearance as possible.

All these stones, prepared in the lodges, had then to be carried to the scaffolding and set in place upon the wall. As has been explained earlier, the principle of masonry construction is to build the two faces of the wall and fill in the space between with the spalls removed during the dressing of the face-stones. In the case of very thick walls, however, in which the spalls hacked from the stones would have been insufficient to fill the core of the wall, rubble or flint was brought for this purpose. Second-hand and spoilt stones were also employed. The very thick walls of fortifications were sometimes built of rubble throughout; if masonry was employed as a facing, the stones were often supplied ready-hewn at the quarry, and merely laid in position by setters on the job.

This sort of work, which is not true 'free' masonry—that is to say, masonry executed in freestone—was presumably executed by local wall-wrights or rough-masons, who would work either in rubble stone quarried in the district or ready-dressed stones sent by a quarry.

In the case of rubble masonry, it is necessary to have the external angles of the building erected in freestone; a mason would presumably have to be found who would set them out and plumb them, after which the straight pieces of the wall between would be filled in with rubble. At the same time, masons would have to be consulted over details such as door and window casings; only a very humble stone building indeed could have been erected without some form of supervision by a skilled trades-man.

The external angles of the building, which, if badly built, are likely to fall down, are therefore always its weakest point. Thus, even with the most primitive forms of stone building, careful attention must be paid to the angles. Before the science of masonry was understood in this country, stones for the strengthening of angles were set, not coursed as in true masonry, but on end, apparently in a misguided effort to imitate the angle posts of a timber building. If an angle is built all of stones on end, these will quickly topple down; the primitive builders, therefore, found that they had to set alternate stones horizontally, building them into the wall so as to tie-in the angle. This is the origin of that curious feature of Anglo-Saxon architecture known as 'long-and-short' work (Plates 46, 145). A variation of this, popular amongst provincial builders during the eleventh century, consists of standing large square facing-stones on end with each alternate stone faced to the opposite side of the angle. The jambs of arch openings of this period were often faced with stones of this description alternating with those laid flat to provide the 'bond'. The ancient church of St. Verone at Leefdael, near Louvain, has the square piers of its nave arcades fashioned on this principle.

In districts such as Sussex, where the local craftsmanship was good but freestone difficult to obtain, the angles of twelfth- and thirteenth-century rubble-built churches were often beautifully constructed, not merely with quoins, but with properly built masonry angles in well-dressed stonework. Bricks from ruined Roman buildings were used for the same purpose until well into the twelfth century.

An approximate guide to the age of walling is the nature of its core. Early masons had little appreciation of the value of providing a good compact centre to their wall; they were only interested in its faces, and threw in their stone 'spalls' anyhow, regardless of size. Also they were apt to be economical with the matrix, which was often more earth than lime. Later masons built their walls far more carefully; making a compact concrete of small spalls, or even properly laid stones, set in good lime mortar. The decreasing proportion of wall to opening made this desirable.

That part of East Anglia least well supplied with local building stone is its seaboard. This district, however, has a plentiful supply of flint nodules found in the local chalk. These can be used for walling, but it is impossible to form angles. It was, therefore, absolutely necessary to procure proper stone for these. When it came to a tall structure such as a tower, in which the proportion of angle to the wall-face was excessive, the local builders were forced to erect their towers on a circular plan (Plate 149).

At the end of the Middle Ages, however, flint workers had developed a great skill in the use of 'knapped ' flint, that is to say, flint nodules broken in half with the break employed on the face of the wall. This flint facing, which was held in position by reason of the fact that the length of the nodule lay at right angles to the wall-face instead of along it, proved so satisfactory that it became developed as a craft; the face of each flint being squared up until what was almost a miniature masonry style had been developed. In the fifteenth century, pânelled devices were formed of thin stone tracery and the panels themselves neatly filled in with flint 'flush-work', which the stone framework helped to retain in position (Plate 11).

It is, of course, an elementary principle in the laying of stones that vertical joints must not come immediately above each other; this is known as the 'bond'. When brickwork came into general use—to be laid by 'red masons', in place of the 'white masons' who had laid stones—the former found that their task in this respect was greatly eased by the fact that the bricks were all the same size and a standard bond could be worked to.

In addition to the normal members of the mason's team, there were other workers in stone. Chief of these, of course, was the carver, a highly skilled craftsman who followed his own bent and worked almost independently of the mason. Another specialist was the turner, who with his heavy stone lathe turned the columns and—more particularly in English architecture—the slender shafts which form such a delightful feature of mediaeval design.

As the walls rose, the mason began to meet his colleague, the wright. First of all the latter would be in demand for the erection of scaffolding; later, for the construction of 'centering' upon which the mason could turn his arches. At last would come the time when the mason himself could step aside to criticise the construction of the roof, which, in England, remained always the sole province of the craftsman in wood.

When examining an old stone building, it is as well to remember that what one is seeing to-day may perhaps represent but the skeleton of what existed in mediaeval days. Such a building as, for example, a large stone hall may look very beautiful now that it has been cleared of the impedimenta which littered it at the time when it was in full use. But the beauty of mediaeval buildings is often largely fortuitous; the stone arcades which delight us to-day were in fact merely the designer's device for supporting the wide roof. Within this roofed area, however, were possibly a number of rooms, separated one from another by timber partitions which a later age has ripped out in order to display the beauty of the masonry work. Thus we have lost much which would have enabled us to obtain a clearer insight into the domestic lives of our ancestors.

When the building itself was completed, therefore, it was then necessary to call in the wrights once more, in order that the internal arrangements could be set out with partitions. In the finest buildings, these were of wrought boarding or 'bratticing'; in humbler structures, they were framed in half-timber and the panels filled with wattling and plastered.

The machinery connected with mediaeval building was of the simplest form. It was probably limited to the large iron pulley-wheels used for hoisting to the scaffold the cauldrons of mortar. The smith, however, would always be required to prepare the ironwork connected with the hanging and fastening of doors and windows, and, later in the mediaeval period, the iron 'stanchions' and 'saddle-bars' to which the leaded glazing of the windows was secured. The hoist would, of course, come very much into use when it became the turn of the plumber to haul his heavy rolls of lead to the summit of the building. Finally, the glazier would display the skill of his craft in fixing his painted windows to the iron bars provided by the smith and built into the work by the masons as the walls rose.

During the Middle Ages it was, of course, the mason who was principally concerned with the erection of large buildings. When it came to the economic life of the country, however, it was the wright who remained throughout the universal tradesman. In particular, it was he who had to come to the aid of the soldiers when it was necessary to construct the enormous and complicated engines of a variety of descriptions which accompanied the operations connected with the assault of fortifications prior to the invention of fire artillery.

The engineer who planned buildings was also the man who exercised his inventive genius in the improvement of these engines; as newer and more destructive machines came into use, the engineer, again, had to modify the designs of his fortifications to meet their assaults.

At the other end of the social scale, the part played in the creation of our beautiful mediaeval buildings by the ordinary labourer must not be forgotten. These wretched folk fetched and carried and dug for all. More often than not, their services would have gone unrewarded. Feudal lords —or even the Crown—would impress the peasant for the purpose of digging the deep ditches of their castles and carrying the earth in baskets to raise the mounds and ramparts.

Much of the labour employed in building the great churches was probably executed, without earthly remuneration, by the humble labouring folk who dwelt in the shadow of their walls.

25. The cylindrical pillars of Leominster church in Herefordshire are typical of Western churches

24. Crudely 'ordered' arches in a Western nave. St. John's church, Chester

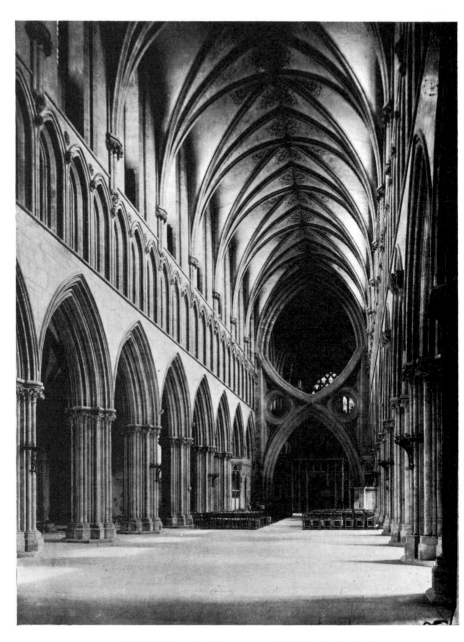

26. The Early Gothic nave of Wells Cathedral

CHAPTER IV

Constructional Problems

Mediaeval planning technique was of the very simplest description. Each building was planned as a simple rectangle; or, in the case of a complex of individual rectangular units, each of these was considered separately. Each unit was roofed with a simple pitched roof; there was no combining of them side by side, as in Renaissance planning, beneath a single wide-span roof.

Excepting the case of great churches planned on a monumental scale, the principal entrance to a mediaeval building, or a unit of such, was invariably sited in one of the long lateral walls; this wall then became the 'front' wall, and its opposite number the 'back' wall. The entrance was never placed centrally in the front wall, but close to one end of it. The position of the entrance determined which of the two ends of the building was to be the 'upper' and which the 'lower', as the entrance into an apartment was always near its lower end.

In the constructional planning of a building, the primary consideration is the span of its roof; this is true whether one is concerned with timber beams, coupled rafters, stone arches or vaulting. The span, therefore, is the first dimension which has to be set out.

When considering the length of a building, however, constructional difficulties do not enter into the problem, which then merely becomes one of convenience or economy. Ever since building science came to be properly considered, however, it has been found necessary to employ some form of building unit by which structures can be set out and the relation of one part with another governed; in other words, to devise a building ordinance.

The Byzantine architects of the sixth century, who had achieved such marvellous structures as the centralised churches of that period, seem to have been puzzled at how to deal with the long barn-like buildings which were the prevailing form of church employed in the sphere of Roman influence. It was probably at this time, therefore, that the architects of the embryo Lombardic school introduced the building unit which we know as the 'bay', indicating this externally by repeating the main arcade as a form of wall ornament. The pilasters alone, with the arcade itself omitted, served to indicate the bay arrangement; by the end of the first millenium this device had been introduced into England to become a feature of Anglo-Saxon architecture (Plate 72). After the Conquest, these strip-pilasters became sturdier (Plate 123); by the Gothic era they had become replaced by buttresses, so that towering pinnacled masses of masonry continued to indicate the architectural bays of the building.

The 'bay' principle in building design introduces the factor of architectural punctuation; once adopted in this country, the principle of dividing-up a building into bays and stories, and indicating the divisions by some architectural feature, remains a constant factor in the ordinance of monumental buildings. In the case of early timber buildings in this country, the bay unit was represented by the spacing of the principal posts. It is said that this distance represented the amount of space required by a team of four draught-oxen; it is interesting to note that the modern German architectural word for our 'bay' is *joch*, which means a yoke.

Although the principle expressed by the employment of bay design was fundamental to mediaeval architecture, small and unimportant buildings, of no great length in proportion to their width, were not necessarily always conceived in bays. Domestic buildings, in particular, were generally set out—probably as ordered—in accordance with their internal dimensions, the subdivision into bays being arranged afterwards. This is particularly noticeable in the case of stone buildings in which the internal supports are provided by timber posts.

In stone buildings supported by piers or pillars, the bay is obviously represented by the distance between the centres of these. In aisleless structures the bay division may be marked by the principal supporting members—beams or arches—of the roof. In advanced construction, where vaulting has to be allowed for, the setting-out of each building bay has to be very carefully considered.

It must not be supposed, however, that the principle of bay-design is inseparable from the use of aisled structures. The designers of the early Christian churches of Rome took no account of it; their longitudinal layouts were never concerned with any transverse element. It is, moreover, clear that the Anglo-Saxon provincial builders knew nothing of this refinement. The measurements of their arcades were taken from solid to void; not from centre to centre of either, for this would have been too difficult for them. This method of setting out is also noticeable in the case of the post-Conquest churches of the backward West. It is only the Anglian school that exhibits a properly expressed bay-design.

It is noticeable that in many aisled buildings of the twelfth century the overall projection of an aisle from the main structure often equals the bay-unit or 'module'. The actual span itself, however, although originally set out to equal approximately twice the module, varies this proportion considerably; probably for the reason that the factors governing the span were too important to form the subject of a mere metrological formula. Moreover, as Gothic architecture progressed, and bays became wider, the main span of the building, for obvious reasons, could not always have been increased in proportion.

It was not until Elizabethan days that standard units of measurement came to be employed by the designers of buildings; before this, every locality had its own version of the appropriate unit required for each purpose. A study of the metrology of mediaeval buildings is to-day much overdue; until this has been done it is impossible to state with any degree of accuracy the variations which each district produced.

Two different phases of measurement must be considered. The first concerns the setting-out of the plan of the structure upon the site. For this purpose, it is safe to say that the ordinary agricultural unit known as the rod or pole was employed. This was nominally sixteen feet in length; it is said that in mediaeval days it was customary to stop sixteen men as they entered the church porch and make each place his right foot behind that of his neighbour, in order to assess the length of the local pole. For building purposes, a stick four feet in length seems to have been used (possibly this was the first yard, as this word, in fact, means a stick, and 'cordwood' to-day is still four feet in length).

It seems fairly certain that the Anglo-Saxon foot was approximately the same as ours, for the pole of sixteen modern feet and its 'yard' subdivision of four feet occurs frequently in the plans of their buildings. Many of the great buildings of the end of the eleventh century and the beginning of the next, however, seem to have been laid out on the module of a pole equal to about eighteen of our feet in length. The Tower of London and Norwich Cathedral are examples.

There are a number of other indications in the measurements of post-Conquest buildings to suggest that the standard foot was equal at that time to nine-eighths of ours. The internal dimensions of the mid-twelfth-century great hall at Farnham castle, if transposed on this assumption, become exactly sixty feet by forty; the well-known hall at Oakham castle also has the same dimensions.

By the end of the twelfth century, however, the modern foot seems to have come into use. The most common span employed in ordinary domestic work is twenty of our feet.

A study of the plans of such elaborate buildings as the great churches will often produce evidence as to the principles adopted by their designers (Fig. 2). The bay-unit, of course, was usually indicated by the spacing of the piers or pillars of the main arcade. The main span (centres of walls) was often twice this, another bay-unit giving the projection of the aisle. Transepts, also, were planned in bays; in eleventh-century great churches, the gable walls of these, two bay-units in width, conformed with the scale of the structure by being divided into two by a strip-pilaster.

The factor which originally determined the setting-out arrangement of a great Ottonian church was probably the existence of the series of cross-vaults which supported the floors of the galleries above the aisles. The early method of 'centering' these—before the invention of vaulting ribs—was to set out the shape of the vault with a number of poles or small beams, propped up from below; the modern method of constructing a properly-framed centering is of later date. It was, of course, convenient to have all the vaulting bays equal in size and shape, so that the same timbering could be used for each. From the existing evidence, it seems probable that the setting-out may have been achieved by using a square

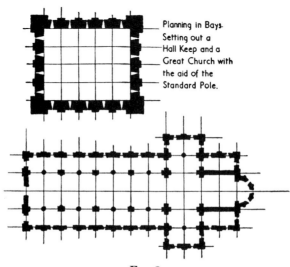

Planning in Bays.
Setting out a
Hall Keep and a
Great Church with
the aid of the
Standard Pole.

FIG. 2

frame of poles, braced with a diagonal, and having the length of each side equal to the standard 'pole'; it would then have been an easy matter to set out a building of any size by simply moving the frame about the site, marking each of its positions by driving in pegs. (This may account for some of the badly-aligned plans of early great churches; nowadays buildings are set-out by alignment, not by fixing points and joining these up afterwards.)

Great halls and other domestic buildings also maintained the bay principle in their designs. The Tower of London is five bays long and four wide. As a general rule, the span of a building was approximately twice the bay-unit; this facilitated vaulting plans, especially in the case of a ground storey having its vault supported by a row of pillars down the centre. Aisles were easily vaulted in square bays; by coupling these, the main span, too, could be vaulted without too many complications.

Constructional Problems

Once the building site came into the hands of the masons, however, a new unit of measurement came into force: that which was marked upon the iron squares of the hewers. Again, it will take intensive metrological research to determine the variations which each district produced. Although it seems fairly certain that the inch formed the basis, the writer's personal examination of a number of buildings has only served to demonstrate that even in one building the variations in the inch seem to have been unlimited. In the original west front of Lincoln Cathedral, however, an inch equal to nine-eighths of the modern unit definitely appears; this seems to fit accurately with the pole of eighteen feet which is found within the same building and suggested by the bay-units of a number of contemporary structures.

The supervision exercised by the master-mason may have been relaxed when isolated structures such as piers were being erected; in these, the courses did not have to meet others which might have been undergoing construction by other masons. It appears, however, not outside the sphere of probability that the masons' inches varied so much that each of the courses in the main structure had to have its own template.

In setting-out a building, rectangularity was probably achieved by comparing diagonals with the aid of a cord. Some buildings are very noticeably rhomboidal on plan; this may have been due to the fact that they were erected round existing buildings the presence of which made it impossible to take diagonals. The replacement of timber churches by masonry successors probably often produced this result.

The first adjunct to the plan of a simple building probably came about when this was expanded laterally by means of aisles, as suggested in principle by the plans of buildings supported by rows of timber posts. Byzantine architecture, based as it was entirely upon the skilful use of arches, must have brought this feature to the knowledge of builders in stone at a very early period. It is an obvious thing to do to hack a hole in a wall in order to give access to an adjoining compartment; a row of such holes becomes, in effect, a primitive arcade.

It is, however, more skilful to consider how to construct a wall which is from the first supported upon a row of arches. This entails the building of masonry 'piers' and the turning of arches joining the tops of these. The early Roman churches, which at first employed the classical device of a row of closely-spaced columns supporting stone lintels, later increased the intercolumniations and spanned them with arches. In north-western Europe, however, there was neither the facility for acquiring second-hand columns nor equipment for turning these. The solid pier was, therefore, the natural support for an arch; it is true that, during the ninth century, a few churches in the Rhineland were built in the Roman manner, but these appear to have been exceptional. In England, the

73

Constructional Problems

earliest aisled churches—which appear to have been Mercian—developed the rubble-built pier until it became a fine architectural feature, as is seen in the last great Mercian church, that of St. Albans Abbey, where the piers are built of bricks taken from the ruins of the Roman town nearby.

The domes of the large Byzantine churches were supported upon eight massive piers of masonry. The outer portion of each building, between the central feature and the enclosing wall, was divided into two stories by means of galleries. The fronts of these were carried across between the great piers by means of small arcades supported by slender columns. The architects made use of the contrast between massive pier and slender column; even in the Roman 'basilicas' the combination of pier and column began to creep into the colonnades.

The Rhenish builders of the Ottonian era adopted the 'duplex' bay system of alternate pier and column and introduced it into western Europe. Before 1050, it is known to have been employed in Westminster Abbey; after which it appears, in various forms, throughout the east and south of England, reaching its grandest form in Durham Cathedral (Plate 23). The twelfth-century churches of the Anglian school (Plate 22) all show the effect of this important architectural principle the last vestige of which is seen in the alternation of circular with octagonal pillars in simple arcades.

English mediaeval architecture belongs to what is called the 'arcuated' style; that is to say, its openings are spanned, not by lintels—as in the 'trabeated' classical and ancient styles—but by arches. In turning an arch, all that is really needed is a strongly-made and firmly-supported 'centering' of timber. If the wall above is very thick, however, the centering will have to be of the same width; thus, in their attempts to economise in centering, the English builders of the eleventh century discovered that they could turn their arches in widening rings, known as 'orders', each order acting as a centering to the slightly wider one above it, until the full thickness of the wall above was attained (Plate 24). English builders developed this principle with great effect, and much of the success of early English Gothic is due to it. The French, on the other hand, were very backward in employing the ordered arch, possibly because they had developed their arcaded style from that of the early Roman churches with their slender columns and consequently narrower bays requiring less centering.

A striking feature of Byzantine architecture is the employment of galleries above the subsidiary parts of the building. Entering the Rhineland at the time of Charlemagne, the galleried system of church design established itself in those parts. By the tenth century, galleried churches were becoming common in this country and by the following century they were universal in the case of the larger buildings. In France, how-

74

ever, church-builders continued to remain faithful to the Roman style, so that the Byzantine galleries did not penetrate very far into the country from the north-east.

The principal feature of Byzantine architecture is the arch (including its roofing form, the dome). In the case of the early Christian architecture of Rome, however, emphasis was given to the *range* of arches which is called an arcade. Byzantine arches were of a considerable span, and sprang from massive piers; 'Romanesque' arches were of much smaller span and generally rose from slim columns. The aesthetic development of arch support throughout mediaeval architecture appears to be concerned with attempts to make it lighter in form, compared with the arch above, than had been the case with the early arches first constructed in north-western Europe.

The appearance of the arch itself was considerably improved when the primitive semicircular form gave place to the pointed Gothic shape. A form of pointed arch had already been in common use since Anglo-Saxon days in timber buildings employing pairs of curved braces; thus English architecture was fully prepared to accept the masonry form. Pointed masonry arches were in use in Armenia by the second half of the first millenium (Plate 6); large and very graceful ones may be seen in the cathedral at Ani. It appears probable that Armenian architects introduced the form into Syrian churches and that it reached this country as a result of the Crusades (Plate 5).

The first supports were, of course, wooden posts. These were invariably, in accordance with the ancient custom of all builders in timber, set with the root end of the wood uppermost. This end was generally left thick, so as to allow plenty of bearing for the beams; posts of this description—which continue in use until the end of the mediaeval period—are known as 'teazle-posts'. In late Anglo-Saxon and early mediaeval days, posts were generally planted upon a foundation formed by horizontal timbers or 'sleepers' of considerable scantling. The posts had to be kept upright by raking struts morticed into post and sleeper; the junction between a pair of posts and the beam joining their tops was supported by braces secured in a similar fashion.

It seems probable that the general form of monumental timber building in this country at the end of the Anglo-Saxon period was of a type now exhibited by the early timber churches of Essex. In these, two sleepers, each about two feet square in section, pass parallel to each other down the axis of the building; each sleeper supports two posts, so that the four together form a square. The tops of the posts are joined by beams in all four directions. Above the sleepers the stiffening is arranged by means of braces, some of which are arranged to cross each other, saltire-fashion. In some examples there is a lesser post, mounted upon the sleeper midway between the two greater, assisting to carry the lateral beam in a manner recalling the duplex bay system of stone-built churches (Plate 73).

Across the building, however, the bracing is always provided by means of large curved members sweeping to meet each other in the form of a wide pointed arch. In later examples, such as at Stock, the raking struts supporting the posts are replaced by framed buttresses; the longitudinal ones being formed by saltires one above the other, while small timber arches, contrived by crossing two curved struts, are introduced across the narrow lateral aisles (Fig. 3). These devices buttressing the four angles of the central structure would be connected to somewhat smaller posts

FIG. 3

forming part of the framework in which the bratticed outer walls were set. Each corner of the building would have two of these in addition to the actual angle posts; thus there would be twelve small outer posts altogether.

Only at Greensted church in Essex are there any remains of the timber walling formed of the boards cut from the logs when they were squared and set, flat side inwards, into heads and sills (Plate 9). At Greensted, only the centre portion is original, the ends—possibly those outside the innermost of the wall-posts—have been formed of inferior timber arranged to match the older woodwork. The wall-posts are missing altogether; they remain, however, in most of the churches which have retained their central structure.

The first masonry arcades were presumably merely the result of cutting holes in the wall of a building to extend its accommodation by adding aisles. Later, a building would actually be erected with aisles, the main walls being supported from the beginning on an arcade rising from

76

28. A 'cradle' roof of the West of England covering Morwenstow church in Cornwall

27. Typical mediaeval roof of closely-spaced 'couples', in this example well braced. Great Bentley church, Essex

30. A Late Gothic roof of flat pitch having a lead covering. Harrow church, Middlesex

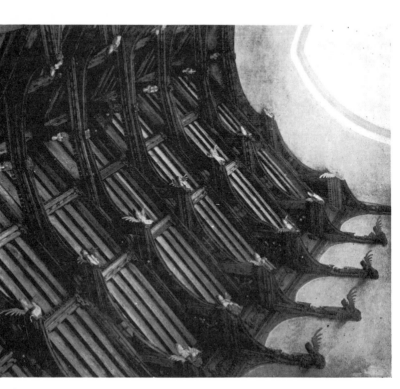

29. One of the 'hammer-beam' roofs which are the glory of East Anglia. Knapton church, Norfolk

massive stone piers which were in effect merely portions of the wall left in position.

The arches spanning between such piers would have flat soffits of the same thickness as the wall itself. When, however, the device of 'ordering' arches came to be employed, the next step was to make the plan of the pier follow the section through the arch. In order to examine how this important feature became developed, it is necessary to consider the nature of the duplex-bay design of the Ottonian churches of the tenth century, in which every other support was a slender column (Plate 20). Occasionally, half-columns were added to the faces of main piers to match these; it was then an obvious development to carry this half-column round the soffit of the arch as an inner 'order'. Even after the columns themselves had been abandoned in bay-design, the half-columns attached to the piers and the corresponding half-round inner order to the arches remain a feature of the church arcades of the eleventh century, and also in single arches, such as at Langford church in Oxfordshire, or Sompting church in Sussex. (See also Plate 81).

The Anglian masons developed the ordered arch, and the 'compound' pier supporting it, until it forms one of the most striking features of arcade design. They soon abandoned the use of the clumsy half-column, substituting, instead, groups of two or three slender half-shafts of much more graceful appearance. The pier itself became lightened by being planned in orders to match those of the arch above; a further refinement was the slender shafts which were fashioned on the angle of each order to soften its contour. Later, when ribbed vaulting came to be more carefully considered in the planning of a church, additional shafts to carry the ribs were added to the pier design.

These compound piers which provide such interest to the churches built in the style of eastern England during the late eleventh century, and much of the twelfth, are derived directly from the masses of masonry with which the architects of Byzantium supported their great stone roofs, and which, re-introduced on a humble scale in the arcades of the early Rhenish churches, have very little fellowship with the columned arcades of Rome.

In central France, however, where the 'Romanesque' style of the primitive Christian churches had established itself, piers of this description were never employed. In this region arcades consisted, from the first, of rows of narrow arches supported upon drum-built stone pillars erected in imitation of the classical turned column. By the end of the eleventh century, architectural taste in the French regions seems to have been unanimous in rejecting for ever the Teutonic square form of pier in favour of the drum-built pillar.

In western Europe, the mediaeval styles may be divided, broadly speaking, into two main divisions. That of the Rhineland and Flanders, rigid in their determination to employ the square pier, may be said to be the 'Doric' of the era; the more prolific French masons, with their circular pillars, producing what might be considered as the 'Corinthian'.

The Benedictine expansion of the west of England which followed the Norman Conquest resulted in the introduction of the beginnings of this latter style throughout these regions. The Anglian masons remained firm in their tradition, continuing to produce fine examples of what may be considered their most important contribution to mediaeval architecture: the compound piers which were the prototypes of such glorious creations as may be seen in the naves of Wells (Plate 26) and other western cathedrals which had been founded, at the time of their original erection, upon the plain round pillars introduced by the French monks (Plate 25).

The early pillared western style is well seen at such cathedrals as Hereford and Carlisle. Exeter, also, was originally built in this fashion; many other great churches, such as Malmesbury, display the sturdy round pillars of the west. During the twelfth century the circular pillar became fashionable everywhere throughout the country, especially for the main arcades of parish churches (Plate 81). The Cistercian builders favoured it as well as the Benedictines; the latter introducing it even in the regions which had long remained faithful to the compound pier.

Generally speaking, the type of circular pillar employed in the 'Corinthianesque' style of the twelfth century was inclined to be sturdy rather than graceful. In the backward regions of the north and west, however, a number of large churches were built with lofty arcades supported by far better-proportioned pillars ignorant of the French type of capital and having instead crudely-moulded tops in a style which might almost be described as 'English Doric'.

At least as early as the middle of the eleventh century the Anglian masons had taken to building arcades on the duplex-bay system, with pillars and piers alternating. The finest example of this style is seen at Durham Cathedral, begun in 1093. That the device was popular is indicated by the fact that even the twelfth-century naves of Norwich, Peterborough and Ely (Plate 22) still show traces of this Ottonian system of bay-design.

The 'Romanesque' ecclesiastical style introduced by the French Benedictines into the west of England made no use of the Byzantine galleries. Thus, although the choirs of the great churches—which were, of course, the first portions of the buildings to be erected—are fully galleried, the naves of Gloucester (Plate 4), Tewkesbury, Pershore and probably many other western abbey churches, dispensed with galleries and raised the main arcade to absorb this storey. This alteration in design is responsible for the enormous pillars of these churches, which are thirty or more feet high and of commensurable girth.

These early western English pillars, however, were not drum-built as were their French prototypes; being simply crude circular constructions of masonry. It was many decades before the English masons discovered how to build pillars of stone drums. The classical example of the true French style in this country is the choir of Canterbury Cathedral, built in the last quarter of the twelfth century; the pillars are properly built of drums.

It seems as if this choir at Canterbury may have inspired the masons of south-eastern England to develop their technique in the design of supports to their arcades. At any rate, about this time we find drum-built pillars, each embellished with four subsidiary shafts of marble quarried in the Isle of Purbeck, appearing in such churches as Chichester Cathedral and its neighbour Boxgrove Priory.

The introduction of these shafts may be a development from the design of the wooden posts employed at the same period in the timber churches. By the twelfth century it seems to have become the practice to surround the main post with four timbers, each with its outer angles chamfered. These four timbers rose with the post and formed downward continuations of the bracing system.

The posts supporting the roof of the twelfth-century castle hall at Leicester were square, and those at Farnham Castle octagonal; both were finished with coniferous capitals in imitation of their stone brethren. At the Bishop's Palace at Hereford, however, the hall-posts have the four subsidiary shafts, each with a coniferous cap; in this building, also, the arched braces have become complete semicircular arches, with an imitation hood-mould worked in nail-head ornament (Plate 31). This example indicates that the slender four-stemmed drum-built pillar (Plate 88) employed everywhere in the parish churches of the mediaeval period derives from the timber post with its four smaller members attached.

The abandoning by the northern French masons of the compound pier in favour of the drum-built pillar had been leading them into difficulties in connection with the support of vaulting. The addition of four subsidiary shafts had helped to some extent; yet the pillars still remained disconcertingly unconnected with the vaulting system above.

By the time fully-ribbed quadripartite vaulting had appeared, the French masons had begun to make the attempt to give some aesthetic support to the ribs by employing groups of shafts. These, however, they balanced insecurely upon the capital of the pillar, as if unwilling to sacrifice its column-like form by concealing this behind subsidiary features. The English masons, well versed in the traditional form of the compound pier, continued to employ it. During the last quarter of the twelfth century, the compound piers once more appeared, in Wells Cathedral, as a cluster of eight groups of triple shaftings (Plate 26). This magnificent achievement sounded the death-knell of the French pillar—English Gothic architecture had gained one more impressive triumph. Thereafter, the normal form of support to be employed in the great churches became the clustered pier; the multiplying riches of its mouldings were soon to be echoed in the graceful arches above. Hence it is to insular English obstinacy and devotion to tradition that we owe the great superiority in detail and refinements our thirteenth-century buildings display by comparison with contemporary French examples.

By the first half of the thirteenth century, the circular pillar of masonry had become almost ubiquitous in parish-church architecture (Plate 81). Thereafter, however, throughout the Middle Ages, the ordinary simple pillar which supports the arcade of the parish church came to be of the four-stemmed type described above and suffers little change except in the form of its mouldings, which vary with the taste of the period. One factor, however, is noticeable: whereas the pillar nearly always remains of the same thickness as the wall it supports, the tendency is always to endeavour to lighten it by reducing the other dimension, along the axis of the arcade, by as much as was deemed safe.

After this brief consideration of walls, and their principal structural features, the supports of any arches which may be cut through them, we can now consider the roofs which it is the primary duty of those walls to support. The fundamental member met with in all roofs is the rafter. Roofs in this country are formed of rafters inclined towards each other. The feet of the rafters rest upon a horizontal timber known as a 'plate'. In the earliest form of roof employed in monumental architecture, rafters were opposed in pairs pegged together at the apex.

The chief constructional problem in roofing of this description is how to prevent the weight of the roof-covering forcing the apex of the roof downwards, so that the feet of the rafters slide sideways off the top of the wall. This thrust was met by employing various methods of bracing to each pair or 'couple' of rafters. The Scandinavian method seems to have been for each rafter to have been doubled so that the roof had different 'pitches' inside and outside, the shorter rafters crossing each other and meeting the longer rafters at some little distance down from the apex of the roof. A later variation of this was to raise the feet of the shorter rafters so that these formed, in effect, cross-braces to the main rafters. The final form, employed in most early mediaeval roofs, is to substitute for these cross-braces a single horizontal tie known as a 'collar'.

A development of these 'collar-roofs' was produced by combining the use of braces and collar (Plate 27). A further improvement was to employ two wall-plates, one to support the foot of the rafters, and the other to

31. The arched brace of a twelfth-century Western roof. The Bishop's Palace, Hereford

32. A primitive example of a framed 'principal'. Sedgeford church, Norfolk

33. The tie-beam developed into an architectural feature. Kelvedon church, Essex

34. The 'king-post' introduced as a prop beneath the 'collars' of a 'close-couple' roof. The Old Parsonage, Marlow, Buckinghamshire

35. An elaborate example of wainscot concealing a cradle roof. Llanrhaidr church, Denbighshire

36. Purlins stiffened by arched bracing in a Western roof. 'The Tribunal', Glastonbury, Somerset

39. Detail of an East Anglian 'hammer-beam' from Banningham church, Norfolk

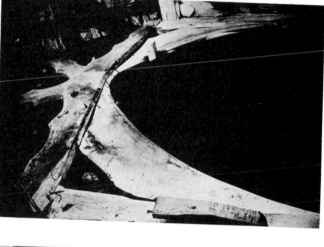

38. An elaborate form of Western 'truss' developed from the primitive 'cruck'. Amberley Court, Marden, Herefordshire

37. The 'jetty' of a fifteenth-century East Anglian house at Lavenham, Suffolk

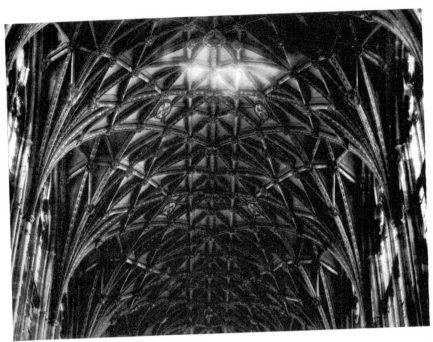

40. A 'lierne' vault of exceptional complexity above the choir of Gloucester Abbey, now cathedral

41. A primitive 'barrel' vault of the time of the Conquest. Westminster Abbey

support a short vertical timber, called 'ashlaring', which was, in effect, a brace between the foot of the rafter and the top of the thick mediaeval wall. With this treatment there was later provided a short timber 'sole-piece' tying the ashlaring to the rafter-foot and resting on the two plates.

A properly-framed roof, however, should not consist of pairs of 'couples', but should have a ridge timber against which the rafters on each side of it can lean; for, if this 'ridge' can be supported at either end, it entirely obviates the necessity for tying the rafters together (assuming, of course, that they are in themselves strong enough to support the weight of the roof-covering without sagging).

It is obvious that no timber can be found which will run in one piece from one end of a building to the other. Ridges must therefore be supported, at suitable intervals, by some structural device. The large curved 'crucks' of the primitive buildings of the north and west are an example of this device, but it seems probable that it was as a result of the Crusades that there was brought into this country the stone 'flying arch' which forms the principal supporting feature in the roofs of Parthian buildings in Syria. There are, however, few examples of these arches in English architecture, possibly owing to the great amount of timber centering that was needed for their construction. The tower keeps of Scarborough and Hedingham castles have fine examples; more graceful flying arches of the Edwardian period remain in the Great Hall of the Archbishop's Palace at Mayfield in Sussex.

The west of England, however, developed 'trusses', to support the ridges of buildings, based on a lighter form of the primitive timber cruck. As cruck design improved through the employment of angled timbers which could combine the functions of the truss and its supporting posts, elaborate timber frames were developed which during the Late-Mediaeval period formed interesting ornamental features passing across many a western building (Plate 38). Such trusses are not provided merely to support ridgepieces, but also other longitudinal beams called 'purlins' which help to stiffen the rafters and prevent their sagging under the weight of the roofing material; this, in the case of slates formed of a fissile rock, might be very considerable. Under the same pressure there was a danger of the whole structure collapsing longitudinally; thus most of the western roofs are also stiffened by pairs of small arched braces—incorrectly called 'wind braces'—joining trusses and purlins and forming a pattern below the rafters (Plate 36).

As far as timber architecture is concerned, the most backward part of England seems to have been the south. The early achievements of the builders of the eastern timber churches were probably forgotten when the local masons stole most of the high-class trade from their colleagues, the wrights. The western Midlands, late in developing a masonry style,

F

devised, instead, a fine timber technique which culminated in the 'magpie' architecture of the sixteenth century. The south of England, however, seems never to have had an opportunity of achieving a really fine timber style at all.[4]

What the primitive cruck was to the west, the tie-beam was to the east. After the roof had been removed from its timber posts and placed upon stone walls, tie-beams were often inserted to tie the wall-plates together and prevent their slipping off the wall-tops. By providing a longitudinal 'cat-beam', passing under the collars joining the rafters, and supporting this by short posts, called 'king-posts', standing upon each tie-beam, a makeshift substitute for the arched truss of the west was devised (Plate 34). In domestic buildings having high-pitched roofs covered with thatch or tiles, the octagonal king-posts with their curved struts meeting the cat-beam are features which continue in use until the very end of the mediaeval period. Such roofs do not, of course, have purlins or ridge-pieces.

A ridge-less rafter system, however well it may be braced, is always a source of weakness in a building and may even overturn the walls upon which it is raised; hence during the mediaeval period most of the original open roofs were strengthened by the insertion of tie-beams and king-posts.

Such obstructive features were not however to the taste of the roof-carpenters of the greater buildings. In eastern England a substitute for the cruck was devised by framing together a system of rafters, collar, and braces to form what is known as a 'roof-principal' (Plate 32). These features were established at half-bay intervals across the building and served to carry ridge and purlins: eventually the joiners improved the design until each principal appeared as an arched truss although in fact framed together in a series of short timbers.

Generally speaking, however, it was the tie-beam which played the chief part in the development of the eastern roofs. The absorption of the king-post within the design produced a type of principal similar in construction to the roof truss of Classical days (Plate 33). Eventually the universal employment of lead as a roof-covering and the consequent reduction of the roof-pitch to a negligible degree enabled the tie-beam alone to perform the function of principal (Plate 30).

The West refused to consider the use of the tie-beam. Their buildings were lower and the wide roofs exercised less thrust upon arcades often lacking a clerestory (Plate 87). The western carpenters were thus able to avoid obstructing their interiors by framing up each rafter-couple to form a miniature arched principal; the 'cradle roofs' they thus created are magnificent features (Plate 28) forming a striking contrast to the lofty creations of their eastern colleagues.

In open roofs of the end of the fourteenth century the tie-beam is sometimes found to be supporting miniature pairs of crucks. In East Anglia a remarkable variation of this is to omit the portion of the tie-beam which is not actually carrying the crucks and stiffen the ends of the beam by inserting beneath them strong timber brackets, known as 'hammer-beams' (Plate 39). Sometimes the arched crucks were made smaller and another pair of hammer-beams inserted between their feet and the original pair; the roof is then said to be of 'double hammer-beam' type (Plate 29).

The framework of timbers forming a mediaeval roof is only the skeleton upon which the actual roofing material is supported. Primitive thatches such as turf or heather—mediaeval straw was too short for thatching but reed was available in some eastern areas and in Somerset—were merely tied to horizontal battens pegged to the rafters; similar battens, set more closely together, were used to support the clay roofing tiles which appeared in eastern England at the end of the twelfth century. The proper way of covering the roof of an important building is, however, to provide a complete sheath of timber boarding upon which the outer waterproofing material is laid.

A common Anglo-Saxon roofing material was shingles, long pointed tiles made of split wood and pegged to the boarding in such a fashion that the pointed end completely covered the joint between the two shingles of the course upon which it rested. Boarded walls, also, were covered with these shingles, which made a curious scale-like pattern often recognisable in contemporary illustrations.

England was fortunate in possessing, in Derbyshire, lead-mines which, from Carolingian times onwards, provided the material for covering a large proportion of the great churches of western Europe. Very probably it was the fact that this material was so comparatively cheap in this country which encouraged the development of magnificent timber roofs to carry it.

The need for providing no lodgment for the heavy snowfall of northern Europe causes the pitch of its roofs to be normally very acute. Lead, however, is such an excellent material for keeping out the wet that it was found possible to build roofs of a much flatter pitch than would have been necessary with a less efficient covering. The disadvantage of lead is its lack of rigidity; it will lie very well flat, but if tilted up too much upon end, the sheets sag and 'creep'. It is for these reasons that, in the course of the Middle Ages, it became the tendency to reduce roof-pitch more and more until roofs became almost flat.

As the pitches of roofs lowered, so did the whole character of Gothic architecture change with them. Thus, after the zenith of the style—towards the middle of the thirteenth century—the soaring arches begin to droop, by very gradual degrees, lower and lower, to conform with the general reduction from that characteristic acuteness which is so typica of the architectural style which we call Gothic.

The aesthetic reason for lowering of the pitch of arches was the resul of the widening of the bay-unit. Unlike the French Gothic builders, who had been concentrating upon height, the English church-designers wer less ambitious concerning this monumental factor. Instead, they ha been planning for lightness and economy of structure, wider bays an more slender pillars. If a pointed arch is to be employed in connectior with a wide bay, the springing line must be raised in proportion to th width of the span, or the arch, perched upon low, disproportionate pillars will look overpowering and ridiculous. Widening a span without modi-fying the springing line, therefore, necessitates a reduction in the pitch of the arch or the raising in height of the whole feature.

It must not be forgotten that, for every large monumental mediaeva building, there were scores of timber structures—some of them possibl of considerable size—provided for such purposes as the storage of farn produce. By the end of the mid-Gothic period, the soaring arched brace of the time of the Conquest had probably all given place to much les obstructive timbers, smaller in size and set at a much flatter angle be tween post and beam. This development, also, would tend to 'debase' th arched effect of the interiors of timber buildings.

After the thirteenth-century aesthetic climax, mediaeval architectur tends to become in many ways more efficient. Thus, for example, it i much easier to fit the 'debased' form of arch into the panelled treatment in both wood and stone, which was becoming popular in the later medi aeval period.

The lowering of the roof-pitch resulted in the development of th trusses which supported it. In East Anglia, particularly, beautifull joinered features were built-up on the foundation of the tie-beam (Plat 33). As the pitch became almost flat, however, it was found that the tie beam alone made a sufficient truss.

Thus the underside of the roof had become so nearly level as to be, i effect, a ceiling. The joiners then diverted their skill from the ornamenta tion of the trusses to the decoration of the underside of the boarding sup porting the lead roof; this they embellished with every form of panellin device, many of their designs deriving from the stone vaults of an earlie era.

Boarded ceilings were employed in those great churches which coul not, for some reason or other, have their main spans vaulted, in order t conceal the ugly jumble of roof timbers. The Anglian cathedrals of Ely and Peterborough have ceilings of this description, dating from th twelfth century. It is sometimes stated that vaulting was invented ir order to render the roofs of churches fireproof; there could hardly be a

43. Twelfth-century ribbed vaulting over the aisles of Peterborough Abbey, now cathedral

42. A 'groined' or cross vault. Ely Abbey, now cathedral

44. Exeter Cathedral: perhaps the finest surviving example of the Mid-Gothic style

more inflammable form of treatment for the roof timbers than to cover them with a wooden ceiling.

Even as early as the reign of Henry III, the bedchambers of the royal palaces were being ceiled. The method adopted was to cover with soft-wood boarding, specially procured from the Continent, the undersides of the rafters, collars and·braces. This produced a sort of timber variation of the barrel-vault, except, of course, it was not semicircular but a series of flat surfaces. Owing to its resemblance to the tilt of a wagon, the boarding which was used to make these ceilings was known as 'wainscot' (Plate 35).

It seems probable that many of the western builders were several decades behind their eastern colleagues in lowering the pitch of their roofs. By the time the East Anglian joiners were constructing their flat timber ceilings, south-western churches were being covered with ceilings equally magnificent, but still having a coved section (Plate 87).

As has been mentioned before, the timber floor was practically unknown in Saxon England; indeed, it was not until, probably, the twelfth century that they were brought into use in this country. It was at this period that the two-storied Byzantine private house began to make its appearance in England. Such houses, however, would have been owned only by individuals of the upper classes, or by foreigners (such as Jews) of more civilised manners than the Englishman of the period.

A wooden floor was known as a 'solar'. The word should probably be pronounced *soller* which is to-day the name for the wooden platforms in mine-shafts; the derivation is perhaps from the French *solive*—a floor-joist. 'On the solar' becoming 'in the solar', the word is used eventually to describe an apartment situated on an upper floor.

The first floor-joists were in reality large beams of square section. The timber 'solar' floors were however often supported by a row of pillars passing down the middle of the ground-floor apartment; these pillars carried cross-beams or 'summers' and thus reduced the span of the actual floor-joists from the width of the building to the distance between the pillars. Reduction in length suggested economy in the section of the floor-joist; late in the mediaeval period the section was modified to a rectangular form like that of the rafter.

The early wrights were so ignorant of the mechanics of their material that they always laid timbers on their sides. Although this gave a better bearing, it meant that, instead of the timber being employed in the strongest way possible, it was so laid that its weight made it sag. Thus all mediaeval floors were apt to be springy.

When it became necessary to build upper stories of timber framing, this was supported on the ends of the timbers of the floor itself. Thus, if any movement took place upon the floor and made it 'whip', the movement was transmitted to the whole of the upper part of the house; this, in a structure of this nature, would probably result in much cracking—possibly even the falling of plaster and similar material. It therefore became the fashion to project the ends of the floor timbers outside the walls of the lower storey, supporting the timbers of the upper storey upon these ends, so that its weight would counterbalance any weights moving about inside the house. It is these 'jetties'—as these projecting portions of the upper storeys of timber buildings are called—which give such character to the houses of the fifteenth and sixteenth centuries (Plate 37).

In monumental buildings, such as churches, upper floors were always paved and supported upon vaulting; such are the galleries above the aisles of the great churches of the late eleventh and early twelfth centuries. In a private house a floor of this description was known as a 'stone solar' (Plate 122).

The simplest form of vaulting is the tunnel-like variety known as the 'barrel-vault', which is simply a long stone arch. Vaulting of this primitive type can be seen beneath the mid-eleventh-century buildings of Westminster Abbey (Plate 41), and in many castles, where the walls were thick enough to resist the tremendous overturning pressure exerted by this type of vaulting.

A variation of the barrel-vault in which some of the strain is taken by heavy transverse ribs—very common in France—is hardly ever met with in this country. The best example is perhaps that beneath the mid-twelfth-century chamber of the Bishop's Palace at Norwich; the arches occur at half-bay intervals. Like all other barrel-vaults, this example springs from immensely thick walls; its form of construction probably makes for no economy in this direction.

The main problem in connection with barrel-vaulted structures, however, is that it is difficult to provide space for windows; unless these be set low-down beneath the springing of the vault so as not to cut into this. The solution is to divide the building into bays; each roughly equal in width to its span. Each bay can then be covered, in addition to the main vault, with a transverse vault passing *across* the axis of the building. The combination of the two vaults produces that feature, known as the 'cross-vault', which forms the nucleus of all mediaeval vaulting systems. The sharp edges where the two vaults intersect are the 'groins'; this type of vault is thus often known as a 'groined vault' or 'groining' (Plate 42).

The principal difficulty met with in constructing a groined vault is the very considerable amount of wooden centering which this requires. Profiting, therefore, by their experience acquired in the construction of arches with 'orders', the late eleventh-century builders constructed the lines of the groining in narrow stone arches, thus forming ribs upon which the vaulting itself could subsequently be constructed (Plate 43).

By the beginning of the twelfth century, by which time the vaulting of the smaller spans of a building—such as, for example, beneath the galleries over the aisles of a large church—was a common practice, buildings were being purposely designed in bays, the proportions of which would assist in the setting-out of the vault. Each bay was generally marked out by means of a large transverse arch, the area bounded by the two walls and two adjoining transverse arches being roughly a square, so that each section of the vault web would be approximately the same. A simple form of church layout was to make the span of the nave equal to twice that of an aisle, and provide one vaulting bay to match two of the aisles. The Ottonian duplex-bay system, as employed in the main arcade, suited this layout admirably; the twelfth-century cathedrals of the Rhineland were all planned with this end in view.

In the Lombardo-Rhenish style from which our own architecture was developed, the original purpose for which the vault was employed was to provide an upper floor. Throughout north-western Europe the roof of a building was always in timber. The Byzantine style, however, which was always before the minds of the early masons as the finest architecture of all, employed a stone roof which was, in addition, an internal ceiling, giving a far greater dignity to the interior than did the maze of timber beams supporting a western roof.

Thus it was always hoped that the masons would be able to ceil their churches in stone; in other words, to throw a stone vault across the main span of the building. The difficulties were enormous. Quite apart from the matter of the mechanics of the structure, there was the problem of providing a centering of the size required and fixing it into position high above the floor. But the invention of the vaulting-rib assisted the English masons, and by the middle of the first half of the twelfth century they had succeeded in vaulting the whole of the great cathedral of Durham. The church, however, had not been planned for the purpose; this makes the achievement all the more remarkable.

The area of the vault which extends between its ribs is known as the 'web'. There are two ways of laying the stones forming this. The French method was to continue to form a perfect arch across each vaulting compartment, as had been the case before the invention of ribbed vaulting. English masons, however, 'swept' their stones together, laying them at right-angles to the lines bisecting the sides of the vaulting-bay and the ridge-ribs; with this system the joints of the vaulting webs, approaching from either side of the vaulting compartment, met at the summit to form a serrated line. This, although an example of clever masoncraft, seems to have been considered unsightly; early in the thirteenth century, therefore, a 'ridge rib' was introduced to mask the junction. The longitudinal ridge-rib was followed, at the middle of the century, by another passing transversely across the building in the centre of each vaulting bay.

Constructional Problems

The type of vaulting hitherto described is that known as 'quadripartite', from the fact of its having each bay vaulted in four compartments separated by diagonal ribs. A development from this was to introduce another transverse rib; thus completing the bay-design of the building by tracing two smaller arches on the side walls instead of the large one which had existed in the case of the quadripartite vault. Each narrow transverse vaulting compartment, or 'severy', was covered with its own vault; the section of this was so acute and the distortion at the springing so noticeable, that this 'sexpartite' vaulting is often known as 'ploughshare', from the shape produced at this point.

The sexpartite vault was introduced into Canterbury Cathedral during the last quarter of the twelfth century, at the time when the old 'Romanesque' style was giving place to such glorious Gothic achievements as, for example, the transept of Lincoln Cathedral, where this interesting type of vaulting may be seen at its best (Plate 101).

Its purpose had been to incorporate into the bay-design of the building the large vaulting-bay of the central span, which had, until then, been equal in width to twice the bay-unit of the building. With the advent of the Gothic style, however, this bay-unit had been gradually expanding, so that it had become far larger than in the buildings of a century earlier. As the span of the building, however, had not been increasing in proportion, this was having the result of creating a main vaulting-bay which much more nearly approached the square without having to incorporate two of the bay-units to attain a suitable longitudinal dimension. Thus the clumsy but dramatic lines of the sexpartite vault had but a short vogue in this country, after which the English masons returned once more to the development of the simpler quadripartite form.

Experiments with the ribs forming the vault framework led the masons to increase the number of these so as to reduce the area of unsupported web. The introduction of the ridge-rib made it possible for lateral ribs to obtain sufficient support from this and thus reduce the amount of centering. The first step was to divide each compartment of a quadripartite vault with a rib—called a 'tierceron'—thus halving the size of the severy; this principle applied to a quadripartite vault produced, in 1350, the glorious vault of Exeter nave (Plate 44). The next stage was to reduce the severy still further by connecting the structural ribs with short lengths known as 'liernes'; attractive star-like patterns were produced by this means.

During the fourteenth and fifteenth centuries it was the west of England which led the way in vault construction; this was probably in no small way connected with the skill which the carpenters of this part of the country had always demonstrated in the design of elaborate wooden roofs. The mid-fourteenth-century lierne vaults of the western churches, such as Gloucester (Plate 40) and Tewkesbury, are perhaps the finest examples of the true mediaeval vault in existence. An important feature of highly-developed vaulting is the multiplicity of 'bosses' masking the rib intersections and providing objects upon which the skill of the carvers could be displayed.

The final phase of stone vaulting—also emanating from the West Country—was reached when the number of ribs, passing in all directions, had been increased to such an extent that there was nothing left to do except combine the rib and web in one stone. The whole mass of masonry then came to be so cunningly constructed that the vault could take any shape desired. By the end of the fifteenth century, just before mediaeval architecture gave place altogether to Renaissance, vaulting was beginning to throw out conical excrescences drooping towards the floor and sometimes ending in elaborately carved finials, from which a multitude of imitating vaulting ribs rose up to meet those springing from the walls themselves. This kind of vaulting is known as 'fan' vaulting (Plate 45).

In churches especially, height was the primary effect aimed at. As walls rose, so did they have to be increased in thickness, in order to support, not only the weight above, but also the thrusts of spreading roofs and vaulting. In small buildings, the gable walls, being higher than the others, are usually the thicker; in the case of vaulted buildings, however, especially where a barrel-vault is employed, the lateral walls often have to be increased enormously to oppose the overturning thrust.

As soon as the groined vault became introduced, however, the thrust of the vaulting became concentrated upon definite points on the walls, corresponding to the bay divisions of the building. This led to the provision of buttresses; thickenings of the wall in positions where point-loads occurred. Aesthetically, buttresses were a valuable addition to the external appearance of buildings; they were the successors to the slim vertical strips which the Lombardic masons had employed for the purpose of architectural punctuation. The indication of the bay layout of a building by its buttresses is possibly the most striking aspect of Gothic architecture.

The externally exposed buttress is a feature which only appears in mediaeval architecture. In origin it is a development from the 'respond' or half-pier which terminates an arcade, or supports the impost of an arch springing away from a wall-face; as, for example, that which, passing over the aisle of a galleried church, helps to support the vaulting above. The first buttresses were merely responds protruded outwards from the external face of the wall against which an arch was thrusting. It appears probable that buttresses are of French origin; some of the early examples are in the form of semi-octagonal responds complete with 'Corinthian-esque' caps.[5]

At first, buttresses held to the same projection throughout their height. Later, however, as the mechanics of the new feature came to be more fully appreciated, buttresses were given a greater projection in their lower courses, the change in face being effected by weathered 'set-offs'. The tops of early buttresses were finished with small gablets; later, the adoption of the pinnacle as a weighting device greatly emphasised the summits of these important mediaeval features.

Structurally, the weakest part of a building is its angles. Twelfth-century buildings are often strengthened aesthetically at their angles by a thickening which as it were echoes the strip pilasters employed to effect punctuation of the elevations (Plate 47). The introduction of buttresses of considerable projection along the sides of the building left its angles, unmarked by any such additions, looking the weakest part of the building instead of the strongest. It was therefore necessary, for aesthetic reasons, to add buttresses—even though these were not needed to support the thrusts of vaulting—at the angles of the building.

During the thirteenth century, when buttresses first came into use, those at the angles were set out in pairs, matching those at the sides of the buildings (Plate 48). From the Edwardian period onwards, however, the pair of buttresses at the angle was abandoned—except in tall structures such as towers—in favour of a single buttress set diagonally (Plate 49); this was less clumsy, and produced an even stronger effect aesthetically.

The higher buildings became, the stronger the overturning thrust produced, and the greater projection needed for the buttresses which met it. As knowledge of mechanics improved, however, it was discovered that the projection of the buttress could be reduced if its summit were loaded with a heavy pinnacle to counterbalance the thrust of a vault or the spread of a roof. As time went on, great play was made with these pinnacles, which, during the hey-day of the Middle Ages, became the most notable features of the Gothic architectural skyline (Plate 183).

When the main walls of a high vaulted building are obstructed externally by the addition of aisles, the former will be thereby prevented from having buttresses built against them, as such would obstruct the aisle itself. It is then necessary to buttress the aisle walls, transferring the thrust of the high vault to heavily-pinnacled aisle buttresses by means of half-arches called 'flying-buttresses'.

In the second half of the twelfth century, when the first attempts were made to vault the main spans of aisled buildings, the flying buttresses were carefully concealed within the roofs of the aisles. Later, however, it became necessary to raise the main body of the building so as to get better lighting through the clerestory walls; the addition of another range of flying buttresses and their exposure above the roofs then became unavoidable. The mediaeval masons, as was to be expected of them, turned this feature, also, to notable aesthetic advantage (Plate 50).

CHAPTER V

The Development of Design

We shall later consider how the types of plans utilised by the designers of the various types of mediaeval buildings were devised and developed. For the present, however, we will consider how these plans were affected, not by the requirements of the user of the building, but by the structural necessities of the individual who had to build it.

As soon as a monumental architectural style began to be firmly established in this country, the principle of the bay-unit became accepted as the best system of design. The bay arrangement of a building constructed in the advanced timber style of, for example, Essex, has already been considered; how each great post was stepped in its assigned position on the sleeper foundation, propped up by struts, joined to its neighbours by tie-beams, and the whole framework stiffened by means of various forms of bracing.

The attention given to bay-design, and the emphasising of this by means of architectural punctuation as devised by the masons of the early Lombardic schools, has been pointed out. The system they inaugurated was that which set the style to be followed throughout the Middle Ages. Whereas the history of the development of classical Greek and Roman architecture is studied by means of the Orders, the development of Gothic architecture is indicated by the changes in bay-design.

Mediaeval architecture is of the form known as 'single-span': that is to say, even the largest building is simply a collection of individual portions, each of which is covered by a single roof having only one central ridge and two planes of rafters. In setting out a vast structure such as a mediaeval cathedral, each portion was marked out on the ground as a distinct entity, capable of being designed as such. Each of these sections would have to be considered, firstly, with regard to the span which could be adopted for it; then the length to which it should attain, and the number of bays into which it should be divided in order to facilitate the construction.

In the case of aisle-less structures, this was simple. There were no lighting problems, and excessive height could be allowed for by providing

91

buttresses of adequate projection. Even in the case of unusually tall, multi-storied buildings, such as castle towers, no structural problems need be encountered provided the walls were thick enough. In such buildings as these, however, a division into architectural bays was nevertheless often made, in order to produce an orderly appearance. The same vertical strips were used for punctuation (Plate 134); often, where it was desired to create an impression of strength, as in a castle tower, or for some other reason to give an impressive appearance, the strips were sometimes made very wide. This is particularly noticeable in the case of the thickened-out angles of large buildings of the twelfth century; in castle keeps and at the ends of the transepts of great churches these thickened angles were often utilised as the sites for spiral staircases (Plate 136).

It was the treatment of the main walls of aisled structures, however, that provided the mediaeval designer with his worst problems. The lofty walls which carry the main roofing span of a great church, when their bases are obstructed by aisles and weakened by arcades provided to give access to these, require careful consideration in order to assure stability. These main walls have two principal stories. There is, firstly, the ground storey which comprises the principal arcade; above this, after a little space has been left to allow for the abutment of the aisle roof, comes the clerestory in which are situated the windows which light the centre portion of the church.

In primitive architecture, utilised by a people who cannot read, lighting within a building is of no great importance; indeed, the presence of openings of any description is apt to make the building less of a protection against the elements. At the end of the eleventh century, however, windows of monumental buildings were becoming enlarged in order to display the skill of the craftsman in painted glass. Thus the fenestration of both aisle wall and clerestory were, throughout the Middle Ages, continually undergoing expansion, at the cost of the reduction of the amount of wall available for supporting purposes. For the same reason, the obstruction to light and view caused by the piers of the main arcade was continually being reduced; again at the cost of the structural stability of the whole towering wall. Broadly speaking, therefore, the history of the development of bay-design may be stated as a continual attempt to increase openings at the expense of supports.

Apart from certain buildings erected during the early years of the eighth century by St. Wilfred in Northumbria—about which such information as we have may, in fact, be unduly embellished and not truly representative of the actual appearance of the structures concerned—the first really monumental churches to be erected in this country were those constructed in the latter half of the tenth century.

None of these, unfortunately, remain, but by analogy with contem-

45. The lofty Late Gothic chapel of King's College at Cambridge

46. An angle formed in 'long-and-short' work

47. Thickened-out angle typical of the twelfth century

48. A buttressed angle of the Early Gothic period

49. Late mediaeval diagonal buttress

The Development of Design

porary Continental examples—such as the church of Soignies in Flanders, built in 965—we are probably safe in assuming that the main arcades of their naves were set out on the Ottonian 'duplex' principle; that is to say, with 'great bays' separated by heavy piers, between which circular pillars of masonry were interposed to mark the lesser bays of the aisles (Fig. 17). Durham Cathedral, constructed more than a century later, provides an example of this system (Plate 23). The great Ottonian churches of the Continent were generally provided with galleries above their aisles, making these two-storied (Plate 20).

Thus we arrive at the probable bay-design of the great church of the late tenth century in England. The main arcade would show the double-bay described above; above this would be another arcade, probably some-

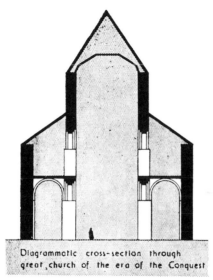

Diagrammatic cross-section through great church of the era of the Conquest

FIG. 4

what lower in elevation, representing the galleries over the aisles. Above this, again, would come a clerestory of small round-headed windows. Internal punctuation—again if we can refer to the Continental churches —would probably be provided by a thick half-shaft passing up the centres of the great piers, but serving no structural function. Externally, the aisle walls would show two rows of windows; the lower of which would probably be somewhat larger than the upper ones which lighted the galleries.

From these late tenth-century churches of eastern England developed the essentially English architectural style of that region.

The next great era of church building came a century later when the wave of Benedictine monks following the Norman Conquest began to employ the loot of a conquered country in enlarging its churches. It seems

93

fairly certain, however, that, apart from modifications in detail, the architectural layout represented by the bay-design of these post-Conquest churches varied very little in principle from those of a century earlier, except as regards the modification of the Ottonian duplex bay (Fig. 4).

One of the most ubiquitous features of Byzantine architecture is a window-opening divided into two by means of a small turned shaft which carries two little arches; apparently a miniature example of the 'duplex' principle of combining piers and columns.[6] The term used by the Lombardic masons for this type of window was *bifora* which, in Italian, simply means a double opening.

During the twelfth century it became customary to provide the clerestory of a great church with a passage, contrived in the thickness of the wall, from which the windows could be cleaned. In order to accommodate this passage, the clerestory wall had to be such a thickness that some consideration had perforce to be given to the treatment of the internal splays of the small windows to prevent the obstruction of too much light. The method adopted was to form an internal arcade which could carry the wall-face across each bay. Each of these arcades was a triplet or *trifora*; the range of these, therefore, came to be known as a *triforium*.

As time went on, any wall-passage having an internal arcade came to be known as a 'triforium', the term being more particularly applied to the arcaded treatments which eventually replaced the arcades of galleries over the aisles of early great churches. It is, however, a mistake to call these galleries, or even the ornamental arcades with which their openings into the church came to be filled, by the name of triforium, as this feature was essentially a wall-passage.

The two-storied aisle is a feature copied directly from the great Byzantine churches of the era of Justinian. In these buildings, the upper arch opening from the gallery into the central space is usually filled by a kind of stone screen incorporating three or four small arches separated by slender stone columns (Plate 1). The same feature may be seen, in a modified form, in the gallery arcades of the large churches of the post-Conquest period in England. Here, however, the inner arcade is usually composed of pairs of arches; the term 'biforium' would thus be a more accurate description of this storey. A purer Byzantine form is seen at St. Bartholomew's, Smithfield.

Galleried churches, of Byzantine origin and popular in the Rhineland and northern France in the latter half of the tenth century and during a large part of the eleventh, seem to have played no part, however, in the architectural style of central and southern France, where Roman architectural influence was predominant.

The centre of culture in France during the eleventh century appears to have been the middle Loire, upon which stood the great abbey of Fleury, the head house of the Benedictines.

The masons of this region seem to have developed their craft independently of the Lombardic school. Their arcades consisted of closely-spaced pillars supporting small arches, the whole resembling a rather clumsy version of the arcade of an early church in Rome. There was no attempt at bay-design nor any form of punctuation. There were no galleries with arcades which could have helped to break up the space between the main arches and the clerestory windows. The portion of the main wall against which the aisle roof abutted was, therefore, apt to be a blank expanse; to obviate this, the French masons ran a blind arcade along it, purely as a decoration. This arcade separating the main arches from the clerestory came to be called by the French a 'triforium'.

The 'blind story', representing that part of the main walls of an aisled structure against which the lateral roofs abut, has from the beginning been an interesting factor in the internal design of churches. In timber structures it was filled by systems of bracing members; in English examples the interwoven braces (Fig. 3), which form such an important feature within the building, were later copied in masonry in the form of interlacing arcading, one of the most ubiquitous motifs in the pre-Gothic architectural ornament of this country which persisted even into the Gothic era (Plates, 203, 204). After galleries were abandoned the blind stories of great churches were treated as open arcades showing two *bifora* openings to each of the great bays.

When the Benedictine monks of the closing years of the eleventh century began to develop the architecture of the west of England, the style which they brought with them was that of central France. Some of the earlier churches in the West Country, such as Gloucester or Tewkesbury, although laid out on a French plan, seem to have been first designed by Anglian masons. Later churches, however, and later portions of the earlier churches, show a very strong French influence, especially in the little arcaded galleries which pass along the upper portions of their walls internally; the transept of Chester Cathedral is an illustration.

As mediaeval architecture progressed, the 'triforium' stage, developed as it was from Byzantine galleries which were never really required in western European churches, shrank more and more until at last it disappeared altogether. As the primary stories were those of the main arcade and clerestory respectively, always one or the other was trying to augment its own dignity by absorbing into itself the triforium. Thus at Oxford Cathedral the twelfth-century arcade rises above and includes the diminutive vestiges of the *bifora* openings; at Pershore Abbey, in the next century, the sill of the internal arcade of the clerestory is lowered to what might have been a 'triforium' level.

In all aisled buildings, the clerestory is of the utmost importance, its function being to provide light to the principal portions of the church. Early clerestory windows were quite small, however; often they were probably merely circular holes. By the Ottonian era, however, the row of round-headed windows was the accepted form of this feature (Plate 54).

In the hands of the Anglian masons of the eleventh century, the clerestory became a fine architectural feature. It was obviously highly desirable that there should be some means of access to the inside of these high windows, in order that the glass might be cleaned; they would otherwise probably soon have become obscured by cobwebs, for instance. Clerestories were therefore provided with passages—triforia—passing within the thickness of the wall, along which persons could patrol and thus keep the windows clean. The existence of these passages again provided an opportunity for some form of arcaded treatment on the inner sides of the window openings.

The method adopted by the Anglian masons was to make a triple opening; the large central one containing the window being separated by two slender shafts from the two smaller flanking openings. In the thirteenth century, a triplet replaced the single central window. This treatment fitted very well into the wall-arch of the vault until the advent of the elaborate 'ploughshare' vaulting so encroached upon the clerestory wall that the triple opening had to be abandoned for a single one. As the width of the bay became greater, and the proportions of the vaulting compartment less suited to the sexpartite vault, this became abandoned for the older form; the return to which, combined with the greater bay-width, enabled much larger and finer clerestory windows to be provided. Eventually, as the windows began to fill almost the entire wall-space available, there became no need for a cleaning passage, as the internal sill of the window served instead; the sills being connected with each other by small openings left in the walling behind the springing of the vault. In later churches, such as York Minster, another gallery was provided passing across the outside of the windows.

Mention has been made of the Ottonian device of punctuating the interiors of the naves of churches with a sturdy half-shaft passing up the centres of the main piers and continuing for the whole height of the wall. This half-shaft is a copy of the half-column employed by the Byzantines as a punctuation device; mounted one upon the other in order to retain something of the Classical proportion, these half-columns appear in many of the great Syrian churches, notably that of St. Simeon Stylites at Kalat Seman. From the Ottonian period onwards the slender half-shaft is commonly employed for internal punctuation within the great churches of the Franks. As it became usual to cover the main span of the nave with vaulting, this feature was found very useful to assist in supporting, both

51. The lofty aisle walls of twelfth-century Canterbury Cathedral

50. The flying buttresses which support the high vault of Westminster Abbey

53. Before the abolition of the terminal gallery the transept-end was two-bayed as here at Winchester Cathedral

52. The three-bay elevation of an Anglian transept-end at Peterborough Abbey, now cathedral

54. Early twelfth-century clerestory and corbel-table at Chichester
Cathedral, Sussex

55. An elaborate chancel arch of the twelfth century at Tickencote
church, Rutland

56. A late mediaeval manor house fortified with 'drop-boxes'.
Compton Castle, Devon

57. A gatehouse with its tower-tops 'machicolated' at Cooling Castle
in Kent

structurally and aesthetically, the main springing points of the high vault.

These half-shafts, however, could only be conveniently employed when a pier was used; a half-shaft passing up the face of a circular pillar —it may be seen in a number of our churches—produces a very ugly effect. The designers of the pillared churches of Normandy and the Ile de France tried to get over the difficulty by balancing the 'vaulting-shaft' on the capital of the pillar; this, however, looks even worse. The surrounding of the pillar by four isolated shafts was a twelfth-century device for improving the situation. With the introduction of the later moulded

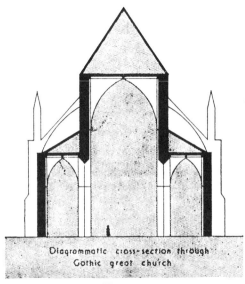

Diagrammatic cross-section through Gothic great church

FIG. 5

pillar, however, which is in effect really a lightened form of compound pier, the vaulting-shaft could, if need be, be incorporated into the plan of the pillar itself; this was, in fact, often done during the thirteenth century. The only really satisfactory method, however, was to cut away the whole of the lower part of the vaulting-shaft below the 'spandrel' of the main arcade, supporting it there on a corbel (Plate 211); this is the common practice from the middle of the thirteenth century onwards.

The main arcades of the eleventh- and twelfth-century churches were low in elevation and rose above sturdy supports. In the thirteenth century the introduction of the moulded pillar, coupled with the raising in height of the arch due to the introduction of its pointed form, completely transformed the main arcades of the great churches (Fig. 5). Romanesque stockiness gave place to Gothic grace.

Despite the gradual reduction in the pitch of arches which took place during the fourteenth and fifteenth centuries, this was more than made up for by the increase in scale, both horizontally and vertically, of the bay-unit. As improved roofing methods enabled the spans of buildings to be increased, so did the advancement of masonry skill enable the arches of the main arcade to be increased, with a consequent enlargement of the bay. At the same time, accumulated experience in building science enabled the designers to increase the heights of their buildings. The great Gothic arches soared ever higher.

The main arcade was always casting greedy eyes upon the obsolescent galleries and triforia above it. At the beginning of the twelfth century, the western designers, French-instructed, had soon made short work of these intermediate stories, which curtailed both the main arcade and the clerestory. Even the masons who built, soon after 1200, the Gothic presbytery of Pershore Abbey, retained the triforium only as a lowered sill to the clerestory windows. A few late twelfth-century churches, such as Glastonbury Abbey and Oxford Cathedral, raised the main arcade to include the 'triforium' openings within its arches.

The Anglian masons, however, steadfastly refused to abandon their graceful *bifora* openings; reducing these in size and doubling them, two to the bay, they turned them into beautiful features such as can be seen at Ely, Lincoln (Plate 101), Lichfield, and many another fine church. But by the Late Gothic period, nevertheless, the 'triforium' stage had disappeared.

Lighting became an important factor in English architecture during the twelfth century. The new stone houses of the period were given windows upon which some care was expended; frequently one such window would be made the principal architectural feature of a house. Fortified and semi-fortified buildings, such as castle keeps and halls, were often lighted by means of a form of clerestory at a high level; the windows being reached by a wall-passage as in churches. There are a few examples of 'fighting galleries', situated high up in the tower and consisting of a row of apertures in the external wall of a similar passage.

As for the outer walls of buildings—which, in aisled structures, are the walls of the aisles—the history of the development of fenestration is one of the improvements of lighting through the enlargement of windows, and the corresponding reduction of the supporting mass of the wall itself.

The large-galleried churches of the tenth, eleventh and twelfth centuries had windows to light the gallery floor; the aisle walls exhibit this two-storied treatment externally (Plate 51). Sometimes each bay is enclosed by a single tall arch of slight projection, introduced to tie the two stories together aesthetically; this is an Ottonian device which continues to be employed as long as the use of galleries continue.

The small arcades which pass along the foot of the walls of so many

The Development of Design

Romanesque buildings, both inside and out, in this country are almost certainly a relic of the 'loggias' by which the early timber buildings were surrounded. These features have been described by many writers from the sixth century onwards; they may still be seen surrounding the eleventh- and twelfth-century stave-churches of Norway. Their purpose was probably to give added protection to the base of the walls from rain which, running down these, might otherwise find its way through the joints of the bratticing and be driven inside the building by a strong wind. The wall arcades of the English Romanesque style were developed still further in the Gothic period; those surrounding St. Hugh's choir at Lincoln being particularly beautiful (Plate 204).

The most important feature in architectural punctuation is the buttress. The slender strips employed by the Lombardic architects became, in English Romanesque of the eleventh century, broad, sturdy pilasters, adding great dignity to otherwise plain wall surfaces. In towers especially, these broad pilasters, made still sturdier at the angles of the building, form the most typical features of the structures of the period (Plate 134).

That these pilasters were employed solely as punctuation is demonstrated by the manner in which they are used at gable ends. The span of a building was generally set out as approximately twice its bay-unit. As the pilasters indicated the bay-unit, it therefore became necessary to place one in the centre of each main gable (Plate 53); all early great churches and towers—including tower-keeps planned with a side of two bay-units—display this awkward arrangement. The western builders, French-taught, made little use of pilasters, but the Anglian masons were rigid in its employment. In the twelfth century, however, they relented a little, obviously becoming impressed with the desirability of having centralised fenestration in gable ends; Norwich and Peterborough (Plate 52) are examples of this convenient lapse from bay-design.

In some parts of the Angevin Empire the church designers permitted the use of tall shafts, similar to those used internally, as features to be employed for external punctuation. This device, however, found small favour in this country; Ripon Cathedral and Steetley church in Derbyshire being twelfth-century examples of it.

The need for the introduction of arbitrary features for the purposes of architectural punctuation vanished with the invention of the Gothic buttress at the end of the twelfth century in order to withstand the thrust of quadripartite vaulting. As the pressure of these vaults were so arranged as to be concentrated on the bay-features of the building, it was an obvious step to construct heavy masses of masonry at these points to withstand the overturning pressure upon the structure.

In order not to obstruct the lighting of adjacent windows, early buttresses were made as unobtrusive as possible by splaying their angles, as at Lincoln Minster; later, they acquire 'set-offs' ('tablements') to increase the projection nearer the ground. The introduction of heavy pinnacles which, at first squat and low, later became soaring spirelets, elaborately decorated, emphasised the punctuation still further; the essential verticality of Gothic composition is chiefly due to the pinnacled buttresses by which the buildings were surrounded.

Such tremendous concentration on striking vertical features, however, necessitated the introduction of horizontal elements in order to tie them together aesthetically.

The plinth, an early device, has been used from earliest times to provide an aesthetic foundation upon which a building can appear to stand firmly. Throughout the Middle Ages plinths became more and more elaborate: increasing in height and multiplying their faces, interpolating large horizontal mouldings at intervals to enrich the design.

In military architecture, great attention was paid to the plinth, for it was the base of the wall which was most exposed to the attack of the enemy by mine, pick and bore. Castle plinths are therefore of great projection, so as to thicken out the foundation at this point. Sometimes there was a high sloping portion, above the actual plinth, known as the talus; often the whole plinth was of this nature. An exceptionally elaborate plinth exists at the base of the tower-keep at Conisborough in Yorkshire. The fine plinths of late twelfth-century ecclesiastical buildings were probably developed from military examples.

The original method of roofing mediaeval buildings was to carry the bottom of the roof over the wall-face in the form of eaves. Eaves being unsightly when viewed from below, important buildings had the upper part of their walling brought forward as a 'corbel-table' (Plate 54); this device probably recalls the Classical 'modillion' cornice. During the thirteenth century, it became the practice to elaborate the corbel-table by forming small arches, sometimes foliated, between the corbels. This treatment is probably Islamic in origin, partly as a decorative form of machicolation and partly a Gothic copy of the 'honeycomb' features encountered in contemporary Moslem architecture.

The roofs of military structures such as keeps, however, could not be exposed for fear of destruction by the enemy's engines. The strong outer walls of the building were therefore carried right up to ridge level, at which was the wall-walk, protected by its parapet. This necessitated the employment of some form of gutter where the foot of the roof met the wall, and the disposal of the rainwater by means of apertures through this.

This is probably the origin of the lead box-gutter which, by the Edwardian period, had entirely superseded the overhanging eaves in more important buildings. The gutter itself was concealed behind a parapet, through which the rainwater was taken by means of gargoyles.

The Development of Design

The parapet itself, forming, as it does, the crowning feature of the wall-face, is an important factor in ecclesiastical architecture. In monumental building it is at first supported on the corbel-table; towards the end of the mediaeval period, however, this feature is often dispensed with, the need for the extra width having been obviated by improved gutter construction.

The aesthetic design of parapets seems to have been capable of any amount of variation, the general tendency having been to repeat the forms of contemporary window tracery in the stonework of the pierced parapets which were the finest form of this feature. The fifteenth-century battlemented parapet with its pierced panels imitating woodwork is the last development.

The wall-walks at the summits of military structures were protected by a high parapet, pierced at intervals by square notches known as 'crenels' in order that the garrison might fire their weapons through these. In the later mediaeval period, the crenels were set closer together until the proportion of void to solid became about the same. It then became a principle of the design to lower the main height of the parapet and raise sections of it to form 'merlons', behind which defenders could retreat if pressed. 'Battlemented' parapets of this description were also utilised as decorative features and by the fifteenth century were appearing upon religious, as well as domestic, buildings.

The disadvantage of having any sort of parapet to a military building is that it prevents the garrison on the wall-top from observing what is going on at the foot of the wall—a serious matter in the event of the walls being attacked by miners. To remedy this, wooden screens called 'hoards' were set out beyond the crenels to protect persons leaning out of these. This obstruction rendering the crenels themselves useless, late mediaeval military engineers set the whole parapet in front of the wall-face on a series of corbels, between which the base of the wall could be overlooked. This Islamic device—known as 'machicolation'—provides the most striking architectural feature of later military architecture (Plate 57).

The use of brick in houses built in pseudo-military style enabled the bricklayers of the fifteenth century to make great play with machicolation. The magnificent example which crowns Bishop Fox's gatehouse at Farnham Castle shows what could be done with this material. A form of machicolation motif was sometimes introduced in later examples of the ordinary corbel-table.

Gothic architecture did not employ the classical cornice. The exposed summits of walls were invariably covered with copings, usually with a high-pitched top to throw off snow. The crenels of a battlemented parapet, as well as the merlons, were always finished in this manner.

From the plinth up to the parapet the strong vertical emphasis in later

Gothic design was counteracted by a form of horizontal punctuation provided by moulded bands known as 'string-courses', in which the skill developed in devising the moulded sections of arches and their pillars could be utilised along the lines of the Classical entablatures of other days.

In the early days of English architecture little attention was given to the provision of light. A building was primarily a protection from all external elements—even fresh air was not greatly esteemed—and light, to an illiterate community, was of no use at all provided the interior of the building was not actually so dark that nothing could be seen at all.

The original windows of timber buildings were merely small round holes a few inches across. The fact that they were considered more of a disadvantage than otherwise is illustrated by the name given to these features; for our word 'window' is derived from the Anglo-Saxon form of 'wind-eye'.

The windows of small stone buildings, even as late as the Conquest, were boards built into the thickness of the wall and pierced with a hole or a series of these. The woodwork was set in the very middle of the stonework, which was splayed away upon either side in order to reduce as much as possible the obstruction to such meagre light as managed to filter through the hole.

This method of filling a window-opening was presumably borrowed from the Byzantines, who employed it frequently in their buildings, often using pierced stone slabs instead of boards. The pre-Conquest tower of Barnack church in Northamptonshire has windows of this description, the slabs being pierced with a fretted design (Plate 147).

A two-light window cut out of a single stone slab remains at Culbone church in Somerset; it appears to be of eleventh- or twelfth-century origin, but another, similar, example, seen in the porch of Bishopstone church in Wiltshire, appears to be two or three centuries later in date.[7]

When cloth soaked in oil came to be provided to serve as a more or less translucent draught-excluder, the hole in the board became enlarged to almost the full area of that portion of the wood exposed within the masonry opening, so as to make the most of this for the introduction of light.

By the time that properly-designed stone window-openings had been accepted as recognised features of buildings, the window frame was then carefully set out as a border of dressed stonework forming an integral part of the wall-face, or lining up with it in the case of rubble work. The whole of the splay, which was still necessary to provide the maximum light, then became internal to the window. Another frame of dressed stonework—the stones of which are called 'scoinsons'—surrounded the internal opening; the two frames being joined by the 'reveals', covered by the 'rere-arch'.

The Development of Design

Such is the typical window of the pre-Gothic period in England (Plate 58). Many were probably entirely unprotected by glass—in large buildings the presence of a few small windows could probably be tolerated—but in some cases there may have been a wooden frame set behind the stone window-dressings.

Military buildings generally had plenty of openings through their walling—provided, however, not for the purpose of firing weapons through them, but in order that a good watch could be kept over the surrounding countryside. In the thirteenth century, an improvement was effected by making slits cruciform; this provided a much wider range of vision without exposing the watcher, who, by moving about within the embrasure of the window, could survey as much of the countryside as if the opening had been as large as the limits of the two slits.

The primitive window formed by building a wooden board into the thickness of a rubble wall has already been described. In situations such as the upper storey of a bell tower, where no protection was required by residents, the Lombardic *bifora* was a popular architectural feature. This, mentioned elsewhere, consisted of a double-opening divided up by a turned stone shaft which supported two tiny arches (Plate 62).

Such a window could not easily be fitted with any sort of protection such as glass, or even a board. By the twelfth century, however, the *bifora* had become modified by giving the early squat shaft a more slender form and bringing it out to the wall-face, where it could form part of the stone window-dressing which had become the recognised form of fenestration (Plate 63).

During the latter part of the eleventh century, it was an almost invariable device in the case of large buildings to set the face of the window back from the wall so as to provide it with an inner 'order'; the angles were ornamented with small shafts.

Throughout the latter part of the twelfth century the *bifora*, with its slender central shaft, was employed to light chambers in the upper stories of private houses; the principal feature of the whole building being generally one such window in the gable overlooking the street or on the entrace front.

At the end of this century, when the semicircular heads of window lights were adopting a 'lancet' form (Plate 59), the central shaft fell into disuse, being replaced by a 'mullion' (Plate 64); in the rebates of this and the window jambs, frames could be inserted to take glass. These frames were generally of iron and, in domestic examples, sometimes had a moveable casement secured to the frame by means of 'hooks-and-bands'.

The two-light window continued throughout the Middle Ages as the form generally employed in domestic architecture. Often the stone mullion has an internal bulge, through which a hole is pierced to take a wooden bar fixed for the purpose of securing the window shutters provided internally against being forced from outside. Mediaeval doors, which also invariably opened internally, were secured by the same means, the bar being slid back, when not in use, into the thickness of the adjoining wall. Attractive features of the windows of thirteenth- and fourteenth-century houses are provided by the window seats which line the embrasure on either side (Plate 68).

Circular windows had been in use from the earliest times, especially in the upper parts of gables. The low clerestory wall of an early aisled building was also a suitable situation for windows of this description.

During the latter part of the twelfth century, large round windows were often constructed having spokes radiating as in a wheel; each spoke was formed by a small shaft similar to that seen in the *bifora* of the period. As window tracery developed, these wheel windows were replaced by large circular windows filled with elaborate tracery patterns; these are known as 'rose windows', and may frequently be seen in the transept ends of fourteenth-century cathedrals, such as at Lincoln.

It may have been the Crusades which introduced to English designers the window formed by a pierced stone slab; this is a very common type of window in Syrian churches, the holes being cut to simple geometrical patterns, generally of a lobed or 'foliated' type. During the twelfth century, it became the practice to fill-in the spandrel above the shaft of the *bifora* with a foliated opening designed on similar lines (Plate 63). This so-called 'plate tracery' is presumably the origin of that style of fenestration known as the 'Geometrical'.

From the earliest period of church-building in stone, large windows had been developing merely in respect of their overall size; towards the end of the twelfth century, the pointed head had everywhere taken the place of the semicircular. At this time, a safe limit had been reached in regard to the width of a sheet of leaded glazing; beyond this span, even the window ironwork could not prevent the glass from being blown in. It was still the custom to place windows centrally in each bay of the building; by the end of the century, however, builders were beginning to site their windows in pairs, sometimes with a small buttress between them, as at Lincoln. By the first quarter of the thirteenth century the small buttresses had disappeared, and the windows were approaching each other until only a very small portion of wall was left to separate them. The enclosure of the pair of windows within a single containing arch, and the reduction in size of the dividing masonry until it merely formed a 'mullion', resulted in the creation of the first large multi-light window.

The greater use of glazing, and the resulting necessity for having glazing bars in the form of stone mullions, necessitated the invention of some scheme for dealing with the upper portions of mullions when these

58. Pre-Gothic

59. Early Gothic

60. Mid-Gothic

61. Late Gothic

64. The coupling of Early Gothics lancets leads to the invention of the mullion

63. The 'spandrel' pierced and the whole covered by a 'hood-mould'

62. Pre-Gothic *bifora* or two-light window

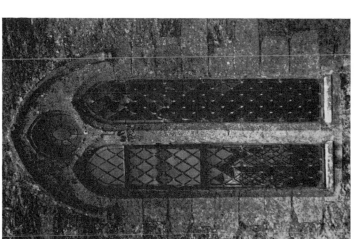

65. An example of primitive or 'plate' tracery

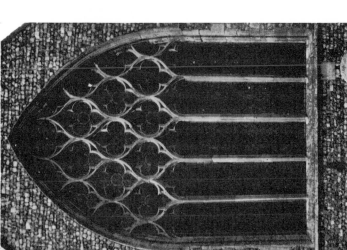

66. The 'reticulated' or fish-net pattern is typical of the 'curvilinear' tracery of the Mid-Gothic style

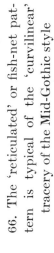

67. The panelled or 'rectilinear' tracery universal in Late Gothic windows

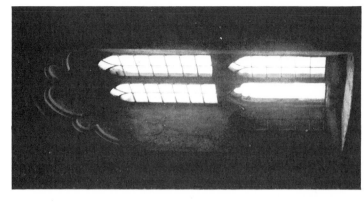

70. The 'transom' enables the lower lights to be made to open

69. An oriel window of the late mediaeval period at Cerne Abbey in Dorset

68. The early mediaeval chamber window is frequently provided with window-seats

reached the curved head of the window. The wrights engaged on the construction of timber churches had been experimenting with methods of improving aesthetically the arrangement of the curved braces with which they were stiffening the posts of their structures. A common form of bracing, frequently met with in the churches of Essex, is the trellis pattern formed by crossing the curved braces over each other (Fig. 3). This is possibly the origin of the 'reticulated' style of window tracery (Plate 66). The great stone saltires sweeping across the crossing-arches of Wells Cathedral and preventing their piers from bulging towards each other under the pressure of the adjoining arcades, provide perfect examples of the adoption of timber forms in masonry design (Plate 26).

The fourteenth century saw windows growing ever larger and requiring more and more stone frameworks of mullions and tracery to assist in holding the glazing together against the pressure of the wind. The masons turned their skill to developing various patterns of tracery bars in the heads of the windows, producing what is known as 'curvilinear' tracery.

An important feature of the window was the ironwork to which the glass was fixed. Every 'light' had one or two vertical 'stanchions', and a series of horizontal 'saddle-bars', the latter bedded at either end in the mullions, and further secured by the stanchions which passed through them. Each pane of glass, whether a plain diamond-shaped 'quarry' or an elaborate piece of coloured glass, was fastened to its neighbour with a grooved lead strip known as a 'calm' (pronounced 'came').

Reference has been made to the foliations which are found in the early geometrical forms of window ornament. These foliations are first met with in the pierced stone slabs forming the windows of sixth-century Syrian churches, and are thus of Byzantine origin. The Islamic builders, much of whose architectural style was derived from the Byzantines, employed the foil as an ornamental treatment to the soffit of the arch; by the tenth century, multifoil arches were appearing in profusion in the great mosque of the Caliphs at Cordova.

Foliated arches, at first trefoiled, first appear in this country at the middle of the twelfth century; they are only employed, however, in connection with doorways. By the beginning of the thirteenth century the trefoiled head frequently appears in wall-arcading; foliations of an undulatory form may also be found in wooden bracing members.

It is not until the middle of the century that foliations come to be generally employed in window tracery. At first the tracery forms are merely geometrical; later, the heads of lights are given foliated heads. The ultimate stage is reached when the foils are distorted into 'flames' and 'falchions', so as to adjust them to the design of the tracery bars; the elaboration of the French 'Flamboyant' style, however, was not attained in this country owing to the supervention of the Black Death and consequent decay in design which produced the subsequent more restrained panelled forms of ornament.

The projecting tooth which separates each 'foil' is known as a 'cusp'. As window tracery developed and glazing bars began to be elaborately moulded as if they had been of wood, attention was given to the form of these cusps. At first they were planted roughly on the soffit of the bar; later they were cunningly arranged to flow smoothly out of its mouldings.

After the change in Gothic feeling associated with the shortage of English craftsmen due to the Black Death of 1349, window tracery was among the features which altered suddenly. The masonic strength of the country appears to have suffered considerable losses, possibly due to the fact that these tradesmen were mostly congregated in towns. The joiners, however, do not seem to have been so badly affected; the designs of roofs and furniture seem to have, if anything, improved. It may have been for this reason that the architecture which followed the Black Death developed the characteristics of joinery; the principal type of decoration became various forms of panelling applied to the wall-faces or repeated in the designs of window-tracery (Plate 67). The very much reduced pitch of roofs and depression of arches assisted with this debased style.

The fifteenth century saw the rebuilding of most of the old naves of those parish churches which had not been so extended during the previous century. In most cases, fifteenth-century naves were accompanied by western bell-towers erected at the same time. Some churches as could not afford a new nave nearly always succeeded in improving the fenestration of the old structure by providing it with large windows in the new style. Most chancels, also, whatever the date of their original erection, were entirely re-fenestrated during the fifteenth century. Clerestories of parish churches are generally of this period.

The principal windows of great mediaeval buildings were either placed centrally in the end gables or, if in the side walls, were centred in the bays of the structure. If the building were aisled, the principal lateral windows have to be transferred to the walls of the aisles, leaving the centre of the church less well-lit. In this event, the fenestration of the clerestory had to be given special attention. The widening of windows—always a feature of the development of Gothic architecture—made it generally desirable, in the interests of proportion, to give them a height commensurate with their width; thus the clerestories of the great churches became ever higher, creating new problems in connection with the thrust of the high vault and the elaboration of the flying buttresses by which it was supported.

A noticeable factor in the development of the parish church plan is the gradual increase in the width of its aisles. At first these were roofed by a downward extension of the main roof and could thus only be of humble projection; only when they were provided with roofs of their own, with a reduced pitch, could they expand laterally without having their outer walling dwarfed until headroom disappeared. The expansion of aisles involved the architects in the provision of clerestories and the provision of larger windows in the aisles themselves.

By the middle of the thirteenth century, the windows of domestic buildings had been considerably enlarged in conformity with the prevalent style of fenestration. In order to allow for opening casements, a stone 'transom' was provided near the bottom of the window (Plate 70); this low-placed transom, an invariable feature of large domestic windows, later found its way into the panelled windows of fifteenth-century churches.

In early aisled churches, where the windows were necessarily small, the most poorly-lit part of the building was the 'crossing' where the nave, chancel and transepts met. It was early realised that the simplest way of lighting this part of the church was to raise the walls of the crossing high enough above the roofs of the building to enable windows, similar to those of the clerestory, to be provided above these. This is the origin of the central towers of the great cathedrals; they were not originally bell towers, but lighting devices known as 'lantern towers'. (Plate 155) By the middle of the thirteenth century, the ranges of windows in the lighting stage of the lantern had often become very beautiful features; later, however, when the windows of the churches had become larger, the lanterns were frequently obliterated through the insertion of the elaborate vaulting which had become so popular.

As the wide-flung dome had been the culminating feature of Byzantine architecture; so were the soaring towers and spires the crowning triumph of the Gothic builders.

Byzantine designers, sophisticated and scientific, had relied for their effect upon the skilful concealment of the structural features behind light screen walls. The profligate Gothic visionaries, however, left all their secrets exposed to view; making, indeed, the most of every available feature by covering it with mouldings and carving, and further emphasising it with pinnacles.

It took the English mediaeval builders more than five centuries to discover what the Byzantine architects had so long concealed from them. Wedded as they were to the long axial 'Romanesque' plans, they would never have discovered the answer had it not been for the determination with which they adhered to the principle of bay-design.

It was probably the vertical punctuation of their buildings which first showed them the way to the buttress, without which their high vaults would never have been possible. As the wall-spaces between the windows shrank more and more with the expansion of the fenestration, the buttresses made up for the loss of mass by protruding still further outwards. The mediaeval engineer was at last discovering the principles of abutment.

The climax is seen in the chapel of King's College, Cambridge (Plate 45), begun in 1446 but not completed until a century later. Here the design is one of great arches, not placed 'in series' as in the case of the early arcaded buildings, but arranged 'in parallel', one to each bay of the structure. These huge transverse arches support the richly-wrought fan-vaulting and the roof above; between them is nothing but great sheets of stained glass.

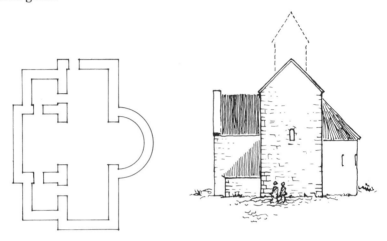

FIG. 6. Attempted reconstruction of early 11th-century church at North Elmham. A timber belfry is indicated.

CHAPTER VI

The Parish Church

In the temples of pagan days, the ancient peoples worshipped their gods in the form of statues of these; the practice being to place the figure in a recess in the wall, so that it would appear to the devotee that the god was emerging, as if through a doorway leading from his home, for the purpose of attending to the wishes of the suppliant.

(The Moslems, whose creed was based, fundamentally, on the abolition of idols, retained the door; siting it, however, in the wall of their place of worship which lay nearest to Mecca, so that they could see, in the eye of the mind, their prophet waiting there. This empty niche, known as the *mihrab*, is the essential feature of all mosques.)

In the days of early civilisations, temples were generally either enclosed in, or their entrances confronted by, some form of sacred enclosure. The early mosques of the great days of the Arab dynasties were simply large courtyards with a *mihrab*, or a series of these, in the Mecca-ward wall.

The Jewish synagogue of Roman days was based on the plan of the pagan temple. It was not, however, orientated towards any quarter, nor were the worshippers within aligned towards any one side or end. Whatever may have been the original arrangement of the Jewish temple, the synagogue of the time of Christ was apparently laid out on a plan the proportions of which more nearly approached the square than had been the case with the axially-planned temples of pagan days (Fig. 7).

The internal colonnades were not arranged in two parallel rows, however—as in a classical temple—but surrounded the centre of the building, thus giving it an aisle on each side. Within the central space was an elevated platform or *bema* from which the learned men interpreted to the surrounding congregation the mysteries of the Law. At one end of the building—on occasion, but not invariably, that nearest Jerusalem—there was the usual niche; in the synagogue, however, this relic of pagan times was enclosed by doors to form a cupboard, the *'aron'*, in which were kept the sacred scrolls.

It seems most probable that the internal arrangements of early Christian churches developed from those which obtained in contemporary synagogues. The principal change was in the abandoning of the centralised plan for the axial. This was probably due to the fact that the altar—which in pagan temples had been always, for reasons of hygiene, situated in the open air—now became transferred to the interior of the building, in order that the ritual Celebration of the Sacrament could be performed thereon in full view of the congregation. The niche, expanded to the scale of the apse which accommodated the magistrates within the basilica, became the focal point of the building; in it the priesthood had their seats, with the altar immediately in front of them. The elevated platform was moved from its central position to a site in front of the apse, where it provided a railed-in space for ceremonial connected with the services and as a choir for the singers (Fig. 7). It is these two features, the apse and the choir, which remain the principal features of the Christian church plan for many centuries. For the rest, plan-development becomes mainly

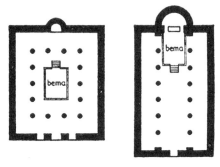

SYNAGOGUE AND CHURCH

Fig. 7

concerned with the improvement of the arrangements for the accommodation of worshippers.

The building itself was originally, presumably, merely a plain rectangular structure with a wooden roof, having no architectural feature other than the apse at its end. As enlargement became desirable, this would have been achieved by the addition to the plan of lateral aisles, separated from the central portion by colonnades (Fig. 1).

The early Christian churches of Rome were, architecturally speaking, very humble structures when compared with the magnificent piles which were erected by the Christians of Byzantium; the only influence which the latter buildings appear to have had upon the design of the former was to expand the end of the structure nearest the apse by providing a transverse arm or transept.

Practically nothing is known of the churches of Roman Britain; the solitary example discovered at Silchester suggests that it was a very diminutive copy of those in Rome.

The designer of a Christian church has to concern himself with two primary factors connected with its accommodation. There must be a nave

110

to hold the congregation, and a sanctuary to house the altar. This plan, which always survived in those parts of the British Isles untouched by the Anglo-Saxon invasions, continues to be used as the basic form of the parish-church plan to the present day.

It has been emphasised earlier that any important building, such as a church, should always display the monumental factor of height. The early Celtic church adhered to this principle; however tiny its buildings, the heights of these were always greatly exaggerated. Churches of this description built at the end of the seventh century as a result of the missionary efforts of Sts. Wilfred and Benedict Biscop in Northumbria still remain to this day. The Durham churches of Jarrow, Escomb and Monkwearmouth are examples. At the same time, however, the missionaries were apparently also erecting humble copies of the Roman and Byzantine churches of their times; these have unfortunately all perished.

Shortly afterwards, at the southern end of the Celtic frontier, St. Aldhelm was also building a few small churches. One of these, at Bradford-on-Avon in Wiltshire (Plate 13), remains. It illustrates the Celtic plan, augmented, however, by the addition of two small lateral 'wings'; these features, which combine the functions of porch and chapel, appear to have been introduced to add a cruciform element to the plan, thus bringing it more into line with current Byzantine practice.

The entrances to Celtic churches were generally in their side walls, not, as was the Roman fashion, at the west end. The lateral porches do not, however, appear again in English ecclesiastical architecture until late in the mediaeval period.

These two missionary expeditions at the end of the seventh century mark the beginning of the permanent Christian settlement of England. A century earlier, however, the Roman monk, St. Augustine, had laid the foundations of the Anglo-Saxon conversion in the course of his visit to Kent, as a result of which Canterbury was permanently established as the headquarters of the faith in this country. St. Augustine founded a number of churches, practically all of them in Kent. Traces of some remain at Canterbury, Reculver, and elsewhere. The most perfect example, however—although only its nave remains—is at Bradwell in Essex (Plate 12).

These very early churches were exceedingly humble in character. They consisted of a small rectangular nave with a semicircular apse at its east end (Fig. 8); the two portions being connected by means of an arcade of three arches. The buildings were executed in rubble and bricks taken from the ruins of the Roman towns in which St. Augustine founded his churches.

A remarkable feature of each building was the wooden portico with which it was surrounded. These constructions were presumably similar in design to those which formed an integral part of all important wooden buildings in the neighbouring areas of the Continent. That the Byzantines used them occasionally may be seen at the church of St. Fosca at Torcello; they were also employed in the seventh-century churches of northern Spain. Perfect examples still surround the eleventh- and twelfth-century timber churches of Norway.

The eastern ends of the porticoes surrounding St. Augustine's churches were built-up with solid walls to form a pair of small apartments known as *parabemata*; these were in the nature of sacristies. The entrances to the naves were at their western ends, where was sometimes built a solid porch. In later years, lateral entrances, also covered by porches constructed within the portico, were sometimes added to the buildings; these additions recall the 'wings' of Bradford-on-Avon.

7th-CENTURY KENTISH CHURCH.

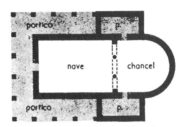

p.p. parabemata

Fig. 8

It was an important feature of St. Augustine's policy to utilise, if possible, the existing pagan temples which were to be found throughout the countryside. Up to the present, no archaeological exploration has succeeded in discovering any remains of these buildings, which were, of course, constructed of wood.

It is now known that, by the third century B.C., the ordinary Classical temple, in a wooden form, had penetrated into this country; the buildings consisted of a very small square, or almost square, *cella* surrounded by a colonnade four feet or so in width. These buildings were presumably perpetuated throughout the Roman occupation, and may very well have existed with but little modification up to the time of St. Augustine. This fact may explain the wooden porticoes which surround his churches: Classical features which, under Byzantine influence, eventually vanished from ecclesiastical architecture. There may also be some affinity between the humble little temples and the Anglo-Saxon 'four-poster' churches.

After St. Augustine's only partially successful attempts to convert the Anglo-Saxons, little is known of ecclesiastical matters relating to the country until the more permanent conversion which occurred at the end of the seventh century. It is clear, however, that bishops were introduced

71. The central feature of this Wessex church is a 'turriform' church of 'winged square' type. Breamore, Hampshire

72. A 'pseudo-cruciform' church of the eleventh century at Worth in Sussex

74. The interior of an Essex timber six-poster, extended eastwards during the twelfth century. Blackmore church, Essex

73. Built in 875, this Rhenish 'six-poster' represents the Carolingian form of the Byzantine church. Abbey of Werden on Ruhr

76. The timber church at Blackmore, Essex, twelfth- or thirteenth-century date

75. The great kitchen of the Abbot of Glastonbury

77. A large parish church of the era of the Crusades at Hemel Hempstead in Hertfordshire

into the country during this century, and dioceses in part organised. It may have been a seventh-century Bishop of Elmham who built the little church, known to-day as the 'Old Minster', at Southelmham in Suffolk; the building is a humble little structure of flint rubble, on much the same plan as those erected by St. Augustine, but with the addition of a small western annexe (Fig. 9).

The inauguration of the Holy Roman Empire by Charlemagne produced great advances in the architectural knowledge of western Europe; England, doubtless, also benefited from this. After his conquest of Lombardy, Charlemagne built, as a chapel to his palace at Aachen, a humble copy of one of the great octagonal churches in the construction of which the Byzantine architects had surpassed themselves. The subsequent Byzantine supremacy in architectural matters throughout the north-western part of the Empire is shown in the design of its churches; the centralised plan, based on a square, circle or cross, remains for centuries

SOUTHELMHAM, SUFFOLK.
THE OLD MINSTER.

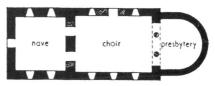

FIG. 9

the popular form, until the long naves of the Roman churches at last intrude upon the designs.

The Aachen octagon seems never to have been forgotten. Every now and again this type of plan crops up, even in the largest churches as, for example, St. Augustine's at Canterbury. It was not until the Norman Conquest that the French-trained Benedictines at last announced publicly that the centralised plan was unsuitable for a great church. Even then, the example of the most venerated church of the Holy Sepulchre in Jerusalem led the Order of the Knights Templars to construct the naves of their churches on a circular plan, as may be seen in London, Northampton, and a number of other places.

It is unfortunate that none of the Byzantinesque timber churches of the ninth century are, so far as we are aware, still in existence. There are, however, a number of representations of them in the art of the period. They seem to have been founded on the principle of four posts supporting a central tower-like structure, surrounded upon all sides by aisles, often with the addition of an outer portico enclosing these. There was presumably always a small timber chancel projecting from the eastern side.

The Parish Church

It perhaps has not been sufficiently appreciated that, while the germ of the English church plan has always consistently remained that of the Celtic nave and chancel, the monumental aspect of the buildings has shared more affinity with the vigorous church architecture of the eastern Empire than with the enfeebled culture of Rome, notwithstanding the fact that it was undoubtedly the latter which supplied the spiritual incentive to produce the buildings concerned.

The long church was gradually forced upon the English builders, who eventually came to accept it as the logical descendant of the Celtic plan. Nevertheless, throughout the period during which English church architecture was being conceived, it was the centralised church of the Byzantine architects which provided the example for a monumental style in ecclesiastical architecture (Fig. 10). The Saxon wrights, and their Con-

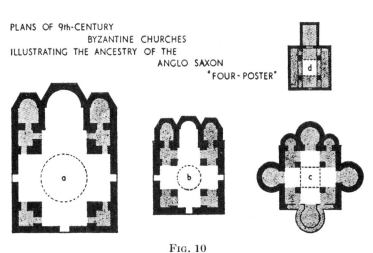

PLANS OF 9th-CENTURY BYZANTINE CHURCHES ILLUSTRATING THE ANCESTRY OF THE ANGLO SAXON 'FOUR-POSTER'

Fig. 10

tinental counterparts, translated this style into timber with their 'four-posters', of which, fortunately, a number of examples yet remain in the twelfth-century wooden 'towers' attached to Essex churches (Plate 76). Stone representations of the form may also be seen in the ninth-century crypt at Repton (Plate 97), and the remains of the twelfth-century chapel of the Bishop's Palace at Hereford.

The headquarters of Christianity in the Rhineland was Trier. The cathedral of this place was in origin a most remarkable structure, the date of construction of which is uncertain. It comprised, however, a square of walls, within which a lofty central nucleus was supported upon four huge piers of masonry, joined to each other and to the surrounding walls by massive arches. The whole structure is, in essence, Byzantine; the construction, however, is very like timber reproduced in stone. It may be that this early cathedral of Trier represents the highest architectural form attained by the 'four-poster' style of the region at the time when it was built.

About the year 810 there was built at Germigny-des-Prés, near Orleans, a church which, although on a much smaller scale than that at Trier, was set out on a very similar plan. It has a lofty central portion consisting of a slender tower supported upon four stone piers. A surrounding aisle makes the ground plan of the building a square; at the highest level, however, the building is roofed in the form of a cross, the tower being flanked on all four sides by short lengths of roof. Emphasising the cruciform appearance of the building were four apses, projecting from the ends of the arms of the cross (Fig. 10c).[8] The whole building, which has now been completely transformed by the addition of a long nave in Roman style, was probably designed as a rough copy of the chevet erected by Justinian in place of Constantine's octagon at Bethlehem. This remarkable edifice, destroyed by an earthquake during the twelfth century, was a tower-like construction surrounded by three apses (see Fig. 21). It seems fairly certain that this 'four-poster' form represents the western European version of the little cruciform churches which were being built in such stone-building countries as the Balkans and Spain.

During the seventh century, the builders of Byzantium and Anatolia were beginning to extend their churches westward by adding a short 'west nave' to the central space which had hitherto provided the only accommodation (Fig. 12). The great church of St. Irene in Byzantium seems to have been the prototype of this plan.

The remains of sleeper foundations existing within the remarkable tower of the church at Barton-on-Humber in Lincolnshire indicate that this had been preceded by a timber four-poster. The building-history of this church suggests a clue to the possible development of the church plan in the eastern parts of England. It is quite clear in this case that a stone chancel and a 'west nave' were first added to the original timber building, which was eventually replaced by the large stone tower (Plate 146), the walls of which probably picked up the ends of the timber beams, thus enabling the posts to be removed and the interior freed from these obstructive features. (This is frequently the manner in which timber structures become replaced by stonework: the new walls, replacing their timber predecessors, take over the task of supporting wooden upper stories and roofs which remain themselves unaltered.)

The replacement in stone of the light screen walls of the humble four-poster buildings seems to have been the first stage in the development of the stone church during the later Anglo-Saxon era, perhaps during the same period as that represented, in the architecture of the greater churches, by Archbishop Dunstan's ecclesiastical renaissance.

Square stone naves of the very end of the tenth century or the beginning of the next may be discovered, as might have been expected, in an area of England which, culturally advanced through proximity to the Continent, was at the same time blessed with a good supply of rubble stone suitable for use in walling without having first to be dressed under the direction of skilled masons. The Northamptonshire church of Barnack (Plate 147)—centre of the quarry area—and the Lincolnshire churches of Broughton and Hough-on-the-Hill, possess early stone naves of this description. All have subsequently been raised, to serve as bell towers to a later nave added to the east of the original structure; the position of the doorway to the latter, rather to the west of the middle of its south wall, in each case indicates its original purpose.

It seems probable that the more backward Saxon areas would have contented themselves with consolidating the walls of their timber four-posters in masonry rather than in conducting experiments in enlarging the buildings either laterally or vertically. The western areas provide plenty of useful rubble stone for this purpose; the Saxons, observing the destruction of the Anglian wooden churches during the holocausts of the ninth century, may well have concentrated on fireproofing their own buildings.

When at last the genius of the Saxon king, Alfred, had brought a semblance of order to the country, a memorial to the final defeat of the enemy was founded, at Athelney in Somerset, where Saxon Wessex met the fringe of the old Celtic Christendom.

From contemporary descriptions, it seems fairly certain that the abbey church which Alfred built about the year 900 was laid out on a plan similar to that of Germigny-des-Prés. Thus it had the same four posts—which may have been of stone, but were almost certainly of timber—and a surrounding aisle; this last must have been stone-built, for a semicircular apse projected from each face. This building, which the contemporary chronicler describes as being 'in a new fashion', seems to have founded the style upon which future Wessex churches were to be constructed.

From the examination of the few remaining examples of tenth-century churches in this region, it seems fairly certain that the plan adopted was one of a fairly lofty square of stone walls, having a small projection on each of the four sides, the eastern of these being, of course, the chancel, with, opposite to this, the 'west nave' (Fig. 11). The projecting portions are not apses but have square ends in the Celtic fashion. The old chroniclers have several ways of referring to these appendages; calling them chancels, porches or wings. It would seem perhaps less confusing if the latter term should be adopted. Nothing remains to show the roofing arrangement of the square central portion; probably it surrounded a tower built up on four posts. It is possible that many churches were built

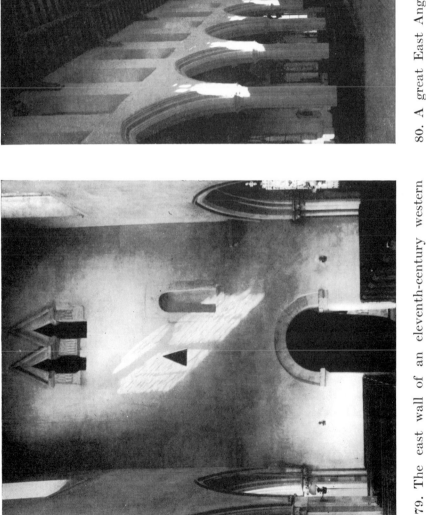

79. The east wall of an eleventh-century western tower, showing the window of its first-floor chapel. Deerhurst church, Gloucestershire

80. A great East Anglian parish church of the Late Gothic period at Blythburgh in Suffolk

81. Primitive pseudo-Classical mouldings round an eleventh-century chancel arch, and twelfth-century aisle arcade. Wittering church, Northamptonshire

82. Eleventh-century nave arcades with arches turned in Roman brick. Brixworth church, Northamptonshire

throughout Wessex, on this 'winged square' plan, but entirely of timber. The central portion of the church of Breamore (Plate 71), in the New Forest, is an illustration of the stone-walled variety. It appears that the lateral wing is a Saxon feature; it is not met with in the Anglian districts.

It has been noted earlier that, although the native taste in architecture of western Europe seems to have been for the Byzantinesque, the origins of the missionary efforts which inspired the erection of the churches were in every case Roman. We may presume, therefore, that influences were always being brought to bear upon the native designers to Romanise the plans of their churches. Moreover, it cannot be denied that the long Roman church provides a far more convenient structure for the purpose of ceremonial than the centralised Byzantine form.

A centralised church-plan, therefore, seems never to have survived for long without the addition of a new nave. It appears probable that, before the tenth century had come to an end, most of these Wessex churches would have had their western appendages, and perhaps even the whole wall on that side of the 'square', removed in order to allow for the addition of a longer and wider nave. The present appearance of Breamore church suggests that its plan has developed along these 'crypto-cruciform' lines (Fig. 11).

There are still a number of these churches, developed from the 'winged squares' of Wessex, remaining throughout the country. The central feature has, of course, long ago lost its original roofing arrangements, and is now an unobstructed open space; the posted interior having been removed after the timber bratticing had been replaced by rubble walls which then came to the support of the ends of the projecting cross-beams.

The four arches surrounding the 'square' may still remain, especially in the case of monastic churches. The two narrow lateral ones may have been deprived of one or both of the wings to which they once gave access; the chancel arch, however, will constitute the principal architectural feature of the church. The western arch joining the central square to the nave—probably the largest arch of the four, may yet remain, or may have been removed, together with the wall in which it had been set, as an obstruction.

Whether or not the central space remains intact, however, we nevertheless have in this development of the winged square what is in effect a cruciform church, planned as a Latin cross; the prototype, perhaps, of the great cathedral of the Middle Ages.

The early eleventh-century church of St. Mary-in-the-Castle at Dover is an example which has all four arches—leading to chancel, nave and the two wings respectively—still intact. The plan spread later into Mercia, where there are traces of it at Wooten Wawen in Warwickshire, Deerhurst in Gloucestershire and—finest of all—the great church of Stow in Lincolnshire, built in 1040. The last two examples, however, are in reality 'great' churches, and not parochial; the large cruciform church was yet too ambitious a structure for the provincial mason to attempt.

It is now generally accepted that the ancient 'crypto-cruciform' church at Hadstock in Essex is that built in 1020 by Canute as a memorial to the battle of Ashdown nearby. The detail of the remaining crossing

DIAGRAMMATIC PLANS OF ANGLO-SAXON CHURCHES

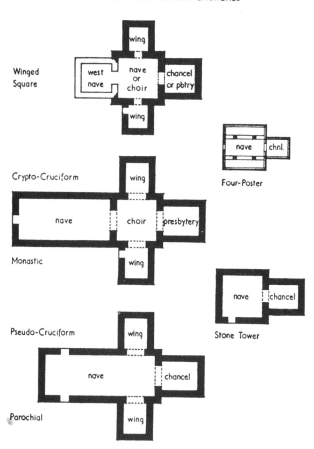

FIG. 11

arch is more advanced than at the larger church of Stow; both, however, show the elaborate plinth mouldings of the period.

By the middle of the century, the central square seems to have vanished entirely from the plans of the Saxon parish churches; the space having been added to the nave, which then forms an unbroken rectangle from the west end to the chancel arch. At the eastern ends of the side walls, however, there still remain the two arches leading to the wings (Fig. 11 'Pseudo-Cruciform'). The entrances to the nave are situated, not in the west wall in accordance with Roman usage, but towards the western ends of the side walls.

Worth (Plates 21, 72) and Stoughton churches in Sussex are good examples of this' pseudo-cruciform' plan, which may be taken as the standard Saxon parish-church plan at the time of the Conquest. There are many other examples; Britford in Wiltshire had elaborate arches leading into the wings.

The culmination of this 'winged' plan was reached when the nave began to be set out with aisles. By this time, the wings and the arches leading to them had become of considerable size; the latter were represented in aisled churches by the enlargement of the easternmost arches of the arcade. Great Paxton church in Huntingdonshire is a notable example of a late Saxon aisled church.

This 'aisled pseudo-cruciform' plan was very popular in Flanders during the first half of the eleventh century, where it is often found in association with a contemporary west tower. The churches of Celles and Hastieres—the latter built in 1033—are good examples.

Although, as an accepted plan form, the 'pseudo-cruciform'—that is to say, the church with wings or transepts but no proper 'crossing'—went out of fashion during the twelfth century, a number of late mediaeval churches still echo the arrangement in their plans; possibly some of these replaced pre-Conquest churches or even still incorporate part of the walling of a primitive predecessor.

By the end of the tenth century, the reorganisation of ecclesiastical affairs sponsored by Archbishop Dunstan had resulted in the classification of religious buildings into four distinct grades. First came the great churches, known as 'head-minsters'; at the end of the scale came the chapels, or 'field-churches', which had no burial ground. Between these two limits were the two types of parish church: the 'middling-minster' and the 'lesser-minster'. It may be that the pseudo- and crypto-cruciform parish churches we have been considering were classified as 'middling-minsters'; the lower grade being reserved for timber churches and perhaps the very smallest types of stone nave-and-chancel buildings which were, nevertheless, of parochial status.

The bell-tower—which formed no part of the accommodation space within the building but existed merely for the purpose of carrying bells —had yet to arrive in this country. Developed in Lombardy during the ninth century, the campanile had been gradually spreading across to western Europe, where it formed, however, a very expensive luxury for the local builders to attempt.

After the end of the first millenium, however, some of the western porches of early northern churches, such as that of Monkwearmouth and Jarrow, had been raised to form slender bell-towers (thus, perhaps, assisting to set the fashion as to the position which this feature—placed any-where in a Lombardic church—should adopt in the plans of English churches; this matter will, however, be discussed later at more length).

The bell-tower eventually came to be established as the crowning feature of a parish church; the Lord of the Manor possessing a church so adorned becoming entitled to the rank of Thane.

Although the fine masonry styles of later days were developed within the districts found at either end of the building-stone belt, the first at-tempts to build stone structures would have been made in regions which produced a good supply of easily-collected rubble suitable for construct-ing rough walls. To this is probably due the important part that what is now Northamptonshire played in the development of a provincial style during the decades immediately preceding the Conquest.

The principal feature of this branch of Anglian architecture is the bell-tower, which appears in this country at the beginning of the second millenium. The first towers were comparatively slender structures. Built at the west end of the nave, their primary purpose was presumably merely to carry the bells. Deerhurst in Gloucestershire—an important monastic church—possesses a west tower of exceptional interest. A curious feature of this tower is the small chapel on the first floor, with its elaborate east window looking into the church; access was originally by means of a wooden stair rising from the interior of the nave to a narrow doorway in the east wall of the chapel (Plate 79).

The Anglian towers in what is now Northamptonshire, however, are much sturdier and more elaborate structures. That of Barnack (Plate 147), with its lateral doorway, is an early stone nave, raised by one storey to form a tower after a larger nave had been built eastwards of it. The tower at Earls Barton, however, which has a western doorway, was probably always a bell-tower, being thus more in the fashion of a raised west porch. Both these towers have first floors which were probably chapels; they were approached by external wooden stairways rising to doorways provided—as in the case of the early naves—in the south walls of the structures.[9]

These elevated western chapels were a common feature of Ottonian architecture; most of the great churches of the Rhineland possessed them. The parish church of Herent, near Louvain, has a fine western tower; the chapel on its upper floor has an elaborate *trifora*—a more refined version of that at Brixworth—looking eastwards into nave of the church. This tower is ornamented externally with a row of interlacing arches; it is just possible that the tower at Earls Barton may have been copied from it.

The enrichment of the eastern side of the tower arch at Barnack illus-trates the important part which the ground storey of the western adjunct was playing in the accommodation within the church. Barnack church, together with many others in east Mercia, apparently began its existence as a square 'turriform' nave of masonry, to which was subsequently added a longer nave extending eastwards from the original building, which thus became a western tower. The Lincolnshire church of Hough-on-the-Hill also illustrates this development, as does the very ancient church of Old Shoreham in Sussex. The development of turriform churches by building on an eastward extension will be discussed at length in the following chapter.

Even at the end of the twelfth century, the enrichment of the tower arch at Etton in Yorkshire—one of the finest arches in England—clearly indicates that the tower-base formed an important part of the church internally.

To recapitulate, it would appear that there were two principal parish-church plans in use at the time of the Conquest. The most common was probably the 'pseudo-cruciform', with its lateral wings but no trace of the central square; this plan would be met with mainly in the Saxon regions of the south and south-east. In Mercia, the 'crypto-cruciform', with the central square and all four appendages, was appearing in the more important churches. This plan, however, is far removed from the true cruciform of later days; except for the nave, the arms of the cross would be smaller in span than the central square.

These two types of plan would have been employed only in the more important churches. The ordinary village church would probably have followed a more humble design, based on the simple square nave in timber or rubble stone. There would also be the 'Roman' rectangular naves, and similar structures, mostly in the Anglian districts, which had been added to square tower-naves.

In the Saxon districts, the western bell-tower would only appear in places near the sea-coast, such as Bosham and Sompting in Sussex. The magnificent tower of South Lopham in Norfolk indicates that the fine central towers of the twelfth century were not far distant; this East Anglian example is surrounded with elaborate arcading resembling the decoration round the walls of the chancel at Cumptich in Flanders.

The central towers of the 'crypto-cruciform' churches were probably at first somewhat light in construction and therefore rather squat. The influence of the late-eleventh-century Benedictine expansion, however, which brought with it the fashion for fully developed cruciform churches with all four arms of equal span and height with each other, resulted in the eventual introduction of this plan into the design of larger parish churches. Cholsey in Berkshire is an early example of the true cruciform church. Such churches as these, however, are probably intended as small-scale copies of the great churches rather than representing a parish-church type of plan.

121

The Parish Church

There can be little doubt that the Crusades of the twelfth century, by introducing to all classes of Englishman the churches of the Holy Land itself, played a very important part in the development of the English parish church.

By the end of the first millenium, the provincial churches of the eastern parts of the Byzantine Empire had adopted a standardised form combining the axial and centralised plans by attaching a stumpy nave to the western side of a lofty central feature (Fig. 12). These buildings were laid out, in the orderly Byzantine fashion, within a rectangle of walls divided by arcades into three aisles. At the east end, a wide bay provided a 'crossing', above which was a low lantern dome flanked by short transepts. East of this feature was an apsidal chancel flanked by the usual pair of *parabemata*; as all three were usually terminated by apses, this type of plan is sometimes known as the 'triapsidal'.

Churches of this type were founded by the Crusaders throughout the Holy Land, sometimes upon the foundations of earlier buildings destroyed by the Moslems. The Crusader churches had their plans 'Romanised' still further by omitting the chancel with its *parabemata* and moving the lantern and transepts eastwards to allow for the provision of a longer nave.

In England, scores of parish churches were built on the same principal; the little 'axial' buildings, of aisle-less nave and chancel separated by a simple lantern tower in place of the oriental dome, represent the English architects' interpretation of the church-plan of the Holy Land (Plate 78).

The popularity of the true cruciform plan for larger parish churches during the twelfth and thirteenth centuries, and even subsequently, may also be traced to Crusader influence. The keynote is the central tower, flanked by transepts of no great length; eastwards is a short chancel and westwards a nave of no remarkable length unless the building were a large one in which case it would probably be aisled in four or five bays. The aisle-less class might be described as being on a 'six-square' plan with two squares representing the nave and the others occupied by tower, chancel and transepts. Some of the aisled churches are very fine: Melbourne in Derbyshire and Hemel Hempstead in Hertfordshire (Plate 77) being notable examples.

The semicircular apse of the early Christian architecture of Rome was never suited to the English plan of nave and chancel, as it made the latter too short. Thus English apses are nearly always apsidally-ended chancels, having the spring of the apse separated from the chancel arch by a short straight-sided portion (Fig. 13). At the end of the first millenium a form of apse appears in Mercia which, being formed of a series of faces, is at least easier to roof than the semicircular variety. The normal

122

The Parish Church

Byzantine apse was trilateral externally. Mercian polygonal apses, of which the best example is that at Wing in Bucks, generally have each external face ornamented with a large arch similar to those of the Ottonian churches.

The increasing French influence—and with it the introduction of Roman fashions—which is apparent after the middle of the eleventh century, caused a revival of the semicircular apse in south-eastern England at this time.

The cruciform churches of the day were occasionally developing transepts of considerable length; these were frequently being provided with

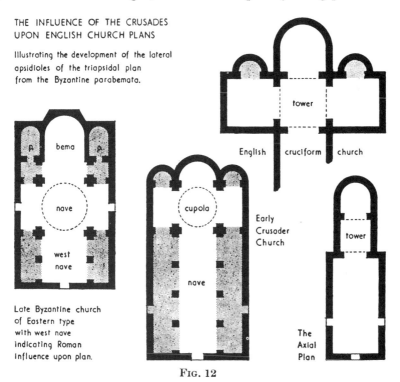

THE INFLUENCE OF THE CRUSADES
UPON ENGLISH CHURCH PLANS

Illustrating the development of the lateral
apsidioles of the triapsidal plan
from the Byzantine parabemata.

bema

nave

west
nave

Late Byzantine church
of Eastern type
with west nave
indicating Roman
influence upon plan.

cupola

nave

English   cruciform   church

tower

Early
Crusader
Church

tower

The
Axial
Plan

FIG. 12

small apses or 'apsidioles', protruding from their eastern walls to provide sites for the altars of side chapels (Fig. 12).

Another reason for the return of the apse was the introduction of the 'triapsidal' plan, universal in the case of the Crusader churches of Syria, by pilgrims and soldiers returning from that country. The lateral apsidioles of these churches—relics of the *parabemata* of their Byzantine prototypes—by the end of the eleventh century had become merely the terminal features of the aisles. In many cruciform churches having nothing but an apsidal sanctuary as eastern arm, the lateral apsidioles were in fact projections from the transepts; hence the arrangement so often met with in English cruciform and pseudo-cruciform churches. In the case of the long transepts of the greater churches, the apsidioles were frequently increased in number to a pair or even three in each transept.

Despite the high standard which had been attained, more especially in the eastern parts of the country, by the Anglo-Saxon masons, there was nevertheless still a vast amount of building in progress which perpetuated the traditional timber style.

In Essex, for example, where there was a complete absence of building stone—or even of reasonably suitable rubble—a fine timber technique was being employed; this is, fortunately, still admirably illustrated by more than a score of churches, apparently raised towards the end of the twelfth century, pyramidal in form and which are entirely constructed in wood. These remarkable buildings have fortunately been preserved by the mid-twelfth-century builders of the later stone churches attached to them;[10] the small wooden structure having been preserved in each case to serve as a western bell-tower (Plate 76).

Some, as at Stock, were four-posters (Fig. 3); there are also larger ones, such as Blackmore (Plate 74) or Margaretting, which seem to have been axially planned like contemporary stone structures, with two rows of posts. The main bays of these structures—which appear to be of earlier date than some of the four-posters—were divided into two by smaller posts, as if in imitation of the Ottonian duplex bay system. The principal bays are marked by large curved braces sweeping across the church to meet each other in a Gothic arch; surely it is in such buildings as these that one can discern the origins of the Gothic style in this country.

These churches have all lost their chancels, but the fine timber chancel arch remains at Stock.[11] Great play has been made with many forms of curved and reticulated braces and saltires.

The original bratticed walls which enclosed the outer aisles of these churches have, with one exception, disappeared. The remaining example, the church of Greensted, has lost its posted interior, but the bratticing, formed from the outer portions of the tree—sawn from it when the great square posts themselves were squared-up—may still be seen in the centre section of the nave (Plate 9); the two ends having been added, in inferior timber, at some later date.

It is unfortunate that the delay in appreciating the date and origin of these remarkable timber churches has caused them to be hitherto neglected; the antiquaries of the nineteenth century were apt to ignore timber structures in favour of the more monumental masonry buildings. A careful examination of the design and construction of these buildings might assist in determining their dates;[12] their association with later stone buildings is an unreliable guide, as timber buildings of this nature are easily taken to pieces, transported to another site, and re-erected.[13]

84. A typical late mediaeval parish church porch at Salle, Norfolk

83. An elaborate example of the twelfth-century type of porch. St. Germains in Cornwall

85. The interior of the Early Gothic chancel of Burgh-next-Aylsham church, Norfolk

86. A spacious nave of the fourteenth century at Cley church, Norfolk

The eleventh- and twelfth-century 'masted' churches of Norway were, of course, all built in softwood; in them, the oaken posts of the Essex churches are represented by tall fir poles. The very late example at Urnes is tricked out with imitation semicircular arches formed with the bracing timbers, and cubical caps have been added to the masts; the whole resembles the efforts of the carpenters who erected the mid-twelfth-century Bishop's Hall at Hereford with details imitating those of contemporary stone buildings (Plate 31).

Some clue to the form of the humblest type of stone church in use at the time of the Conquest is given by the example at Deerhurst, which is known to have been erected in 1056; it is merely a modification of the simple Celtic plan of nave and rectangular chancel. Through the latter part of the eleventh century and the greater part of the following one, hundreds of small stone churches on this plan—some, however, with apsidal chancels—were being erected in the country parishes, as well as those of the more elaborate pseudo- or crypto-cruciform type, with a few large cruciform churches of monastic inspiration.

In all the simply-planned churches it is invariably found that the principal architectural feature of the interior is the arch which leads from the nave into the chancel. In the most primitive churches, openings between the body of the church and its appendages—whether these be chancel, wings, west nave or bell-tower—are in the form of narrow doorways; by the eleventh century, however, these openings have all become open arches of as wide a span as possible. The west face of the chancel arch received great attention during the twelfth century; some of the arches of this period—notably the well-known example at Tickencote (Plate 55) in Rutland—are very fine indeed.

Wherever possible, a carver was also found to ornament the principal entrance doorways of the building. During the twelfth century, even the very smallest churches have doorways exhibiting the greatest elaboration of their many orders (Plate 83).

Until perhaps the eleventh century, the only arches to be met with in the parish church were those of the entrance doorways and the openings leading to the various appendages.

During the seventh century, the timber porticoes of the churches founded by St. Augustine and the other early missionaries were gradually becoming built up with stone walls to form what were termed at the time 'solid porticoes'; the primitive aisles thus created appear to have been principally used for intra-mural interments.

One of the earliest churches with its main walls supported upon an arcade appears to be that of Brixworth (Plate 82) in Northamptonshire. The arches in this example are small, very clumsily constructed of Roman bricks, and rise from heavy masses of walling retained as piers.

125

For the next two or three centuries, the humbler churches were being expanded laterally through crude openings of this description cut through the walls of their naves. It was not until the twelfth century brought the knowledge of how to construct a proper arcade of ordered arches supported upon pillars that the designers began to build the main walls of their naves in this fashion; which must, after all, have seemed a very daring achievement to the early mason. The early aisles were very narrow, often a bare six feet or so in width. The early origin of an aisle having late-mediaeval fenestration is often betrayed by its humble width.

Among the first churches to be constructed with aisles were the Saxon 'pseudo-cruciform' buildings; these had the eastern arch of the arcade built larger than the remaining arches, in order to emphasise the wings. Many early churches—such as that at Brixworth, which has a central square but no wings—had naves of four bays in length. It is noticeable that five in all is frequently found to be the number of bays in the nave of a mediaeval church of average size.

True to Celtic tradition, the entrances to the parish churches of this country—where the inclement climate makes doorways at the end of a building undesirable—were almost invariably situated towards the western ends of the side walls of the nave; only in the monastic churches was the Roman practice of the western portal adopted.[14]

Again, for climatic reasons, the southern of the two lateral entrances was that generally used by the parishioners, unless it should happen that the other was more convenient of access. If only one aisle was to be added to a church, that opposite the entrance flank was the one selected; this caused the minimum disturbance, especially of interments within the churchyard.

The protection of church doorways from the rain and wind by means of porches is met with a century or so prior to the Conquest. The west doorways of churches built under Roman influence would have made the building very draughty without the provision of some form of external shelter. The west porches of these churches—most of which may be found in the north and east—were in some cases raised subsequently to form slender bell-towers.

The lateral doorways favoured by the native builders, however, were not in so much need of protection. Porches, therefore, do not appear in large numbers—even in the greater churches—until well into the Gothic period. By the end of the mediaeval era, however, the church-porch was a universal feature of even the smallest buildings.

During the fifteenth century, emphasis to the church entrance was frequently given by making the porch of two stories in height (Plate 84); the upper room, which generally was reached by a stone stair, often served as a muniment room and a meeting-place for church officers.

The Parish Church

During the eleventh century only the most important churches were aisled. These would generally adopt the classical form of a lofty central nave, raised above lower aisles with a clerestory inserted for lighting purposes. The twelfth-century parish churches, however, could seldom rise to the dignity of this extra storey. In their case, the arcades represented, not so much a means of support for the central portion of the building and its roof, but a system of intermediate props which would hold up a roof spanning the whole structure across its entire width. This humble structural principle will also be met with in the case of the early halls (Fig. 22).

During the twelfth century, the standard Byzantine plan was still in use for the chancels of parish churches. In essence, this consisted of a square presbytery terminated by a semicircular apse of rather lower elevation.

DIAGRAMMATIC PLANS ILLUSTRATING CHANCEL DEVELOPMENT

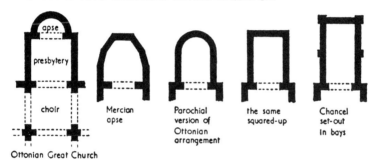

FIG. 13

Few churches of the lesser rank, however, adopted this arrangement without modification. There is either a simple square chancel, or, in the case of axial churches in which the tower might be used as a presbytery, merely the apse itself attached to the eastern face of this.

The commonest form of twelfth-century chancel comprises the combination of presbytery and apse as one structure, of the same height and with no intervening arch (Fig. 13). A later modification consists of the abandoning of the apse in favour of a square east gable, in which case the chancel becomes a rectangle having its ratio of length to breadth as three is to two, the eastern portion representing the sanctuary and the remaining two-thirds the presbytery. The 'priest's door' giving access to the chancel is almost invariably near the west end of the south wall, as in early monastic choirs.

The existence of a wave of building activity sweeping over the country at the end of the twelfth century is chiefly illustrated by the very obvious efforts which were being made at that period to extend the eastern arms of the greater churches. Those responsible for the chancels of parish churches—many of them often, by the way, in monastic custody—began soon afterwards to enlarge these also, in conformity with the growing taste for imposing eastern arms in ecclesiastical planning.

Thus the thirteenth century was a period for chancel rebuilding. Old apses and short single-bay chancels were swept away, and long, graceful eastern arms, two or three bays in length, were erected in their stead. Some were even vaulted; a great many display the evidences of having received the attention of skilled masons, probably imported by monastic patrons to a village which could never have produced anything of the sort without outside help (Plate 85).

To worshippers in the nave, the most important architectural feature in the building was the opening leading into the chancel, the Holy of Holies. In early days this archway was kept small; even when no structural problems dictated its size it was still allowed to retain its air of mystery, a factor which during the twelfth century was enormously augmented by means of elaborate ornament which converted it into a sort of proscenium arch (Plate 55). Chancel extensions of the thirteenth century, however, had the result of removing the altar so far away from the congregation that they could not possibly see what was going on, so openings were often made beside the chancel arch to assist them. The wide chancel arches of later days destroyed much of the effect of mystery, so it became customary to place a 'rood beam' across from side to side and fill up the arch with a wooden partition serving as a background for the rood or calvary. From this developed the 'rood screen' enclosing the chancel and the 'rood loft', a gallery passing before the rood in order to enable the lamps lighting it to be serviced; although most of these features disappeared at the Reformation the newel stair leading to the rood loft remains in a large proportion of our parish churches.

The Edwardian period, wealthy, realistic and progressive, was the era of the great preaching naves copied from the Friars' churches (Plate 86). Older structures, often mean in altitude and with narrow bays and clumsy arches, were replaced by lighter, more graceful, creations displaying ranges of high wide arches rising from slender pillars. Such naves were all clerestoried; by the end of the fourteenth century most old naves allowed to stand were being raised—often by simply altering the roof-pitch without raising the height of the ridge—in order to provide sufficient wall-space for a clerestory.

To the period of the wool boom of the fifteenth century may be assigned most of our largest and most magnificent country churches. In the east they are generally tall stately structures (Plate 80); in the west, however, the churches, while no less spacious, are designed along quite different lines to those hitherto followed in this country. Adopting the

87. A Devon 'hall church' with its cradle roof and elaborate rood-
screen. Kenton church

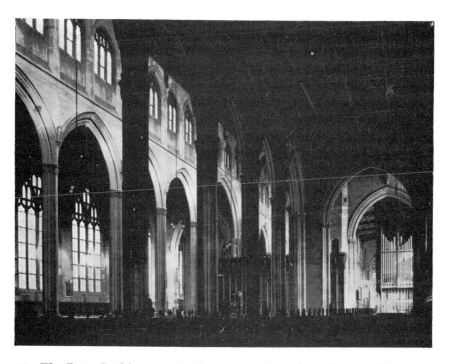

88. The Late Gothic nave of a large town church at Newark, Notting-
hamshire

89. The choir and presbytery of Norwich Cathedral

91. The great apse of Peterborough, re-fenestrated in the Late Gothic period

90. One of the 'apsidioles' of the elaborate twelfth-century 'chevet' of Norwich Cathedral

92. The Early Gothic cathedral of Salisbury in Wiltshire: the central
tower and spire is a later addition

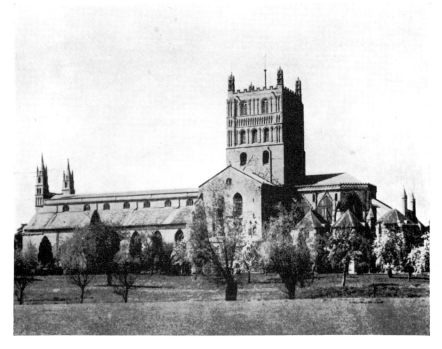

93. A Benedictine abbey church of the twelfth century at Tewkesbury
in Gloucestershire

system evolved by the architects of the German 'hall churches' the western builders, instead of planning a nave with subsidiary aisles, set out their churches as if they had three naves side by side, each with its own pitched roof instead of the lean-to roofs of normal aisled structures (Plate 87). Thus they produced a very spacious effect in their buildings which were, moreover, very well lit by fine large windows, so that the absence of a clerestory is of no consequence.

It was during this era that the two types of church plan, the parochial and the 'great church', began finally to draw away from each other in so far as the relationship between nave and chancel were concerned. Thus, while bishops and abbots were concentrating all their efforts on the construction of huge presbyteries, parish-church designers were building spacious naves (Plate 88) to hold large congregations gathered as closely as possible to the chancel, which was kept to a reasonable size so that the altar should not be removed too far from the people. Perhaps the finest parochial nave in England is that of St. Botolph's church in Boston.

The aisles of this period were very much wider in span than those of the twelfth or thirteenth centuries. It became the custom to provide chapels at the end of these wide aisles, which were sometimes extended for a bay or so alongside the chancel for this purpose. It was a period of good joinery, especially as regards screenwork, and these chapels were frequently enclosed by 'parclose screens' of traceried panels.

As the 'rood beam' which crossed the chancel arch was now frequently supported by a 'rood screen', the fifteenth century saw a system of screens being provided right across the building to enclose both chancel and side chapels. Many screens had galleries—'rood lofts'—above them, reached by a staircase in the aisle wall. The finest of these screen systems are those of the churches of Devon (Plate 87).

In addition to the great church and the parish church there is a third class of ecclesiastical building to be considered. This is the chapel, of which a great many types were in existence during the mediaeval period. There were rural chapels, and those attached to houses, castles and palaces; chapels may be found in the vicinity of cathedrals and monastic houses. There were numerous chapels within the great churches themselves; especially in the transept aisles and round the eastern ambulatory. There were also the chantry chapels connected with family tombs.

The finest chapel of all was the 'Lady Chapel': usually found at the east end of the great church, or beside the presbytery. Some parish churches, also, had their Lady Chapels, almost invariably situated alongside the chancel. Chapels were also built in this position to serve as burial places for important local families.

Even as early as the thirteenth century it had been the practice to provide the chancels of the more important parish churches with one or more aisles, to serve as side chapels. By the fifteenth century, most of the large wool churches were being built with fully-aisled chancels; sometimes, however, the easternmost bay of the building was left aisle-less in order to emphasise the sanctuary itself.

This practice of building aisled chancels led eventually to the abandoning of the separation into two portions—nave and chancel—which had characterised all the original churches of this country. Moreover, the development of the rood-screen had made it possible to indicate the division by this fine architectural feature without having to break-up the lines of the building. The final form of the English parish church, therefore, is that of a long, lofty, aisled hall, within which the chancel and the various chapels are indicated by screenwork. In wealthy East Anglia, in particular, such magnificent buildings as the churches of Southwold or Blythburgh (Plate 80) illustrate this climax in parish-church plans.[15]

Notwithstanding the debased shapes of their arches, and the severe lines of their window-tracery, these great wool churches illustrate in no inconsiderable fashion to what architectural heights the parish-church architects of the Middle Ages had attained. The constructional skill exhibited by the lightness of the walling and the slenderness of the pillars is matched by the brilliance of the fenestration, especially if—as at Fairford church in Gloucestershire—the building should still be in possession of its original coloured glass. In the west, the same tale of magnificence is indicated by the richness of the woodwork.

The most difficult building venture which could be undertaken by any parish would be the erection of a bell-tower. Skill and ingenuity would enable the parish craftsman to construct graceful arcades and span between these with a timber roof; the construction of a high tower, however, involved the transport and elevation of masses of material. Most of our great bell-towers were built during the fifteenth century (Plate 148); practically all of them were paid for out of the profits accruing from the woollen industry which at that period was making all England rich. In certain wool districts such as Yorkshire, East Anglia and Somersetshire, not only were great towers constructed, but often indeed the whole church was re-erected on a magnificent scale and with lavish ornamentation—all paid for by the benefactions which were pouring in from the wool farmers and merchants.

At this period, the town churches also were benefiting from the affluence which the country was attaining through the wool trade. Enormous cruciform churches were being built on cathedral scale in great wool ports such as Hull, Norwich or Bristol.

At the other end of the architectural scale, the small churches of humble parishes which had not come into contact with the wool boom were still being constructed on the simple plan of nave and chancel, the former possibly even aisle-less, or with one aisle only. If the parishioners could not afford a bell-tower, the bells might have to be hung in a simple cote perched on the west gable (Plate 184).

The rector of the parish, who enjoys the revenue derived from its great tithes, is thereby charged with the maintenance of the chancel of his church; the parishioners being held responsible for the rest of the building.

The chancel, employed as an essential feature of the parish church, is generally omitted from small chapels of a private nature, which have no congregation, other than the personal retainers or household of some notable, to accommodate. Such are, in particular, the domestic chapels attached to the palaces of the bishops, of which that at Chichester is one of the finest examples. Here and there in cathedral closes or within the precincts of a monastic house may often be found chapels consisting of one apartment only. The chapels of castles and royal palaces are also of this nature. Some ordinary private houses had domestic chapels so small as to be little more than oratories holding only half a dozen or so worshippers. Many castles have, in addition to the chapel accommodating the garrison, private oratories for the castellan and members of his family constructed in the thickness of the great walls of the fortification, or contrived in an upper storey of a wall-tower.

The domestic chapel is a clearly recognisable type of building, in that whereas the more public chapels—wayside, monastic or garrison—appear as isolated structures, the former is generally directly attached to the residence of which it forms part. The attachment is usually to the upper end of the Great Chamber; even the Norman hall-keeps adopted this arrangement. Domestic chapels, unlike free-standing chapels, were nearly always sited on an upper floor, partly for convenience of access from the chamber and partly in order that nothing should be built above them.

Other types of non-parochial chapels belonging to individuals or institutions are those attached to hospitals, monastic or secular, or reserved for the use of guilds. Towards the end of the mediaeval period, the single-apartment chapel plan reaches its highest form in the vast structures which were built to serve the new scholastic establishments which were founded to replace the monastic sources of education which ceased to function after the Dissolution. Such magnificent buildings as those of Eton or King's, Cambridge (Plate 45), although technically chapels, rival with their striking emphasis on the monumental factor of height many churches of cathedral standing.

CHAPTER VII

Greater Churches

The greater churches of this country are those which, instead of having been built to serve the needs of a parish, were erected as architectural monuments by the members of a priestly or monastic Order, or by a bishop for the dignity of his See.

Some of the buildings discussed in the last chapter should possibly have been included under one of these categories, but their small scale and humble architectural pretensions make it more convenient to consider them as being of parish-church types, rather than structures corresponding with the vast buildings of the great era of the Middle Ages.

There is documentary evidence that St. Wilfred, during his missionary efforts in Northumbria at the end of the seventh century, was building churches which, if the accounts of these can be credited, were much finer than anything remaining in this country either from this period or that of several centuries later. They appear to have been based on contemporary Roman or Byzantine buildings—even the use of columns is mentioned in the descriptions—but of all this nothing remains.

As has been noted earlier, the first English bishops were appointed as ecclesiastical supervisors of a region and had no cathedral churches from which to operate. Indeed, we are specifically told that the fifteen Sees which, at the close of the seventh century, had become established throughout the country, were purposely based on 'country monasteries', in order that the bishop might be protected from undesirable secular influences such as might be encountered in towns.

We are fortunate in still possessing the site of one of these 'country monasteries' with the fragmentary—but extremely valuable—remains of its church. This is the Minster of the Holy Cross at Southelmham, near Bungay in Suffolk, which documentary evidence makes almost certain was once the principal church of the See of Elmham. The minster is a small building of the simplest description. It consists of a rectangular choir with a large apse at its eastern end. West of the monastic portion of the building is a small square nave, the connection between the two portions being by doors on either side of the nave altar (Fig. 9). It is possible that it was originally surrounded by a timber portico.

132

94. The vaulted undercroft of a twelfth-century house, 'Moyses Hall', Bury St. Edmunds, Suffolk

95. The chapel in the White Tower of London

96. The vaulted undercroft beneath the presbytery of a great twelfth-century church. Canterbury Cathedral, Kent

97. The crypt of an ancient 'four-poster' church at Repton, Derbyshire

This extremely important example of a monastic church of the late seventh or eighth century appears to be the sole survivor of its class now standing above ground. A direct descendant of the Kentish churches of St. Augustine, it probably represents the type of church built by colonising Roman monks in this country until the Ottonian renaissance of the tenth century introduced the centralised church of the Byzantine architects. The foundations of the first church of Romsey Abbey remain in part; it appears that its plan may have resembled that of Southelmham minster.

Across the Waveney into Norfolk, the remains of another building connected with the ancient see of Elmham—perhaps the cathedral itself —may be seen at North Elmham. Although subsequently extended westwards with a long Ottonian nave and west tower with first-floor chapel, the original cruciform nucleus, probably very early eleventh century in date, can be detected east of this. The main structure runs north and south, in the manner of a transept, and has an apse projecting from its east wall. Opposite this was a short nave flanked by diminutive square aisles, opening into the transept. These aisles may have been raised to form small flanking turrets of Lombardo-Rhenish type, but this would not have been done until after the addition of the long nave (Fig. 21).[16]

The masonry work of this little church—good squared rubble—is similar to that to be seen in another cathedral church, of contemporary date but somewhat larger scale. This is the important eleventh-century cathedral of Dorchester in Oxfordshire, of which the north side of the nave and part of the western tower, containing its internal stair-turret, remain. In this church, the plan is of the 'pseudo-cruciform' type common to the parish churches of the period; the large arch which led to the northern 'wing' remains to suggest that the cathedral church of the period preceding the Conquest was possibly merely a larger version of the contemporary parish church.

The mediaeval cathedral as we know it, however, is in reality a copy of the *monastic* church of the period. We have already caught a glimpse— at Southelmham—of the planning principle involved in designing such structures. The parish church, as was described in the last chapter, consists, primarily, of a nave and a sanctuary. In the case of a monastic church, however—whether it should be of stone or timber—the parochial nave then becomes the monks' choir, and its chancel the 'presbytery'. If a nave should subsequently be considered necessary—either to accommodate the laity or merely to increase the monumental scale of the building—one would be added, as at Southelmham, at the western end of the choir.

The well-known monastic church of Brixworth, in Northamptonshire, illustrates how such buildings developed. There are no remains extant of the original foundation of *c.* 680; it was probably a simple rectangle with an apsidal termination. Late in the ninth century a square church of considerable span was built, with a fine apse and a 'west nave'. The foundations of the arch leading to this have been discovered, and parts of the windows flanking it in the west wall of the 'square' may yet be seen. When the large-aisled eleventh-century nave came to be built, the old western arch of the 'square' was filled in and two small arches—one on either side of the nave altar—cut below the ancient windows. To-day the whole of the old west wall of the ninth-century church has been removed.

Monastic church plans continued along simple lines, either as Romanesque rectangles or Byzantine squares, until the two came to be finally combined during the period of the Ottonian renaissance at the middle of the tenth century. Although the centralised type of plan lingered on for a century or so, it was obvious that the long Roman nave had come to stay.

The real leader of the country at this time was the energetic Archbishop Dunstan; it was under his direction that England was able to derive the fullest advantage from this era of cultural expansion.

The English centre of this architectural revival came to be the district —adjoining the Anglian building-stone region—in which were situated the important abbeys of Peterborough and Ramsey.

During the tenth century, the accepted plan-form for a 'great church' was developing as a combination of the normal 'turriform' type of western Byzantine provincial church with the addition of a long nave of 'basilica' type: this last representing the contribution of the Romanesque school. Until the last quarter of the twelfth century, by which period the elongation of the *eastern* arm of a church had become the indication of its status, it was the long 'basilican' nave—whether aisled or aisle-less— which differentiated the great church from the parish church.[17]

Before discussing the architectural design of such great churches as those of the East Mercian abbeys, therefore, let us recapitulate what we know of the plan-forms which were being employed at the period in connection with the more important parish churches. The two principal types were those which have been designated 'pseudo-cruciform' and 'crypto-cruciform' (Fig. 14).

The first of these is the Saxon form—probably hitherto the most popular—which was being developed throughout southern and southeastern England; its primary characteristics were the simple rectangular nave with the two lateral 'wings' at its eastern end.

The more monumental plan-form, however, was that which retained the central square, to which the four arms—chancel, 'west nave' and the two wings—were joined by means of four arches pierced in its walls. It was this type of church-plan which was spreading throughout Mercia, and

134

it was probably from this 'crypto-cruciform' style of church that the great tenth-century monastic structures eventually developed.

It should be borne in mind that the monastic church, with its choir, was not primarily concerned with the provision of a long nave; the central square itself probably supplied all the accommodation needed by the monks themselves. It is certain that the choir was originally situated in this, the loftiest, portion of the tenth-century monastic church; the nave being a subsequent addition to the building, provided for the accommodation of the laity.

Let us consider the development of the Mercian central square. It was probably during Ottonian times that the Anglian builders widened the four arms of their churches to the same span as the central area.[18] The enormous advantage of doing this was that the span of all four arches could now be increased to the fullest possible width, unlimited abutment

ANGLO-SAXON CRUCIFORM CHURCHES   TYPES OF CROSSINGS

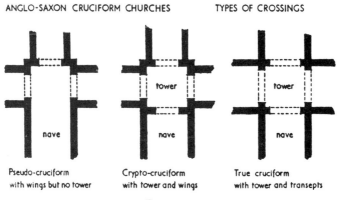

Pseudo-cruciform
with wings but no tower

Crypto-cruciform
with tower and wings

True cruciform
with tower and transepts

Fig. 14

being provided by the adjoining walling. The great churches of the tenth century probably all had properly-designed 'crossings' of this nature; the finest and last example of it may be seen in St. Albans Abbey (Plate 2), erected soon after the Conquest.

The Saxon taste, however, was all for abandoning the obstructive central square—even in the greater churches—in order that the main axial lines of the building should pass unbroken from west to east. Parish churches had already adopted the 'pseudo-cruciform' plan, with the lateral wings represented, in the interior of the building, only by the two arches leading to them.

By the time of the Conquest, even the Anglian builders—leaders of the monumental architectural style of the period—had abandoned the crossing in favour of deliberately running the main longitudinal walls of the building right through from west to east, leaving out the transverse arches altogether and merely retaining the two lateral ones to indicate the position of the transepts (Fig. 19). This feeling is very noticeable in most of the great arches of the post-Conquest period, especially in the west of England. It was not until after the middle of the twelfth century, when the central tower—possibly reintroduced from the 'axial' or 'Crusader' tower of parish churches—came to be employed again as a common feature in the design of a great church, that the properly set-out crossing became finally established.

From the descriptions which remain of the great churches of the late tenth century—the Ottonian era—in this country, it seems clear that, in the eastern districts at any rate, they all possessed some form of crossing. This may have been properly designed, as at Gernrode in Old Saxony (Plate 20) erected in 961; on the other hand, they may have been planned

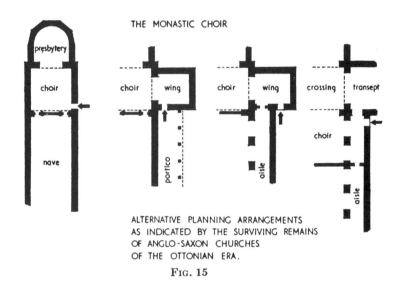

THE MONASTIC CHOIR

ALTERNATIVE PLANNING ARRANGEMENTS
AS INDICATED BY THE SURVIVING REMAINS
OF ANGLO-SAXON CHURCHES
OF THE OTTONIAN ERA.

FIG. 15

on similar lines to the central squares of the Mercian crypto-cruciform buildings, such as that at Stow, built eighty years later. In any case, it is certain that they had central features of some sort or another: probably stone lantern-towers surmounted by timber spires.

The most important of the four arms of the building was the eastern; the presbytery (Fig. 18b). The church of Westminster Abbey, as rebuilt altar was situated. By comparison with contemporary buildings, such as, for example, the abbey church of Flavigny in Burgundy, it seems that the Ottonian presbytery was a square apartment, two bays in length, with an arch in the east wall leading to the apse. The presbytery would probably in most cases have solid walls, separating it from the pair of lateral *parabemata* or sacristies; these might have galleries above them, looking into the presbytery (Fig. 17b). The church of Westminster Abbey, as rebuilt

136

by Edward the Confessor in 1045–50, apparently possessed a presbytery of this description.

While we are considering the plans of the most important of these great buildings, however, it is as well to remember that many of the smaller monastic churches, even at the time of the Conquest, still had only the central square for choir, and a small sanctuary—possibly apsidal —as its only eastern feature. The eleventh-century monastic church of Deerhurst in Gloucestershire is an example. The tower containing the choir would have its western arch filled by a low wall separating the monks' portion of the church from the nave; this appears to have been the normal Ottonian practice. The entrance to the choir was by a doorway near the west end of one of its side walls (Fig. 15).

The 'wings' or transepts flanking the choir were important features of the early great church; without them, the external aspect of the building would have lacked that cruciform central massing which was the primary factor in Byzantine church design. Internally, however, they served merely as chapels flanking the choir itself. In an early cruciform church, the entrance to the eastern portion is generally in the west wall of a transept; doorways in their eastern walls led to the *parabemata* flanking the presbytery. While considering these 'Romanised' great churches with their long naves it is nevertheless well to remember that a number of buildings of equal importance would still have been restricted to the primitive Byzantinesque 'turriform' nucleus with only a short projecting sanctuary. The church of Werden-on-Ruhr, built in 875, is a good example of the state of development to which these buildings had attained (Plate 73). It is a six-poster, the two intermediate posts—or piers, rather, for the building is constructed in masonry—are supports for the lateral galleries recalling those of the Byzantine octagons upon which the church was modelled. It will be noted that the six-poster illustrates the form of bay-design which may be called 'duplex', that is to say in which sturdy supports are alternated with lighter ones.

These large six-posters are important in that they play a large part in the subsequent development of the great church of the Ottonian era. We have seen how the large cruciform building expanded westwards in order to provide increased accommodation in a long nave. Well-established town churches situated in towns—on main street or market place— could not always be enlarged westwards. Thus extension had often to be achieved by building a complete new church to the east of the original square structure (Fig. 16).

This had the effect of leaving the earlier turriform structure rising above the west end of a long cruciform church. To this may be attributed the subsequent development of the western tower as the principal monumental factor in the mass of the Ottonian great church, thereafter to become an ubiquitous feature of the ordinary parish church of western Europe.[19]

A further result of the eastern expansion of the six-poster church was the repetition of its 'duplex' bay ordinance to produce such striking architectural effects in the nave arcades of great churches.

The custom of adding an axially-planned eastern extension to an earlier centrally-planned nucleus became common during the late-twelfth and early-thirteenth centuries in this country. Circular Templar churches became thus extended, as did the early timber buildings of Essex.

Under the influence of the centralised 'crypto-cruciform' plan, Mercian designers seem to have been engaged in developing the transept. It

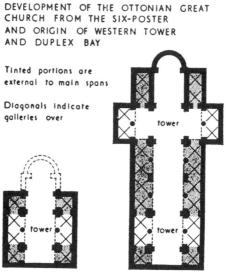

DEVELOPMENT OF THE OTTONIAN GREAT CHURCH FROM THE SIX-POSTER AND ORIGIN OF WESTERN TOWER AND DUPLEX BAY

Tinted portions are external to main spans

Diagonals indicate galleries over

Fig. 16

was probably some time, however, before this part of the building attained its eventual importance in the planning scheme of the mediaeval great church. The first stage seems to have been to make it of two stories throughout, as at Deerhurst; this brought the transept into line with the galleried naves which Byzantine tradition maintained in the Rhenish cruciform churches and perhaps in some contemporary Anglian buildings. When the long Ottonian nave became aisled, the transept appears to have been opened up to the full height of the church for one bay of its length, the remaining bay still retaining its gallery (Fig. 17). Under the influence of the Anglian builders the transept expanded to monumental proportions and developed aisles with galleries above them as well as the terminal gallery; thus the whole vast structure became two-storied in all four arms. By the twelfth century, however, the galleries were being omitted from the transepts, their aisles disappearing with them; the great Benedictine churches sprouting a range of apsidal chapels on the eastern side of the transept in emulation of the multi-apsidal churches of the Holy Land. The Cistercians restored the eastern aisle but divided it up into a row of chapels; later great churches dispensed with the solid partition walls and substituted light screenwork.

By the Ottonian era, the long 'Romanesque' nave had become such a well-established feature of ecclesiastical architecture that all monastic and cathedral churches came to be provided with an elongated western arm. In actual fact, however, all that was really needed for purposes of

DEVELOPMENT OF THE TRANSEPT

Tinted portions are external to main spans
Diagonals indicate galleries over

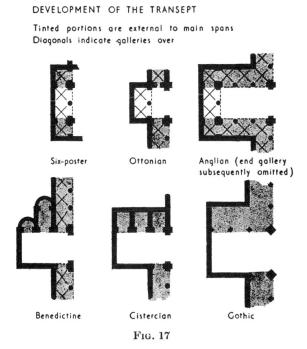

Six-poster   Ottonian   Anglian (end gallery
                                        subsequently omitted)

Benedictine   Cistercian   Gothic

Fig. 17

accommodation was enough room for the choir—which by the time of the Conquest was being set westwards from the central area in order to leave this unobstructed—and sufficient support for the central feature of the building. The first stage in the construction of a monastic church, therefore, generally ended when two to four bays of the nave had been completed.

The Anglo-Ottonian naves were in a number of cases built without aisles; the early eleventh-century cathedral at Dorchester is an example. The more important Benedictine abbey churches, however, would probably have been provided with fully-aisled western arms. In this case, the arcades might have been supported upon massive Mercian piers, like those of Brixworth church; the designers of Westminster Abbey, however, employed the 'duplex' system with the piers alternating with some form of pillar. Aisled naves were probably in nearly all cases provided with lateral galleries, the floors of which would have been supported above the aisles on rough groined vaulting.

A feature of mid-tenth-century great churches which seems to have been recorded by all the contemporary chroniclers is the western bell-tower at the end of the nave. This would probably have had, attached to it, one or two circular turrets containing staircases giving access to the nave galleries.[20]

It is unfortunate that so far the sites of none of the great churches built under the influence of St. Dunstan's ecclesiastical renaissance have been explored. That of Westminster Abbey, founded nearly a century later, is the earliest building of its class of which we have any detailed knowledge. The illustration of the church which appears on the Bayeux Tapestry (Plate 153) is also a remarkable possession, indicating as it does the appearance of the building as it existed only a short time after its foundation by Edward the Confessor.

History books—perhaps unduly prone to over-emphasise foreign influences—have dwelt much upon the Norman favourites of this Saxon king. By the same token, the national architecture of the England of the period has been entirely misrepresented as 'Norman'. But the architect of the Confessor's great church at Westminster was one Godwin Greatside—surely no Norman!

The plan of his church is of interest as illustrating the two-bay transept arrangement usually met with in the eleventh-century churches of eastern England. The end bay of each arm had a gallery passing across it, supported upon a central pillar; the remainder of the transept, within the limits of the walls of the nave aisles, being open to the full height of the church.

These transeptal galleries—the result of Ottonian copying of Byzantine features—were probably in this case used as chapels. The abbey church of Hildesheim in the Rhineland, erected about the year 1000, had similar galleries to all four transepts; access was provided by stair-turrets attached, in true Ottonian fashion, to the middle of the gable walls, recalling the turrets which are found in conjunction with the chapels on upper floors of western towers in contemporary English churches. The priory church of Deerhurst in Gloucestershire had both the two-storied transepts and the chapel in the western tower.

William II's Abbey Church of St. Mary at York, begun in 1089, had transepts three bays in length; the end bay of each was designed as a chapel with solid walls, above which was almost certainly a gallery looking into the transept. At the roughly contemporary Priory Church at Christchurch in Hampshire, these terminal chapels were exactly reproduced, below ground level, as crypts beneath the end bays of the transepts.

98. The row of pillars supporting the first floor of a monastic building
at Kirkstall Abbey, Yorkshire

99. The vaulted undercroft of a thirteenth-century house, now the
'Angel' inn, at Guildford in Surrey

101. The 'ploughshares' of the sexpartite vaulting at Lincoln Cathedral

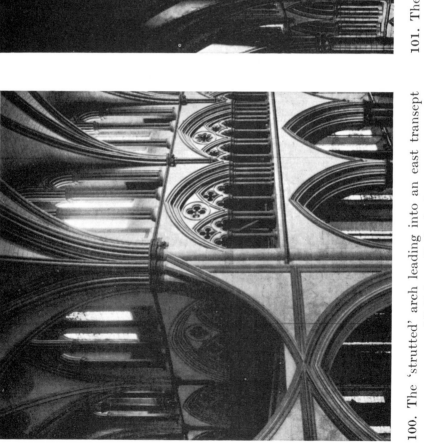

100. The 'strutted' arch leading into an east transept of Salisbury Cathedral

The great three-bay transepts of Winchester (Plate 53) and Ely had aisles on both east and west sides, the galleries above which were joined by open galleries crossing the end of each arm of the transept, leaving the upper parts of the gable walls unobstructed internally, so as not to interfere with lighting.

It is a feature of all axially-planned mediaeval buildings that they have a lower and an upper end, the entrance being at the former and architectural emphasis being concentrated at the latter. In great churches, this emphasis was displayed in the eastern arm of the cross; which, although smaller in scale than the nave to the west, was from the first given special architectural treatment.

DEVELOPMENT OF THE EASTERN ARMS
OF GREAT CHURCHES

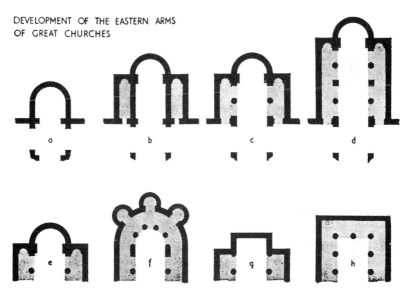

DEVELOPMENT OF THE EASTERN TERMINATION OR CHEVET
Fig. 18

Towards the end of the eleventh century, presbyteries began to be doubled in length; that of St. Albans, begun in 1077, is a notable example. The presbytery of this great church, however, still had solid walls, though there were probably galleries above the very long narrow *parabemata*.

These relics of the old Byzantine church plan, however, during the course of the eleventh century, gradually became abolished in favour of providing better light to the presbytery by giving it lateral arcades through which could be seen the windows in the outer walls; in fact, the presbyteries became, like the naves, fully aisled. In large churches, the number of bays in the presbytery is usually four; in smaller buildings two (Fig. 18).

The general expansionist tendencies of the east end of the building seems to have included the lengthening of the transept by extending its arms so as to provide more space for altars; each in its subsidiary 'apsidiole' projecting from the east wall of the transept. Thus the enormously long presbytery of St. Albans Abbey appears to have been matched with almost equally long transepts (Plate 2).

A feature of the greater churches which has probably been in existence since Ottonian days was the raising of the central portion to a sufficient height above the surrounding roofs in order that a pair of windows, matching those in the adjoining clerestory, could be inserted to light the darkest part of the building. These 'lantern' stories, as they are called, were only made high enough to provide space for a window on either side of the ridge of each arm of the cross. In churches which—unlike that of

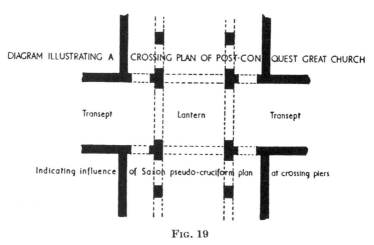

FIG. 19

St. Albans—had not been designed with a proper crossing, transverse arches had to be thrown across the body of the building to carry the east and west walls of the masonry lantern (Fig. 19), the height of which, in order to save weight, is therefore generally reduced to the minimum required for lighting purposes. At St. Albans, however, the existence of a proper crossing enabled the tower to be completed by the addition of a charming external gallery of Rhenish type (Plate 155).

It will be remembered that the Wessex type of smaller church had abandoned the central square feature, retaining the memory of it only by leaving two arches, leading to the 'wings', in the side walls of the nave. It is quite clear that the designers of the great churches of late eleventh-century England were working along the same lines. The main walls of their churches run straight from west to east; each having a row of arches for the nave, another for the presbytery, and a larger arch to give access to the transept. What was left of the crossing-piers was given a fairly generous width from west to east in order to provide some measure of abutment to the main arcades while the crossing was in course of erection. There is no provision for a cross arch continuing and joining the lines of the transept wall except high up in the main walls of the building.

These transverse arches were obviously never intended for the support of a central tower, but merely the low stone walls of the 'lantern' required for lighting purposes. A twelfth-century drawing of Lanfranc's cathedral at Canterbury (Plate 154), compared with the representation of Westminster Abbey introduced into the Bayeux Tapestry (Plate 153), permits us to appreciate two of the forms adopted by the elaborate timber steeples which covered these low stone lanterns of the eleventh- and twelfth-century great churches.

It is greatly to be regretted that none of these fine timber structures, which were probably the masterpieces of the carpenters of the period, remain to us to-day. Fortunately, however, these two contemporary illustrations, which will be discussed in a later chapter, are in existence to give us some idea of their form. Such constructions, which had been placed upon the tower-tops of the Continental churches for two centuries before the Conquest, were in all probability framed-up on the same principles as a timber church of the period. For about a century after the Conquest, they formed the invariable crowning feature of the central lanterns of great churches; doubtless varying, however, in magnificence so that less important buildings may have had nothing more than a pyramidal roof to cover the lantern. The memorial of these vanished timber steeples is the glorious fourteenth-century octagon at Ely (Plate 152).

It is unfortunate that the post-Conquest engineers failed to appreciate the value of a properly-planned crossing. By their employment of the Saxon pseudo-crossing, with its light transverse arches carrying the lantern, they made it a venturesome business to attempt to construct a complete central tower of stone. As a result, the lateral arches, against the lofty piers of which the main arcades of the building were thrusting, were insufficiently weighted to meet the pressure; generations after the Conquest, the central lanterns of many great churches were collapsing for this reason, though some bold designers saved the situation—as at Tewkesbury (Plate 93)—by venturing upon a central tower.

It was the Anglian masons who created the first great churches of the post-Conquest era. It is unfortunate that every single one of the eastern ends of these buildings have disappeared; with the notable exception of the great apse of early twelfth-century Peterborough (Plate 91), which, with its wealth of arcaded ornamentation, alone remains to remind us of our losses. At the very end of the eleventh century, the fully-aisled presbytery of Durham was erected on this Teutonic plan, with the single lofty apse at the east end.

The Durham apse was preceded by a narrow bay, with solid walls separating the presbytery from its aisles at this point. This is a common feature of the east ends of great churches, being provided to give abutment to the thrust of the arcades. The ends of the aisles are nearly always curved, within the space provided by this narrow bay, to form small apsidal terminations in which side altars could be placed.

In the example at Durham, the eastern ends of the presbytery aisles were probably carried up as towers, flanking the great apse. Apses flanked by tall slender towers had been a form of eastern termination very popular amongst the Comacine masons of Lombardy a century before; the device, spreading throughout the Rhineland, had been adopted by the Teutonic designers as the universal form of east end for a great church which moreover provided convenient access to the galleries over aisles. The tower-flanked apse certainly found a home in England also; the finest example of which there are any remains above ground being at Hereford Cathedral, where the lower portions of the towers, but not the apse, may still be seen.

Another Rhenish practice, detectable in the foundations of the original cathedral at Old Sarum, and still visible in great magnificence at Exeter, was the raising of short square transepts to form a pair of great towers flanking the whole centre of the church. Except at the western end of naves, however, flanking towers do not appear to have ever attained the popularity in this country that they did in the Rhineland.

In the eastern parts of England, the result of the Norman Conquest was to encourage the Anglian masons to build, on an even greater scale, their fine long churches with extended transepts and long aisled eastern arms terminating in a great apse. The more backward western parts of England, however, appear to have possessed no comparable native talent. The late-eleventh-century great churches of that region, therefore, were built along different lines from their eastern contemporaries.

It was probably Benedictine monks from the abbeys of the Middle Loire who introduced into western England the art of building great churches.

At this period the design of churches was still being influenced by the much-revered Church of the Nativity at Bethlehem with its elaborate chevet erected by Justinian in the first half of the sixth century (see page 154). This was a square tower supported by four piers between which arches opened into three wide apses. The walls of these were each in turn carried upon a pair of columns above which arches sprang: thus the central feature was surrounded by an aisle forming an ambulatory. It was this impressive planning conception which the French monks wished to introduce into the design of their great apses.

To effect this they had to support the high curved wall of the apse

102. The west front of Lincoln Cathedral

103. Bayeux Tapestry illustration of a Norman stockaded castle

104. Bayeux Tapestry illustration of Edward the Confessor's great
hall at the palace of Westminster

106. A great hall of the Edwardian era at Stokesay
Castle in Shropshire

105. A great hall of the twelfth century castle at
Oakham, Rutland

107. The remains of a twelfth-century monastic infirmary at Canterbury Cathedral, Kent

108. The Late Gothic refectory of a western monastery. Cleeve Abbey, Somerset

upon a row of pillars and arches. This was a dangerous thing to do, as the combined thrusts of the arches would tend to collapse the whole structure outwards. To counteract this thrust, it was the invariable practice to buttress the outer wall of the surrounding aisle with three apsidioles (Plate 90), towards the walling of which the thrust from the main apse could be led by flying buttresses passing across the vaulting of the aisle itself. The whole scheme was probably derived from an examination of the circular and octagonal Byzantinesque churches which had slowly been spreading in small numbers across Europe since the days of Charlemagne's notable experiment with this form of structure at Aachen; these semi-circular eastern ends of the great Loire churches are, in fact, each half a large round church.

Once devised, the semicircular 'ambulatory' passed through several modifications, the most obvious of which was to make the whole structure a complete continuation of the presbytery itself by raising the apse to the same height as this and abolishing the communicating arch through what had been its east wall (Fig. 18*f*).

A craze for the multiplication of chapels is noticeable at this time. By protruding small single-storey wings or transepts from the point where the curvature of the east end began, space was found for an apsidiole in the east wall of each wing.

The perfected apsidal east end with surrounding ambulatory is first found in this country in the chapel built by William the Conqueror shortly after the Conquest in the Tower of London (Plate 95). A year or two later, the king was building his memorial abbey of Battle on the same lines. The new design was speedily adopted in the south-east of England; which, by virtue of the political changes, had temporarily taken the place of the Anglian districts as the centre of culture. The cathedrals of the two Anglo-Saxon capitals, London and Winchester, were rebuilt with the new French east end, as were also two large churches at Canterbury. The church of St. Augustine's Abbey, the Benedictine house at Canterbury, illustrates the standard Continental form, with its multiplicity of closely-spaced pillars. St. Bartholomew's at Smithfield is another good example.

Spreading to the west of England, however, the design, meeting such traditional influences as there existed, underwent a slight modification. The traditional form of apse in this part of England was not semicircular but polygonal. Possibly the great apses of the tenth-century Benedictine churches in this region were of this form, as is suggested by the remains of the humble example at Deerhurst. Be this as it may, the aisled apses of the churches of Gloucester and Tewkesbury (Plate 93) were not semi-circular, but half-hexagons, as are also the apsidioles of the former. The English designers also preferred to reduce the number of supports; which, owing to the scale of these, they were well able to do. Thus some of the western apses have only two medial pillars.

The fashion for expanding the arms of the church by means of aisles included the transepts; thus the great church at Winchester was, towards the end of the eleventh century, provided with aisles, having galleries above, on both the east and west sides of the transept—the ends of which, however, still retained the column-supported galleries of earlier days.

At this period, Byzantine ecclesiastical architecture was adopting an eastern termination set out on what is known as the 'tri-apsidal' plan, in which the great apse is flanked by two smaller ones at the ends of the aisles or *parabemata*. The contact between east and west provided by the Crusades had the effect of introducing this eastern termination into a few English aisled churches; practically all the Crusader churches of the Holy Land and Syria follow this plan, but the buildings are more closely related to the rectangular Byzantine pattern, and not the elongated and extended cruciform plan common to western Europe at the time.

Despite the efforts of the Roman Church to insist upon the apse as the only suitable background for an altar, the Celtic east end had, by the beginning of the twelfth century, reasserted itself in a great many churches, even those of which the details were being influenced by French design. At the very beginning of the century, Southwell Minster was being built with its east end squared-up to form what might be described as a square apse; west of the two bays occupied by this feature, the remainder of the presbytery is aisled, the ends of the aisles having small apses indicating the influence of the tri-apsidal school of Syria.

The reformed monastic Order known as the Cistercian rejected the semicircular apse from the outset; the earliest churches of the Order in England had 'square-apse' presbyteries, two bays in length, with a flat east wall. Nor do they show apsidal chapels in the east wall of the transept; which is, instead, furnished with an eastern aisle divided into its bays—of which there are normally three—by stone walls, thus providing chapels between these (Fig. 17). There are no galleries in any part of the Cistercian churches.

Once it had been decided that the standard east end of any church was to be on a square plan, the next stage was to consider whether this should be provided with an ambulatory similar to that which had surrounded the original great apses of the late eleventh-century churches. This was, in fact, achieved. The abbey church of Romsey has a fine early twelfth-century presbytery which is fully aisled, across the square east end as well as along its sides. The later Cistercian churches, such as that at Byland, included the square ambulatory in the plans of their eastern ends.

146

In the second half of the twelfth century, the eastern transept—originated by the Benedictines of central France in connection with their elaborate aisled apses but slow in arriving in this country—is found included in the east end of the plan of the greater church by the time that this has adopted the square English variation from its French prototype. If the presbytery should be a long one, the eastern transept may be sited where it would have been had the east end been apsidal: that is to say, between the end of the presbytery and its apse (Fig. 20). In the case of a short presbytery such as that at Hereford Cathedral, however, the east transept forms a transverse extension of the actual ambulatory itself, giving the east end of the church the form of a T. This feature was later developed into such magnificent eastern terminations as can be seen at Fountains Abbey and Durham Cathedral.

Towards the end of the twelfth century, the east end of Lincoln Cathedral was rebuilt with an eastern transept, with two apsidioles in each arm; a trilateral Mercian apse, surrounded by an ambulatory of the same shape, projects eastwards from this. The extreme end of this remarkable presbytery—which has unfortunately disappeared—was completed by a hexagonal tower flanked by two stair turrets; the sides of the ambulatory had, in addition, an apsidiole each. The whole feature may have been based on the very elaborate east end of Canterbury Cathedral; the apse itself, however, is of Teutonic type.

From the earliest period of the Christian era, it had frequently been the custom to found churches over the burial places of saints and martyrs, the altar being sited approximately over the actual tomb. As early as the seventh century in England, small chambers were sometimes provided under the chancels of churches to accommodate the tomb of a saint; such chambers frequently had narrow passages passing round them in order that the tomb might be seen by pilgrims. The crypts of Ripon and Hexham are examples of this. The early eleventh century apse at Wing in Buckinghamshire has a similar crypt, shaped to suit the polygonal apse which was built above it, and entirely surrounded by a passage.

A four-poster church at Repton in Yorkshire was built over a stone crypt set out on the same plan, having a vaulted roof supported on four stone columns. This crypt (Plate 97), which probably dates from the end of the tenth century, is now beneath the chancel which replaced the original church; this having been at the same time extended westwards to provide the rectangular nave always popular in the north. There is another fine four-poster crypt at Lastingham in the same county. Probably of mid-eleventh-century date, the crypt extends beneath the short apsidal presbytery as well as the church; which has suffered the same transformation as that at Repton.

The fashion for providing a crypt under the whole of the presbytery seems to have been at its height at the time when the Benedictines were building their great aisled apses at the end of the eleventh century; most of these were raised over crypts, the floor over the main span being supported by two rows of columns (Plate 96), though the early example at Winchester follows the secular arrangement of having one central row only.

In the early Christian church, the choir of the singers had been sited immediately adjoining the apse. In the great churches erected in western Europe towards the end of the eleventh century, the eastern end of the church had been extended by inserting a square presbytery between the

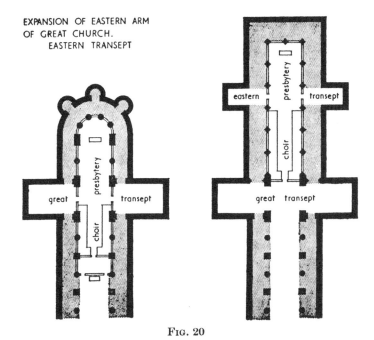

FIG. 20

choir and the apse; this presbytery had, throughout the centuries, been getting longer and longer. In the Ottonian churches, the choir was established in the centre of the building under whatever feature—stone tower or timber steeple—existed at this point. As the naves of the great churches grew ever longer, the choir began to move westwards into the eastern ends of these (Fig. 15).

In the twelfth century, therefore, the ritualistic arrangement of the monastic church was that the choir-stalls were sited, facing each other, along the easternmost bays of the nave, being moreover joined, at their western extremities, by a row of stalls passing transversely across the building and facing east; these stalls—known as the 'return stalls'— provided seats for the higher ranks of the fraternity. At the back of the re-

109. A Cistercian refectory with a fine pulpit at Beaulieu Abbey in Hampshire; it is now the parish church

110. A late mediaeval great hall with its panelled screen at Penshurst, Kent

112. Its interior is vaulted from a central pillar

111. An Early Gothic chapter house of cathedral type at Lincoln

turn stalls was the choir screen with its central doorway. This screen was not, however, the actual division between the nave and the monastic choir; this being effected by a low wall entirely crossing the building a bay west of the choir screen. The wall formed the reredos of the nave altar, on either side of which a small doorway led out of the nave into the space between the two screens—known as the 'retro-choir'—in which infirm monks could take part in the service without having to stand in the stalls within the choir (Fig. 20).

The division wall which—possibly owing to its use as a reredos to the nave altar—is sometimes known as the 'rood screen', only occurs in monastic churches. In cathedral churches there is only the choir screen with its central doorway. In the days of the great late-mediaeval presbyteries with the choir situated entirely within them, the choir screen becomes a magnificent architectural feature, as at Exeter (Plate 44); these elaborate masonry structures were known by the designation of 'pulpitum'.

The pulpitum may be a development from the curious architectural feature introduced by the Friars into their churches as a division between the choir and the great preaching nave. In place of a transept, two walls were built right across the building from side to side. The space between these walls, known as the 'walking space', was connected with the eastern side of the cloister and formed the entrance to the choir; a slender bell-tower, generally of octagonal form, was usually raised above it.[21]

By the beginning of the thirteenth century, when the power of the episcopacy was beginning to vie with that of the great monastic Orders, many cathedrals were having their eastern ends extended. The plan followed by the designers of these new structures was a kind of confirmation of that which had been developing during the preceding century by a process of evolution. Thus the choir of Salisbury Cathedral for example, has a presbytery, east of the central tower, of five bays; the two eastern of which are formed by the east transept (Plate 100), and its own eastern aisle. Still eastwards of this point is what may be described as a great square apse surrounded by an ambulatory.

Improved knowledge of building thrusts and how to meet them by means of abutment systems enabled the designers of the aisled square east ends to dispense with the surrounding apsidioles which had been universal features of the early semicircular aisled apses. A number of thirteenth-century cathedrals, however, retained the eastern of these; extending it to form a chapel of Gothic proportions, with, of course, a square east end. Thus Salisbury Cathedral has a 'Lady Chapel' of this description projecting eastwards from its ambulatory to complete the whole *chevet*. In some early thirteenth-century churches, this projecting eastern chapel was raised to the full height of the building.

As a result of the elongation of the eastern arms of the Gothic

149

churches, the high altar was beginning to retreat to too great a distance from the old monastic choir in the east end of the architectural nave; by the Gothic period, therefore, the choir was beginning to be moved into the architectural presbytery east of the crossing.

It seems more than probable that the earliest extensions of the presbytery were due to a wish to move the choir into the eastern arm—as at Canterbury in 1096—and thus leave the crossing and transepts open to the public. An early twelfth-century non-monastic church such as Southwell may have always had its choir sited at the west end of the long four-bay presbytery. By the thirteenth century, the choir had moved into the presbytery for good; new churches such as Salisbury were so planned. The reproduction of the transept at the eastern end of the choir may be the result of trying to achieve the same space effect as had existed when the stalls were west of the crossing (Fig. 20).

A further excuse for exaggerating the length of the eastern arm was provided when bishops and abbots began to find it of good commercial value to provide space for the interment of important personages in elaborate tombs aligned beneath the arcades. Of still more value was the presence of the shrine of some local saint, such as, for example, St. Hugh of Lincoln; to accommodate which the High Altar would be set back several bays west of the east wall, leaving a fine chapel for the saint between this and the back of the reredos of the High Altar itself.

The French designers of the period were adhering firmly to the great apse with its ambulatory and ring of chapels. Mid-thirteenth-century Westminster is an example of the style. In the west of England—still to a considerable extent under the influence of French architectural practice—Pershore Abbey constructed, about 1230, a similar chevet surrounding a trilateral Mercian apse.

Again, under French influence, some of the great Cistercian abbeys forsook their habitual austerity in planning, and returned to the use of the aisled apse at the eastern termination of the church. The important Cistercian abbey of Pontigny in Burgundy extended its east end in this form at the very end of the twelfth century; instead of a ring of apsidioles, however, the aisle is surrounded by yet another aisle, this being divided up, in the same way as the eastern aisle of the Cistercian transept, with solid stone walls separating each bay, thus making a ring of chapels of Cistercian type. The church of Beaulieu Abbey in Hampshire was of this form. The wealthy Cistercian abbey of Hayles in Worcestershire, however, rebuilt its east end in the most elaborate multi-apsidal form in order to enshrine a relic of the Precious Blood.

As the thirteenth century wore on towards the great days of Edwardian England, the tendency to simplify the plans of the eastern arms of great churches in conformity with those of the western portions is every-

where noticeable. Thus the earlier confused assemblage of eastern transept, ambulatory and various protruding chapels all tends to be swallowed
up in one vast aisled hall extending from the central tower to a lofty east
wall.

It may be that the expansion of window area for the display of
coloured glass had some effect upon the obvious desire to simplify the
mass of the building and provide unobstructed areas of wall, such as now
existed at the extreme east end of the building, suitable for the siting of a
great traceried window. York Cathedral, the choir of which was built at
the end of the fourteenth century, is an example of the extreme simplicity
of the noble presbyteries of the period, in which the lack of Early Gothic
refinement in its architectural detail is counterbalanced by the glories of
the fenestration.

It is greatly to be regretted that none of the late tenth-century monastic churches of eastern England remain to-day; probably their naves,
short though they were compared with their vast successors of a century
later, possessed a simple dignity such as is exhibited by the contemporary
church of Soignies in Belgium. It is not until the very end of the eleventh
century, however, that the fine nave of Ely (Plate 22) was achieved, to
remind us of the skill of the Anglian masons during the period when
Anglo-Saxon England was beginning to settle down under Norman
government. There is nothing comparable with this vast structure remaining anywhere in the world. There is an immense dignity in the sweeping arcades; the supports of which, it will be noted, vary alternately
between compound pier and circular pillar, thus recalling the Ottonian
duplex-bay system. Above the main arcades are the arches of the galleries
above the aisles; each arch having its *bifora* with the slender central shaft.
Above is the clerestory, threaded by a wall passage, having a *trifora*, in
each bay, looking into the interior of the church. The nave is covered by
a wooden roof, the timbers of which are concealed by a boarded ceiling.
Finally, at the extreme west end is a magnificent façade crowned by a
bell-tower, again in the old style of eastern England—the whole spreading
frontispiece continued across the entrance end of the church by a western
transept.

During the Middle Ages, eastern England could once exhibit a number
of magnificent naves of this description; those of Peterborough and Norwich are examples of the seemingly interminable halls which were built at
the very beginning of the twelfth century. On the other side of England,
however, there were, at the same period, no masons capable of performing such wonders. Under the influence of the French Benedictine monks,
however, strange parodies of the Romanesque naves, such as can be seen
at Gloucester (Plate 4), Tewkesbury or Pershore, were erected. In place
of the turned monolithic columns of Rome, or the drum-built pillars of

early Benedictine French copies, the western masons constructed huge cylinders of masonry towering to thirty feet or more in height. These western naves were short compared with their eastern contemporaries, and, as there were no galleries above the aisles, there was no large second-storey arcade.

The late-tenth-century introduction of the western bell-tower into England resulted in many of the great churches of the eastern counties being provided with one. Contemporary accounts of the great churches of mid-tenth-century date in this country make it clear that the single western bell-tower had captured the fancy of the English designers. By the second half of the eleventh century, however, it was becoming more fashionable to have two western towers flanking the central entrance in the west front. Eastern England, however, adhered to the earlier practice and concentrated on the broadening of the whole western end of the building, in the fashion of the Byzantine narthex, rather than by attempting to emphasise the vertical factor with a pair of tall towers.

Whether a lantern crowned by a wooden steeple or a fully-developed central tower surmounted by a belfry stage, the lofty transept-flanked nucleus forms the keystone of the external mass of the pre-Gothic great church. Though we have to-day lost the primitive spectacle of the two towers riding tandem along the high ridge, it is quite clear, from contemporary descriptions of the great mid-tenth-century Benedictine churches in this country, that these nearly all exhibited them and probably the two pairs of transepts as well, as may still be seen at Hildesheim.

A number of twelfth-century Anglian great churches still continued the Teutonic tradition of the western transept.[22] The finest of these once existed at Bury St. Edmunds Abbey; it has all but disappeared, but the remains of that at Ely, with its magnificent tower—one of the finest things of its kind in the world—provide some small indication of what has been lost through the destruction of that great Suffolk building which was probably once the largest church in Christendom.

At Lincoln (Plate 102) and Peterborough, the spreading western transept remains, in an abbreviated form, masked by later façades. In both these examples, however, the massive medial tower has been abandoned in favour of the pair of smaller ones over the ends of the aisles. Both single- and twin-towered west transepts are common throughout the Rhineland.

The important feature connected with the development of the west front of the great church is that it forms, in English architecture, the first attempt to provide any portion of a building with a façade. Buildings—even the finest—had hitherto merely been planned as accommodation. Such architectural treatment as might be considered necessary had been confined to experiments with the bay-design—mostly in the interior of the building—little attempt had been made towards treating any part of the external elevation as an architectural entity.

Entrances at the end of a building were unpopular during the Middle Ages; the doorway nearly always being at one end—the 'lower'—of the principal *long* elevation or 'front'. The lay-folk's entrance to the nave of a great church was opposite the westernmost of the doorways leading out of it into the cloister. But the Roman influence strongly encouraged the use of the western entrance as a processional doorway; hence its gradual incorporation into a fine façade, framed by the pair of towers which became essential to the finest churches of the later mediaeval period.

The western church-designers seem to have been unable to venture upon towered west fronts or any other of the features employed by the Anglian church-builders for the embellishment of their entrance façades. Nevertheless, the simple west front of Tewkesbury Abbey, with its single huge arch, may indicate the type of frontispiece which once gave dignity to other great churches of the West Country.

The development of the west front was probably in part due to the need for providing a bell-tower. In such churches as those of Tewkesbury, Norwich, or St. Albans, where the central tower had been raised in height to include a belfry stage, the builders seem to have been content to do without a western entrance feature to their naves.

The huge structures, monastic and cathedral, which we have been considering, were seldom conceived all at once or designed on any comprehensive plan. First to be built would be the presbytery; if this included the central tower, the transepts—or, at least, those portions of them which immediately adjoined the crossing—would have to be built at the same time to provide support to the central feature. The first two, at least, of the eastern bays of the nave would have to be erected for the same reason. The building of the great nave itself, to say nothing of its western complex of façade and towers, might not be completed for many decades after the foundation stone of the church had first been laid.

The building programme might be organised in several ways. Perhaps the central portion would be erected before the aisles, the arcades being blocked by temporary walling.[23] If the whole width was to be erected together it might be the aisle walls which were raised first, then the piers or pillars supporting the main span. These would be built in groups, for an arcade cannot be turned arch by arch. Perhaps centering would be economised by constructing first one arcade and then that opposite to it across the building. Scaffolding had to be raised stage by stage; as the work rose the difficulty of lifting material to the working level became proportionately more acute. Sometimes the main span was stopped at clerestory level; often the stone vaulting of galleries was abandoned and their arcades included within the main range so as make the aisles taller

153

but single-storied. It is no wonder that the original design of a structure suffering vicissitudes of this description is only with difficulty appreciated to-day.

The first extension which the church would undergo would be the enlargement of the presbytery; this would almost certainly involve the complete removal of the original eastern arm. It is for this reason that, while so many fine early naves remain to us, practically nothing of what must have been fine contemporary presbyteries is visible to-day. The rebuilding of the rest of the church would probably start with the transepts and crossing; these reconstructed, the matter of the nave itself might then be at last attempted. By the time this had been completed, it might then be found that the presbytery was due to be rebuilt, for the second and final occasion, as a spacious well-lit hall matching the new nave.

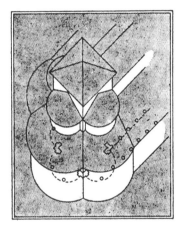

Fig. 21. Axonometric diagram illustrating Justinian's *chevet* at Bethlehem.

CHAPTER VIII

The Hall

The home of the nomadic tribesman is, necessarily, a portable shelter of some sort, generally a tent. The headquarters of the tribe will be the somewhat larger tent occupied by the head of that tribe, partly as a home for himself, but, more particularly, as a tribal council chamber.

This is, in effect, the origin of that most important feature of the social organisation of the Middle Ages—the Hall. The early civilisations of Mesopotamia or Egypt had no such structure. They were settled peoples; each man lived in a permanent house, however humble this might be. The king had his palace; the people had the market place.

Buildings of the nature of halls first appear when civilisation begins to penetrate into inner Europe, during the era of the cultural domination of the Aegean world; behind its littoral, most of the interior of Europe remained in a nomadic condition, only just beginning to show signs of settlement.

Anglo-Saxon England during the period of the Heptarchy was still in process of transformation from the nomadic tribal state of economy towards the feudal organisation which, under an aristocracy having at its head the king, formed the basis of the civilisation of the early Middle Ages.

The origin of the actual building known as the hall is still enveloped in mystery. As, for many centuries, halls were constructed of timber, most of these have perished long ago.

The existence of a permanent building replacing a removable tent postulates a change from the pastoral to the agricultural. The early agriculturalist, however, especially if he were a man of substance such as we might suppose the first builders of permanent structures to have been, would have required, in addition to a home for himself and his family, barns for the storage of produce and shelter for certain draught animals such as horses and oxen. Some authorities, therefore, believe that the first hall-like building was a combined house and byre. It seems possible that examples of a similar type of building which yet remain in Scandinavia may give a clue to the nature of the structure concerned.

We can at any rate visualise a building planned on a rectangular form and having a ridged roof—possibly rising direct from the ground—to throw off the snows of the north. Very probably, this roof received additional support from two rows of posts which ran longitudinally down the building, and between which the animals were stalled.

The theory is that it was at one end of such a building that the primitive farmer first began to find a permanent home; this would include, as required by the climate, a hearth upon which a fire could always remain alight when required to warm the occupants during winter.

Developing this theory: the ejection of the animals, and the housing of these in a separate building, would leave the original structure looking very like the hall as we begin to find it at the beginning of the second millennium.

It is almost certain, however, that, at the same time as the animals were ejected from the original building, this was reduced in size to save the space previously occupied by them and at the same time to release material for the erection of their new shelter. Thus the first true hall might not have been a long building at all, but one more nearly approching the square. Such a building might very well have been constructed on the same 'four-poster' system that we have already discussed in connection with early churches; researches which have been conducted into the subject of early Germanic legal codes suggest that by the time when England was being colonised by the Saxons this may have been, in fact, the case.

In this connection, it is interesting to note that the principal building of the Aegean world during the great period of its architecture—the second millennium B.C.—was a square apartment, known as the *megaron*, the roof of which was supported by four columns. The form to which these ancient halls had at that time attained might well be the same as that of their successors in the barbaric west two thousand years later.

Everything considered, it seems probable that we may imagine the Saxon hall during the latter part of the Heptarchy as being on the same four-poster plan as that of the church; without, of course, the projecting chancel. The elevation of the hall would naturally have been on an economical scale and not attain to the monumental height of the contemporary ecclesiastical building; the finest examples of both structures, however, might possibly have been surrounded by timber porticoes as additional protection against the elements.

It should be understood that the aisled type of plan employed in the classical basilica or the mediaeval great church is the result of a desire to increase the width of the building, beyond the possible span of a single roof, by supporting the main walls of the structure upon an arcade or colonnade; the aisles thus added to the plan became entirely separate structures.

113. The hall porch and bay window of a late mediaeval great house at South Wingfield, Derbyshire

114. The south-east angle of the cloister of Cleeve Abbey, Somerset, showing on the left the monks' house and on the right the refectory

115. An archbishop's great hall of Edwardian days at Mayfield Palace, Sussex

116. Traces of the roof of the chamber stair can be seen passing up the gable wall of this house attached to the end of a hall. Stokesay Castle, Shropshire

The Hall

The early timber halls, however, would have adopted the aisled plan as a form of construction. The two rows of supports passing down the building were inserted to assist in carrying a wide roof which was spanning the whole building including its aisles (Fig. 22).

The earliest timber-supported halls—with, however, stone outer walls —of which traces remain at this day, were certainly four-posters; they are those of the Bishop's Palace at Hereford and the episcopal castle at Farnham, Surrey, both of which date from the middle of the twelfth century. In these examples, however, the buildings are not square but have been slightly elongated to give them an axis; this indicates the transition between the true four-poster technique which postulates a square plan, and an axially-planned structure which however retains the four supports and thus becomes a building of three bays in length.

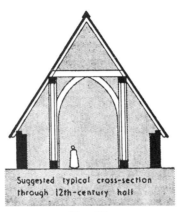

Suggested typical cross-section through 12th-century hall

FIG. 22

The remains of these two buildings may give a clue to the probable form of scores of similar structures which were being erected on the feudal estates at the time of the Conquest. At Farnham, only a large octagonal post, with a coniferous cap, remains; at Hereford (Plate 31), however, the post is square and surrounded by four half-round shafts, each with a similar cap.

It is the latter hall which is notable as still possessing one of the arched braces which originally spanned each bay of the 'arcades' and joined each opposing pair of posts. These arches are formed out of specially-selected pieces of timber, exactly cut so as to form perfect semicircular arches. The finishing touch to what is obviously intended to be an imitation of stonework is provided by imitation hood-moulds carved with nail-head ornament.

This extremely valuable building is of unique interest in indicating the manner in which the western timber-workers were endeavouring to

157

imitate, in their material, the forms employed by the masons who were constructing the larger buildings of the day.

On the other side of the picture, however, we can see how the development of the uninhibited timber technique—as seen, for example, in the approximately contemporary church at Stock—was gradually beginning to introduce into masonry architecture the soaring lines which were the very essence of the new Gothic style. That these arched timber braces were already being employed in the most important buildings at the time of the Conquest is indisputably indicated by the Bayeux Tapestry illustration of the hall of Edward the Confessor's palace at Westminster (Plate 104). In order that the nature of the great curved braces beneath which the king is seated should be clearly appreciated, the artist has indicated the grain of the wood.[24]

It is impossible to lay too much emphasis on the great significance of this important contemporary illustration of an Anglo-Saxon timber building. From it, one can appreciate that the English Gothic style, which appears in masonry work at the end of the twelfth century, was in fact already in existence as a timber style more than a century earlier.

The long hall, with its stone arcades and lateral aisles, makes its appearance in this country after the Conquest. The hall at Westminster was reconstructed in this fashion by William II; its dimensions were probably never surpassed in a mediaeval domestic building in this country. It has as many bays as the nave of a great church; its arcades, however, have long been removed and it is now spanned by a magnificent fifteenth-century timber roof which covers the whole span.

Notwithstanding the existence of a number of fine stone buildings, it was probably the wooden hall which remained the universal form of this structure. Apart from the twelfth-century examples already described, however, no recognisable timber halls of the period remain to-day. It seems most likely that the constructional form of the timber hall was much the same as that of the church; except that whereas the latter was a lofty building having two stories of timbering (Fig. 3), the hall would invariably have been a much lower structure of one storey only.

The history and regional distribution of the building style which employed 'cruck' construction has so far not been fully explored.[25] In the Midlands, however, there are small Tudor manor houses having cruck-built halls which may be of greater antiquity; some of the well-known 'cruck houses' may once have been halls. It is more than possible that large numbers of the Anglo-Saxon halls were actually of this form, and that the large curved braces which make the 'Gothic' arches crossing the four-poster churches may have been derived from crucks. It seems difficult to escape from the supposition that the wooden cruck is the origin of the Gothic arch.

The Hall

Prior to the twelfth century, timber halls may have been of the true four-poster type with an aisle on all four sides; it was possibly only after 'Roman' influence had been brought to bear on these buildings that they came to resemble such stone structures as the naves of the contemporary churches.

In stone, as in timber, the principal difference between the two buildings would always be that the hall would have no clerestory but would have nave and aisles all under one roof; thus the masonry arcades of a hall would be lighter than would be the case with the nave of a church having a clerestory.

At Exeter, in the more backward West, the late twelfth-century hall of the Bishop's Palace, with its magnificent doorway, was unprovided with stone arcades. Although fifty feet in width and close on eighty feet in length, its roof was supported by the usual four timber posts.

In the complete masonry hall, however, the transformation from the wooden four-poster to the axially-planned structure is clearly indicated by an increase in the number of bays (Fig. 23). Thus, although the two halls of Farnham and Oakham (Plate 105) are of exactly the same overall dimensions, the latter example replaces the three timber bays of the former by four bays of masonry.

Four is the usual number of bays exhibited by a great hall of the twelfth century; such was Henry II's palace hall at Clarendon in Wiltshire, and the once-beautiful hall of St. Hugh at Lincoln. By the next century, however, the number of bays in the finest halls had been increased to five.

The loveliest of the aisled mediaeval halls now remaining is the well-known example at Winchester Castle. Completed in 1235, its graceful arcades—lighter than those of any church of the period—are supported by pillars of Purbeck marble. Another five-bayed hall of almost identical dimensions existed at the Bishop's Palace at Wells; it has lost its arcades, and only a shell remains.

Such fine buildings as these may be considered as representing the crowning achievement of the designers of the early-mediaeval aisled type of hall. These thirteenth-century structures, sixty feet or so in width and twice this in length, covered a considerable area and accommodated a very large number of people. By the Edwardian period, however, times were changing; the feudal era was giving place to the commercial, and there was no more need to erect these glorious barns.

Within the aisles of the early mediaeval halls were accommodated the resident staffs of their proprietors. Probably the pallets of these servitors could usually have been observed ranged against the walls. Certain officials—such as, for example, the 'bakers' and 'butlers' who served in the pantry and buttery—might have been provided with partitioned-off cubicles, in much the same fashion as that in which the corporal in charge of a barrack room sleeps to-day. By the late-mediaeval period, these people had all been provided with proper lodgings; the thirteenth-century

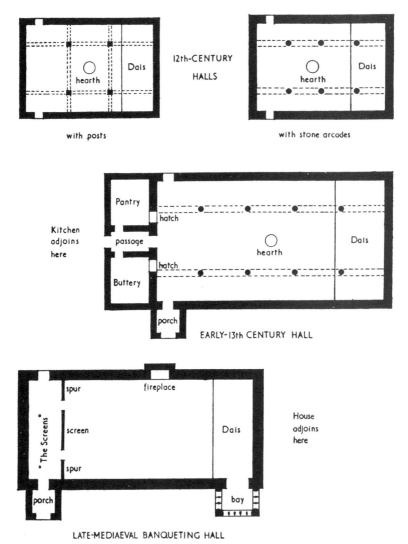

DEVELOPMENT OF THE GREAT HALL

12th-CENTURY HALLS

with posts

with stone arcades

EARLY-13th CENTURY HALL

LATE-MEDIAEVAL BANQUETING HALL

FIG. 23

hall, however, must have been a very untidy apartment, with all kinds of muddle always present along the aisles, and only the central portion kept clear for taking meals round the central fire.

The fine 'banqueting hall' of the later mediaeval period (Plate 106) was not provided for the permanent housing of its owner's retainers, but

117. The 'week-end cottage' of a late mediaeval abbot of Glastonbury at Meare, Somerset

118. A twelfth-century house of unusual type at Boothby Pagnell in Lincolnshire

119. The gable wall of a mediaeval house at Box-grove Priory, Sussex, showing the remains of the vault over the vaulted undercroft

120. The gable wall of a mediaeval house at Castleacre Priory, Norfolk, with a Late Gothic oriel

121. Undercroft below the great chamber of an abbot of Peterborough

122. Undercroft below the great chamber of a bishop of Salisbury

123. The remains of the street front of a large twelfth-century town house. St. Mary's Guild, Lincoln

124. A twelfth-century town house with a fine doorway and elaborate chamber windows. 'Jew's House', Lincoln

for the entertainment of the retinues attached to visiting notables. The designers of these great halls sacrificed accommodation to magnificence, so that the height-factor is apt to become exaggerated far beyond actual necessity. The reduced span obviated the need for aisled construction; the buildings, however, were still kept equally lofty, with high buttressed walls, well-lit, supporting fine timbered roofs.

The great hall of later mediaeval days became, in fact, of the same class of structure as the monastic refectory (Plate 108); the aisled type disappears altogether. (The older plan was retained, however, for the hospital wards or 'infirmary halls' (Plate 107) of monastic houses.)

Except in gable ends, entrances in the centre of a wall are very rare in mediaeval building; they are nearly always placed near the end of a lateral wall. Most mediaeval apartments, therefore, tend towards having a 'lower' or entrance end and a more remote 'upper' end.

The doorways to good domestic buildings are often their best feature. During the latter half of the twelfth century, considerable attention was being given to them; the carver who ornamented the fine doorway to the Bishop's hall at Exeter was indubitably the same as was employed on the original Lady Chapel at Tewkesbury Abbey.

In mediaeval days, the hall doorway, as well as that of the church, was frequently covered by a porch. Indeed, it seems possible that the porch was regarded as more essential to residential buildings, possibly for the reason that the only way to make a fireplace of those days draw was to leave the door always open. At the close of the twelfth century, large two-bayed porches such as those of the Bishops' halls at Norwich and Lincoln, with their elaborately-arcaded and vaulted interiors, could not, perhaps, have been found in any church of the period other than a very magnificent minster.

Throughout much of the mediaeval period, the floor of the hall, whether paved or of the natural soil, was usually kept in a very dirty condition, and used in a very primitive fashion. Layers of rushes or straw would be added from time to time, and occasionally it would doubtless be necessary to clean the whole place out like a stable. An expression occasionally used by mediaeval writers is the 'marsh' of the hall.

When gunpowder had become a commercial commodity, in request for use in fire artillery, the saltpetre required for manufacturing the explosive was obtained by digging up the floors of the mediaeval halls; this practice no doubt assisted, moreover, in preventing epidemics caused by the appalling condition to which these great barn-like buildings were apt —especially in rural districts—to degenerate.

The mediaeval hall always had a lower end and an upper. At the latter end, those of the higher rank ate their meals; at the other end of the two side walls were doorways, one of which was the principal entrance, whilst the other led to the shelters in which the food was prepared.

In order to endeavour to keep the floor at the upper end of the hall somewhat cleaner than the 'marsh', the former was almost invariably paved, and generally somewhat raised in level. This is the origin of that important mediaeval feature, the 'dais'.

The feudal hall was the most important secular building of the Middle Ages. At its upper end the dais indicated the place where the feudal magnate sat to administer justice among his tenants; this portion of the building, therefore, often received special architectural treatment, such as, for example, a wall arcade similar to those which surrounded the interiors of great churches. It may be that tapestry was sometimes hung round the walls of the upper end of the hall. Indeed the Bayeux tapestry itself may have been created for this purpose. The roof above the dais occasionally had a ceiling of 'wainscot'; towards the end of the mediaeval period, when more furniture was being used, the high table in the hall of a very important house or palace would often be covered with a canopy.

An essential feature of the hall was the central hearth, upon which a fire burned in winter to warm the large building; the hearth was usually sited somewhat nearer the upper end of the hall, in order that those on the dais might receive most benefit from the heat.

At the Norman Conquest, Anglo-Saxon timber halls must have been the only secular buildings of note. On the Continent, however, magnates had for some time been constructing timber *houses* in which to live. As will be described in the next chapter, the principal difference between an early house—that is to say, an important house—and a hall is that the principal floor of the former is raised well above ground level.

William the Conqueror's first residence in London was probably the structure which is known as the White Tower. Although this building is of that fortified type which we call a 'keep', it is, nevertheless, in reality a house, which has, however, been specially designed with a view to the protection of its occupants from attack. These massive stone fortified houses, of which the White Tower was presumably the prototype in this country, will be described in more detail in a later chapter. It is interesting to note that the largest apartment on the principal floor may have served as a hall for the garrison.

Many castles had timber or stone halls of the unfortified type described earlier. Nearly all castles, however, except those designed purely for military purposes or as temporary structures serving a campaign, possessed a house for the accommodation of the castellan. Some of these houses, like so much else of the period, were probably constructed of timber; there are, nevertheless, a number of stone houses yet to be seen.

It is not generally appreciated that the monastic refectory is, in reality, the 'great hall' of the monks. Monastic refectories, which were almost invariably on the ground level, were seldom, however, aisled as were their secular counterparts. The great monasteries had better facilities for erecting high stone walls and covering them with wide span roofs than had the ordinary layman; thus large halls could be built without the need for aisled construction. The refectories had their upper and lower ends just the same as any other mediaeval halls, with the entrance from the cloister at the lower end and the high table at the other.

In all probability it was the contribution to the study of hall design supplied by the monastic architects of the twelfth century which led to the final abandoning, by the middle of the following century, of the earlier type of hall with aisles. Some of the Cistercian refectories, such as that of Rievaulx Abbey in Yorkshire, were truly magnificent halls, rivalling any contemporary secular structure. That of Beaulieu in Hampshire (Plate 109) is now a parish church.

In the greater houses, especially those of the Benedictines, the abbot sometimes had his own private hall, in which he could entertain his more important guests. Generally, however, such apartments were on an upper floor and thus, although called halls, were in reality 'chambers'.

By the end of the twelfth century, the bishops were beginning to rival the abbots in wealth and power. The episcopal palaces, from the first, had fine halls, generally aisled, in which the bishop kept a state in every way equal to that of his secular counterpart, the mediaeval noble.

Some of the finest of all aisled halls were those which were constructed as hospitals for the sick and aged. Every monastery had one such 'infirmary', as it was called; the ruins of the thirteenth-century hall at Peterborough show fine arcades of the usual contemporary ecclesiastical character. The Canterbury infirmary (Plate 107) is of the twelfth century. The ward of the modern hospital, although to-day unencumbered by pillars, is nevertheless the descendant of the monastic infirmary hall, in which the beds were placed on either side of the rows of pillars.

Architecturally, the finest apartment in the mediaeval monastery was the hall in which the governing body or 'chapter' met. The term employed in describing these structures is 'chapter house'; they are, however, in reality halls (Plate 112).

Some monasteries had large apartments provided for the accommodation of visitors. Although such are usually called 'guest halls', they are generally situated on an upper floor, and thus come into the category of houses rather than halls (Plate 119).

The 'house' type of structure was very different in design from the form generally followed in planning a hall. The former was a compact rectangular building, of no great span, and *two stories* in height. The hall was, generally speaking, as spacious as possible, and its floor was, more often than not, as much of the soil as was that of the barn from which it was descended.

By the middle of the twelfth century, however, the more important stone halls of palaces and castles were beginning to settle down to a standard plan and associate with this certain essential appendages. Chief of these were two storage apartments (Fig. 23). One of these, the bread store, was known as the pantry, whilst the other—generally the larger— was the buttery in which drink was kept. These two apartments came to be attached to the lower end of the hall, access to them from which was achieved by means of two hatches in its end wall. Between the pantry hatch and the buttery hatch there was generally a doorway leading into a passage separating the two stores and leading to the kitchen. Occasionally, as at Northborough manor house in Northamptonshire, the hatches were replaced by doorways, making a group of three of these at the lower end of the hall.

In early mediaeval days much of the cooking was probably done over an open fire built in some sort of shelter provided outside the back door of the hall. Even before the Conquest, however, kitchens or 'fire-houses' were in existence. They were a universal feature of the monastic house. The kitchen was always placed near the lower end of the great hall or monastic refectory; to which access was either through the 'back door' of the hall or, in the case of well-planned secular halls, through a doorway specially provided, as at Farnham Castle, in the middle of the lower end wall of the building.

The mediaeval kitchen was originally merely a square structure of stone, built to surround the central fire-hearth; it was covered with a pyramidal roof, having at its apex a louvred turret, similar to that provided over the hall-fire, to carry away the smoke and fumes. Even as late as the end of the fourteenth century, by which time the domestic chambers of houses had been provided with wall-fireplaces for three centuries, the great kitchens still retained their central hearths. The finest example remaining in this country, that at Glastonbury Abbey (Plate 75), is vaulted and roofed in masonry in order that the stone-work could support a fine smoke-turret.

By the fifteenth century however, when wall-fireplaces were everywhere beginning to replace the old hearths, and chimneys, with their far more efficient drawing propensities, replace the roof-turrets as conveyors of smoke, the great kitchens also were provided with wide fireplaces in their walls. Great stacks to take the flues from these were added externally. The end of the mediaeval period saw the romantic turrets of the Gothic heyday replaced with the more practical but still ornamental chimney stack which, surmounted by its clusters of shafts, still provided that element of verticality so sought after by mediaeval designers.

125. The roofless dormitory of Battle Abbey, Sussex

126. The ruins of the monks' house attached to the south transept of
Netley Abbey, showing the entrance to the chapter house

127. The long house of the lay-brothers at Fountains Abbey

128. The undercroft of the lay-brothers' house

The Hall

The early mediaeval planner was incapable of laying out a complex of building units. Excepting in the case of castles or monasteries, where enclosure was a fundamental factor, the Oriental courtyard finds no place in western European domestic architecture until the end of the mediaeval period. Thus the early mediaeval royal palace was an untidy collection of buildings—houses and offices—scattered about in the vicinity of the great hall which formed the focus.

The layout of buildings situated within the fortifications of castles is always influenced by those structures which are, by their very nature, the most important in this class of architecture: that is to say, the curtain walls with their towers. On unfortified sites, a hall and its subsidiary buildings can be set out as may be most convenient, having regard for their respective functions; in the restricted 'bailey' of a castle, however, the accommodation has generally to be ranged at the back of some great curtain, perhaps incorporating one of the towers in its layout.

As the hall progressed along the road from the barn to the magnificent apartment of the end of the mediaeval period it began to take on the character of the house by having its floor raised above the ground on a storage basement.

If the deep ditches which formed the principal defensive features of an early castle should be found, upon its enlargement, to be unwanted obstructions, they were occasionally utilised as the sites of such elevated great halls. The finest example of the later castle hall is perhaps that at Kenilworth, built at the very end of the fourteenth century; it has huge windows in each bay as fine as those of a great church but displaying the low transoms which were introduced into all domestic windows to enable opening casements to be provided.

The culminating glory of the fenestration of the later mediaeval hall was the great window which gave light to the dais at its upper end. Even in Edwardian days it had become the practice to make this dais window the largest in the hall; by the fifteenth century, however, it had become protruded in the form of a 'bay' window (Plate 113), perhaps in imitation of the well-lit apsidal endings of some of the later mediaeval churches. Throughout the Tudor period the great bay remains the principal feature of the hall; it was sometimes made a kind of complementary wing to the porch which projected from the lower end of the hall.

Towards the end of the twelfth century, it was becoming a practice to design the windows of chamber floors in houses so that persons could sit in the embrasure and watch what was passing outside (Plate 68). The bay window of the late mediaeval hall represents the first attempt to provide a ground-floor window for the same purpose.

Throughout most of the mediaeval era the life of the hall centred round the fire burning on its central hearth, whence the smoke, drifting upwards, filled the roof space; to find its way out, eventually, through an aperture in the roof generally protected by a turret or some similar architectural feature.

It was nearly always necessary to leave the hall door open if the smoke from the fire was to be allowed to escape. Thus the porch soon became an essential feature in the hall plan; it protected the entrance and greatly added to the comfort of the occupants without obstructing the air supply to the fire. Hall porches, at first outstripping those of churches, by the Edwardian period had fallen into line with these; the two-storied church porch of the fifteenth century is frequently to be found repeated in the hall (Plate 113). Some late mediaeval hall-porches were raised to form what are, in effect, tall towers.

Another feature, introduced as early as the thirteenth century for the protection of the occupants of an apartment from the draught entering through a doorway which had to be left open to make the fire draw, was the short wooden screen or 'spur' built out from the side of the doorway, between it and the middle of the room. The early halls had two such spurs, one to each outer door. After the Edwardian abandoning of the aisled hall, it became possible to introduce another—sometimes movable —screen, between the two spurs; carrying on the line of these, it left two openings through which persons could pass.

Towards the end of the mediaeval period, the two spurs and the centre screen had been combined to form one continuous permanent feature having two doors in it. (Plate 110). During the fifteenth century, considerable skill was lavished on the decoration of these hall screens which became such magnificent architectural features that even the Renaissance architects could not dispense with this treasured relic of Gothic days. Many of the monastic great halls, or refectories, boasted their hall-screens.

Below the screen, a passage had been created joining the two doors of the hall. This passage became known as 'the screens', and was used as a servery; in it was sited an important article of mediaeval furniture known as the 'dresser'. In particularly important halls, the screens' passage was ceiled over and a gallery provided above it in which musicians could perform during banquets.

Although, as has been remarked, the purpose of the elaborate joinery feature at the lower end of the hall was connected with the existence of a central hearth, it was not abandoned when the latter was replaced in the fifteenth century by monumental fireplaces constructed in the walls of the hall. Towards the end of the mediaeval period the skill of the stone carver was called in to decorate the baronial fireplace; it was often made the site for a display of heraldry.

In the next chapter we shall see how was being developed, parallel with the hall, the two-storied mediaeval private house. During the early period before the advent of the great 'banqueting' hall, every manor possessed a hall of some description. Most of these were of the humblest form, low in elevation and of so small a span that aisles were unnecessary. It was possibly in connection with these simple halls that the idea was first considered of saving cost by building the house of the owner of a hall up against its end wall. As it was, for obvious reasons, the upper end which would be selected for this addition, it was soon found convenient to provide access from the chamber to the hall, so that its owner could reach it, from his house, under cover. This L-shaped plan, with the two-storied house built across the end of the single-storied hall, became the standard arrangement for the manor house of the thirteenth century onwards.

There are some examples of houses which were provided by building a chamber over the service rooms—the pantry and buttery—at the lower end of the hall; the thirteenth-century Bishop's House at Lincoln, now mutilated to form a chapel, was so constructed, possibly to take advantage of a magnificent view.

Chambers being invariably on upper floors, stairs had to be provided for access. Sometimes, as at Stokesay Castle in Shropshire, a wooden stair wound up from the end of the hall to the chamber door (Plate 106). By the Edwardian period, however, when the side walls of halls had increased in height, it had become the practice to provide a stone spiral staircase, enclosed in a turret attached to one of the angles of the building.

The large rambling palace of early mediaeval days seldom followed such an orderly plan. The twelfth-century palaces had their various houses scattered all over the site, perhaps with penthouse-covered alleys connecting some of the more important with the hall door. With the arrival of the turreted chamber-stair to replace the 'grand stair' of earlier days, however, it soon became the practice to join hall and house together by arranging for them to share, if not a whole wall, at least the angle containing the stair turret.

Beneath the chamber was the ground-floor apartment upon which it was raised. This storey was usually unoccupied, being used for the storage of the owner's goods. It is seldom entered from outside; usually there is a stair of some description descending to it from the chamber itself. In the case of a house attached to the upper end of a hall, however, the lower storey is occasionally entered through a door leading from the dais.

From the end of the twelfth century to the beginning of the fifteenth, there were probably scores of manor-houses, scattered throughout the country, which consisted of stone houses having attached to them timber halls. A number of the houses remain but the halls have vanished, leaving only faint traces upon the wall of the house against which they once abutted. Many of these isolated stone houses are to-day called, in error, chapels; their two stories, however, indicate the purpose for which they were built.

It was unusual, in the case of most early mediaeval houses—especially those in rural districts—for there to be a ground-floor entrance to the storage basement beneath the living floor; access to the former was almost invariably by means of an internal stair descending from the latter. Towards the end of the early mediaeval period, however, at which time it was becoming customary to attach a house to the end of the hall, the entrance to the lower storey was occasionally direct from the hall. Thus the presence of a mediaeval doorway in the lower storey of an early stone house may be, in fact, the only surviving indication that the building was once attached to a hall.

During the Tudor period, the great halls of England achieved a magnificence possibly unequalled in the contemporary world (Plate 165). Their lofty walls were crowned by glorious roofs of the greatest elaboration imaginable, and enriched with a fenestration the climax of which was attained in the great bay window with its wealth of painted glass. Externally, buttresses equal to those of a fine church added to the dignity of the elevation, which was closed at either end of the entrance front by the great bay and the entrance porch, the last probably with a chamber above it.

Halls were not always associated solely with domestic occupation, however. Guilds and fraternities, apeing the nobility, frequently employed the wealth acquired from trade or craft in erecting fine halls in which to hold councils and banquets.

Reference has been made to the difficulties experienced in siting the larger domestic buildings within the confined space of an early mediaeval castle. By the Edwardian period, however, new castles were being designed on an orderly rectangular plan, which greatly facilitated the layout of the buildings within. These rectangularly-planned castles became, in effect, powerfully fortified houses surrounding a courtyard (Fig. 37).

From this evolved a house designed on a courtyard plan, the nucleus of the whole complex being the great hall. The courtyard was not always completed on all four sides, but there was a tendency for wings to be built out from either end of the hall as if about to enclose a courtyard. That at the 'lower' end would contain the buildings associated with the domestic offices, whilst the other might provide accommodation for guests.

We shall see in another chapter how, as far as domestic architecture is concerned, the great hall tends to diminish in importance and eventually become absorbed in the general structure of a late mediaeval mansion.

It was in the great colleges of the Tudor period, which replaced the dissolved monasteries, that magnificent halls are found associated with complete courtyards surrounded by lodgings for the students and generally entered through a fine gatehouse.

In the ordinary dwelling house, however, the hall begins to shrink. The lowering of the roof pitch which accompanied the end of the mediaeval period resulted, as we have seen, in the popularity of fine ceilings, which eventually became almost flat. This abolition of the elaborate open roof in favour of the ceiling made it an easy matter to build another storey above the hall; thus this once lofty apartment shrank still further within the structure of the house.

The hall had been designed, originally, on strictly functional lines. At the upper end was the dais, eventually lit by the projecting bay window; at the other end was the entrance, protected by a porch which only approximately balanced the bay window. Such rough symmetry as existed, however, was marred by the fact that the entrance was at one end of the elevation.

The Renaissance architects were concerned, above all, with strict symmetry of elevation. Thus they had no use for the mediaeval hall. Very soon, therefore, they ejected it altogether from their plans.

CHAPTER IX

Private Houses

The hall is a symbol of organisation; the house represents the individuality of its owner. Surrounding the great tent of the sheikh are the humbler shelters of the tribesmen. The early civilisations of the Middle East had a population which had advanced considerably beyond tribal status. However humble they might be, men lived in private houses. When the pastoral nomads of Europe settled down likewise to agricultural pursuits, they, too, constructed houses of timber, rubble, or both, as has been described elsewhere.

Monumental buildings of the Middle East tended towards the use of the courtyard as a planning feature. In domestic architecture this device reached its highest form in the great houses of Rome with their graceful columned peristyles. The addition of the peristylar internal portico to the courtyard was of great value in that it enabled the occupants of the house to pass between the doors of their rooms under cover. From the descriptions of early writers, it is clear that fine timber houses of western Europe were, as early as the sixth century, surrounded by *external* porticoes or loggias; these were probably used for the same purpose as the Roman peristyles and, in addition, served to protect the lighter walls of the timber structures from the weather.

Of the houses of Roman Britain, nothing remains but foundations. It is clear, however, that they echoed the classical Roman plan wherever the building was large enough to contain a courtyard; if not, there was generally a loggia along one side of the building. From the ruins of Romano-British houses it would appear that these were not of very sturdy construction. Probably they followed what has always been the national building style and were of timber framing; raised, however, upon a foundation of stone or brick to protect the wood from rot. It was presumably the nature of their construction which caused their complete obliteration during the Anglo-Saxon invasion.

At the end of the Roman regime in Britain, civilisation, and with it private houses, passed away from the country for some centuries. On the continent, however, timber houses of some magnificence were undoubtedly still being built. These structures, despite the nature of their material,

170

were probably greatly influenced in their design by Byzantine models, for the eastern Empire was ever gaining in cultural prestige whilst the old Rome was decaying.

At the middle of the first millenium the typical Byzantine house was a two-storied structure divided into two by a cross wall something after the fashion of a Norman hall keep. On the upper floor of the main portion was the great chamber or *megaron*; lesser chambers were collected under a lean-to roof flanking the main block. The ground floor was used for storage and stabling. The principal front often had a two-storied loggia passing across it.

The sixth-century descriptions of Rhenish timber houses are highly complimentary, but unfortunately are lacking in details as to their planning. Soon after the Norman Conquest of England, however, a house was built at Ardres in Flanders of which a fairly detailed description remains. Although entirely constructed of timber, this fine house, which was situated within the fortifications of a castle, had two storeys and an attic. The ground floor was given up entirely to storage. The principal floor was divided into two portions; in one of these—presumably the larger—was accommodated the male servants of the household. The other portion was the 'chamber'. This comprised, primarily, the 'great chamber' proper in which slept the lord of the castle and his wife; partitioned off from this apartment, however, were two other rooms, one of which served as the bedchamber of the maids and the small children, whilst the other contained the fireplace. In the attic bedrooms above, which were separated into two portions for the segregation of the sexes, slept the adult children of the castellan; here, also, lived the watchman who guarded the castle at night and who needed a quiet place to sleep in during the daytime. High up on the eastern side of the house was a chapel. The whole building was surrounded by a loggia.

By translating this house from timber into stone and omitting the loggia, one arrives very closely at the plan of one of the great stone tower houses which were built within many castles in England after the Conquest, and of which the finest is the Conqueror's own house—the Tower of London.

The architectural significance of these great structures seems hitherto to have eluded proper appreciation. At the time of their construction they were the only stone structures, apart from minsters and monastic houses, to be found in western Europe. Only in the regions colonised by the Normans are they found. While in plan they conform to the standard Byzantine form they resemble nothing to be seen in Christendom and certainly cannot have been invented by the Normans themselves. It is to the far more cultured Moslem regions that we must turn to discover their prototypes. The early-tenth-century palace towers of Mahdia in what is now Tunisia but which during the twelfth century formed part of the

Norman empire may well have supplied the models for the great keeps of the West.

Such magnificent structures as these great stone tower-houses, however, were a long way in advance of the times as far as this country was concerned. Even among the invaders, stone houses had not yet come to be common features. The Anglo-Saxon private residence was, of course, still little better than a hut, although the timber halls of the period doubtless showed the way towards the construction of private houses on the Continental principle.

It has been emphasised that the primary function of a mediaeval house was to provide an upper floor upon which persons could sleep away from the ground. The wooden board as we know it to-day does not appear to have been an object commonly employed by the Anglo-Saxons, who used the rounded portions left over from the squaring of logs for the bratticed walls of their buildings. Nevertheless the time must have arrived when someone conceived the idea of making a boarded floor by laying planks across the horizontal members of roof-timbers. In some parts of the Continent, barn-like buildings often have a loft of this description contrived upon the tie-beams at the end of the structure farthest from the entrance—perhaps something of this nature provided the Anglo-Saxon reply to the chamber floor of the 'Norman' stone house.

The first stone houses, including a number of early twelfth-century castle 'halls', certainly had 'solar' floors of timber boards. Their joists strengthened by beams, arranged at bay-interval, spanning across the building, and probably often propped up in the middle by wooden posts.

A possible origin of the private house may be found by studying the development of town houses. It seems probable that it would have been town-dwellers who first were able to procure the necessary building labour for their housing. After the Conquest it became the practice for building sites in town streets to be divided by fireproof party walls of stone; a byelaw of Henry II makes this obligatory in London. The spanning of the space between these by beams supporting boards would easily provide a solar floor and thus create a two-storied house with its gable on the street-frontage; the improvement of the latter by making it of stone would probably follow as soon as means permitted.

The important timber house of Ardres is certainly of Byzantine origin. Whereas the Oriental and Roman houses were a series of long low ranges set round a courtyard, the Byzantine two-storied structures were cubical in mass and often divided into two portions by a medial wall, each division of the house having its own pitched roof. The Norman 'hall keep' is certainly the masonry successor and last survivor in western Europe of this 'turriform' type of dwelling-house.

It is an axiom of western mediaeval design that buildings are not set

129. Twelfth-century cloister arcade supporting rafters of penthouse roof covering alleys. Canterbury Cathedral, Kent

130. The late mediaeval vaulted cloister of Norwich Cathedral, Norfolk

132. Fifteenth-century inn at Glastonbury, Somerset

131. A fifteenth-century shop front at Lavenham, Suffolk

side by side—except in the case of rows of small town houses with their frontages jammed tightly together—in order to avoid the awkward gutter which would lie between their roofs. Thus the turriform house was inacceptable to the English builders and by the middle of the twelfth century was dying out for good.

In contradistinction to the family residence of the end of the first millenium was a specialised type of house: that which housed the hundred or more monks of a great Benedictine monastery. These houses were narrow two-storied structures of great length having the dormitory of the monks on the upper floor. It was from these huge buildings that the private houses of the post-Conquest era were developed.

The standard plan of a small twelfth-century house was a rectangle of which the length was about one-and-a-half times the span, thus making

EARLY MEDIAEVAL HOUSES

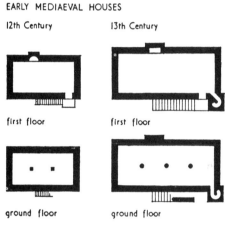

FIG. 24

a structure three bays in length (Fig. 24). Larger houses, however, such as those of the bishops, were often longer; the mid-twelfth-century example at Norwich Palace was four bays in length, subdivided, in the basement, into eight vaulting bays covered by a heavily-ribbed barrel vault. It was in this form that the Byzantine house, with its vaulted ground floor and its *piano nobile*, came to be introduced into mediaeval England (Fig. 25).

By the middle of the twelfth century it had become customary to divide the ground-floor spans of two-storied buildings, such as castle keeps or monastic dormitories, by introducing a row of pillars down the centre line. (Plate 98). Each bay then became covered by two quadripartite vaults—similar to those supporting the galleries over the aisles of great churches—and these would support a stone floor, upon which, if necessary, a fire could be built, in the apartment above. To facilitate the vaulting construction, it was customary to adhere to the common early mediaeval practice of making the bay-unit equal to half the span (Plate 119).

By the end of the twelfth century, many houses were being provided with 'stone solars', or floors supported upon the vaulting covering a lower storey. The wooden posts of the earlier houses became replaced by stone pillars; thirteenth-century examples of these may frequently be met with in the cellars of old houses, especially in our mediaeval towns (Plate 99).

The 'chamber floor' of one of these houses provided the total living accommodation. This apartment had—like all mediaeval domestic buildings—an upper and a lower end. At the lower end of one of the side walls was the entrance doorway, outside which was a primitive timber balcony, supported on a pair of brackets, and known as an 'oriel' (perhaps from a fancied resemblance to an ear). From this balcony, a ladder-like wooden staircase led to the ground; by the thirteenth century, when houses were

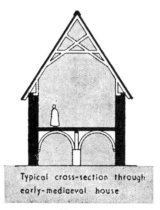

Typical cross-section through early-mediaeval house

FIG. 25

being greatly improved in design, the timber stair would often be replaced by a stone one. The site of one such stair can be detected outside the chamber at Stokesay (Plate 116).

It seems difficult to appreciate that the total accommodation of a good stone house, at the time when the vast cathedral churches of the twelfth century were being constructed, might possibly be only a single room measuring about 16 feet by 24. In this small area, the whole family —and possibly a domestic servant or two—would have to be accommodated.

A clue as to the possible arrangement is given by the description of the large Flemish house already referred to. In the simplest type of dwelling-house, the owner and his wife would certainly sleep at one end, the children and indoor maids being accommodated at the other end near the entrance doorway. If the floor were of stone, there might be a fire-hearth near the middle of the long wall opposite the entrance; a timber solar would require a wall-fireplace, in which case this would have to be sited between two of the windows towards the upper end of the chamber floor.

The general indications are that the middle section of the chamber floor formed the daytime living space of the family. The tripartite layout suggested by the owner's bedroom, general living room, and 'nursery', suggests a reason for the three-bay system of planning which appears to have been the normal arrangement followed by the designers of small family houses of the twelfth century.

In the large 'dormitories' of the houses provided for the monks of the mediaeval monasteries (Plate 125), each occupant was eventually allowed to sleep in his own cubicle, separated from his neighbours by timber partitions. Very probably, the chambers of private houses came to be similarly divided; no traces of such partitions, however, remain to-day.

The royal palace of the twelfth century consisted of a cluster of houses of this description scattered haphazard around the nucleus formed by the great hall and its domestic appendages. There would be a house for the king himself, possibly one for the queen, and also houses for the king's married sons and for his principal officers and their families.

It may possibly have been the fact that the provision of a wall-fireplace would require this to be sited between the upper and middle bays of a three-bay house, instead of nearer the middle of the long wall, that caused the later houses to be planned, in the case of the more important late twelfth-century examples, in four bays. Most large non-family houses, such as those in palaces occupied by the king, the queen, bishops, and similar notables requiring to maintain some state, were of this class. By the second quarter of the thirteenth century, the long four-bay house seems to have become universal except in small houses.

The largest houses of the early-mediaeval period continued to be those which accommodated the members of a Monastic Order. These houses were designed on exactly the same principle as the private house but were of a considerable length, the beds of the occupants being placed side by side along the main walls of the dormitory. Each monastery had a large house of this description, raised on the inevitable vaulted basement, attached to one of the transepts—usually the southernmost—of the church (Plate 126). The lower end of the monastic dormitory was approached from the cloister by a wide stone stairway; another, used by the monks during the night, led directly, from the opposite end of the long apartment, into the church itself.

By the thirteenth century, the standard type of two-storied house was becoming common throughout the country. An interesting example —now badly-damaged by the Germans—may be seen at Great Yarmouth It has an elaborately-ornamented entrance doorway, before which is an Edwardian porch or forebuilding from which the 'grand stair' leads down to ground level. At the angle of the building next the entrance doorway is the original turret containing the spiral stair which led down from the chamber to the storage basement.

These turret stairs were important features of the early mediaeval houses, as it was not customary to provide a ground-floor entrance to the basement which housed the owner's valuables. When it became the fashion to attach the house to the hall, it was often only by this turreted angle that the junction was effected, in order that the stair could also provide communication between hall and chamber. Thus the turret stair, from being merely a means of internal communication between floors, sometimes became the principal means of access to the chamber, in place of the 'grand stair' passing up the outside of the wall. By the end of the mediaeval period, the junction of house and hall had caused the straight wooden stair to be sited inside the latter in order to provide undercover

LATE-MEDIAEVAL PALACE PLANS

Hall tinted.　　　Chamber solid block.

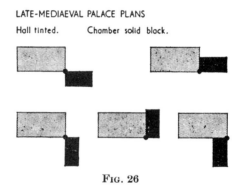

Fig. 26

communication between the two buildings but the enlargement of the turret stair eventually resulted in the abandoning of the grand stair altogether and its replacement by the late-mediaeval feature of the octagonal angle-turret containing a spiral stair.

The larger houses, such as those of the bishops, were seldom joined on to their halls in the simple manner which was adopted in the smaller manor-houses. Generally it was the lower gable-end of the house which was attached, either to the upper gable-end of the hall or the upper end of one of its side walls. As often as not, however, the two touched only at the staircase angle (Fig. 26).

From earliest times the principal architectural feature of the great chamber was the lord's window at its upper end. During the twelfth and thirteenth centuries this was usually an attractive *bifora*, perhaps eventually enriched with tracery. In the later mediaeval period, however, this was often replaced by a projecting type of window, similar to the great bay of the hall but supported out from the wall on brackets or a large corbel and thus known as an 'oriel' window (Plate 69). The oriel was

176

133. The shell keep of Carisbrooke Castle in the Isle of Wight

134. A great tower-house or 'hall keep' of the twelfth century at Castle Rising, Norfolk

136. The tower-keep at Hedingham castle in Essex

135. Henry II's experimental tower-keep at Orford in Suffolk

always at the upper end of the chamber—either in the gable-end (Plate 120) or in a side wall—and a south aspect was invariably avoided, if possible, owing to the popular mediaeval superstition that the plague was borne on the south wind.

It has been mentioned earlier that the actual sleeping chamber of the owner might generally be enclosed by some form of internal partition. The well-known house at Boothby Pagnell (Plate 118), which was built at the very end of the twelfth century, has a separate bedchamber at its upper end, with a wall of masonry dividing it off from the remaining two bays of the chamber floor.

The simplicity of the notions governing mediaeval planning are well illustrated by the plans of private houses which have received additions of any description. Each of these will be a separate structural entity, either built up against the wall of the nucleus or else attached by an angle. If

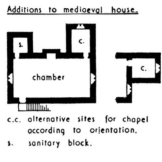

Additions to mediaeval house.

c.c. alternative sites for chapel
according to orientation.
s.   sanitary block.

FIG. 27

the former, only the back wall was used as a basis for expansion; the front and two ends were in mediaeval times kept free from excrescences in order not to block the principal windows in the gables (Fig. 27). It will be remembered that additions to the hall were made at the ends.

Some mediaeval houses possessed—again always at the upper end— a small chapel or oratory. Often this was formed in a small tower or even in the thickness of a wall. The great chapels of the bishops' palaces, however, were separate structures, joined to the house in the same fashion as this had been attached to the hall. These large chapels being usually at ground level, the junction was often similarly effected by means of a turret stair.

An important feature of the mediaeval house was its sanitary block. This was always attached to the 'lower' end of the building and was reached by a doorway from the chamber. Usually it was in the form of a small tower having the latrine on the upper floor and a shaft passing through the lower storey to the ground. Here there was either an external opening for cleaning, an excavated cesspit, or, in rare cases, communication with a sewer and a natural waterway or moat. Sometimes the addition was large enough for the first-floor apartment to be used as a wardrobe, in which case the latrine would be partitioned-off from this. An euphemism for the mediaeval sanitary tower was 'wardrobe tower'—hence the Victorianism 'garderobe' for latrine—the sanitary arrangements of large castles and palaces were often combined into one large wardrobe tower with a latrine on each floor. The sanitary buildings of the monastic houses were huge structures which will be dealt with later.

There were no hotels in mediaeval England. Important personages travelling about the country generally spent the night at a monastery. Neither the monks' dormitory nor their refectory (which had no dais) was a suitable place in which to accommodate, for example, the king. Thus it became the practice for abbots to provide an apartment for this purpose on the upper floor of the western range of buildings which stood on the opposite side of the cloister from the dormitory and parallel with it. This range of buildings was almost invariably of two stories; its basement being usually the principal storage space of the monastery. Except in the case of Cistercian monasteries, where the upper storey of the western range accommodated the lay-brothers, there might have been a certain amount of wasted space in this part of the premises. It was thus an easy matter to set aside a portion as a 'guest hall' for the abbot's more important visitors.

The end six or eight bays of the upper storey of the western range might be assigned to the abbot's hall. During the twelfth century, it gradually became customary for the abbot to use this part of the monastery as a private house for his own accommodation. Sometimes he divided off part of the hall to form a small chamber; perhaps with an opening through which he could communicate with the church. By the thirteenth century the abbots were building fine houses, projecting westwards from their halls, with commodious chambers on the upper floors. Even the Cistercian abbots, who were strictly enjoined to sleep in the monks' dormitory, constructed wings projecting eastwards from these, having chambers in their upper stories which formed, as it were, annexes to the dormitory itself. The western range of a Cistercian house was the house of the lay-brothers.

Throughout the monastic period in England, the houses of the abbots grew ever more magnificent. Sometimes there was a fine stair, or a two-storied porch equal to that of a manor-house. The prior's great chamber at Castle Acre in Norfolk (Plate 120) has two of the finest oriel windows in the country.

Castles had been provided with stone houses, of the normal unfortified type, in addition to the great tower-keeps, soon after the beginning of the twelfth century. Often the castle had at this time no hall, so that the whole of the garrison had to be accommodated within the house; which would then, however, be considerably larger than the ordinary private house. There was thus no proper seclusion for the castellan himself and his family; this was often remedied, however, by separating off a portion of the upper end of the house in order to provide a 'great chamber' at this point. The later type of 'house within the castle'—or 'hall', as the principal domestic building, whether of one of two stories, was usually called —was frequently designed upon the two-compartment principle, which thus provided, as it were, a hall and chamber end to end.

By the very end of the twelfth century, ordinary private houses were beginning to be built with their upper floors divided up in this manner into a larger and a smaller portion; the former serving as a small hall, and the latter becoming the 'great chamber' of the owner, as at the Boothby Pagnell house already described. By the thirteenth century it was more usual to design hall and chamber as separate entities, keeping the former down at the ground level—a much more convenient situation for this public part of the house. Some mediaeval houses, however, were designed with the hall and chamber end to end but of different spans.

The abbots' houses excepted, few houses were developed by expansion from a first-floor hall; more often the chamber with its basement below was added to an ordinary great hall, possibly of timber construction.

It is difficult to follow the development of the domestic buildings within the fortifications of a castle, however magnificent the former may be, owing to the restrictions imposed by the design of the defences upon the arrangements within. Moreover the builders of even the finest castles of the twelfth century, for instance, seem to have been far too much concerned with the military side of their architecture to be able always to pay sufficient attention to the residential factor. It is, therefore, the unfortified palaces which display the best examples of the domestic architecture of the twelfth and thirteenth centuries. The most interesting of these are the palaces of the bishops.[26]

The great halls of the episcopal palaces have now all fallen into disuse and are either ruins or—as at Salisbury or Exeter—incorporated within houses constructed after the mediaeval period. Some of the great chambers of the bishops remain, however; that at Lincoln has had its stone floor, with the vaulting beneath, ripped out and the whole building converted into an excessively lofty modern chapel. In many cases the undercroft of the great chamber remains; that at Salisbury (Plate 122) is an example. The bishop's palace at Peterborough (Plate 121) was once the abbot's house; the undercroft of its great chamber remains.

An interesting feature of bishops' palaces is the retention of the custom of setting the great chamber over the storerooms at the lower end of the hall. At Lincoln and Wells—the latter of thirteenth-century date

—the two buildings form a well-planned entity which at Wells is enclosed within a fine façade-wall having a staircase turret at each angle so that the whole composition resembles a castle in itself. The reason for this unusual arrangement—which is, however, sometimes met with in late manor-houses—may be due to the fact that the bishops generally had two chambers, one of which was the council chamber, often called by some humorous designation such as 'Paradise' or 'Heaven's Gate'; it may be that these lower-end chambers are not in fact the actual residential chambers.[27]

The fortifications of a castle, obstructive though they might prove to the orderly layout of the house within, made up for this by supplying, in the interiors of the wall-towers guarding the stone curtains, numerous rooms which could be used as chambers for the accommodation of members of the household, garrison or for guests. Bearing in mind that only the poorest people slept upon the ground, the ground floors of such accommodation would probably almost invariably be used for storage purposes only. Occasionally they might be used as prisons, which, however, were generally sited so as to be accessible only by means of trap doors, access to which from the floor of the prison below would have been practically impossible without a ladder.

The mid-twelfth-century practice of raising tall keep-towers within the more important castles set a fashion for the tower as a secular structure. Prior to the Conquest, the tower had been considered as an edifice designed solely for carrying bells; the development of the strongly-fortified house into a three-storied residential tower, however, had begun to make this type of structure a symbol of seigneurial splendour. The large 'lord's tower', containing his bedchamber, became a feature, not only of completely fortified castles, but even of such humble manor-houses as that of Longthorpe in Northamptonshire, to the thirteenth-century chamber of which has been added a fine tower of Edwardian date. The lord's tower at Stokesay Castle is, of course, well-known.

The awkward plans upon which most of the early castles were laid out were due to the deliberately chosen difficulties of the sites, these being nearly always upon high ground surrounded by slopes. Towards the end of the thirteenth century, however, when the importance attached to water defences caused newly-built castles to be sited on level ground within a moat, the buildings could then be laid out in an orderly fashion on rectangular plans. The house within the fortifications could thus be set out with as much formality as if the site had been unrestricted.

During the latter part of the thirteenth and beginning of the fourteenth centuries, many manor-houses were acquiring from the king a 'licence to crenallate', so that protection could be provided to the house by surrounding it with curtain walls guarded by towers. Many of our later castles, therefore, display within them as nucleus the hall and house as originally occupied, prior to the erection of the surrounding fortifications (Fig. 37).

As in the countryside, so did the little two-storied stone houses of the twelfth and thirteenth centuries line the narrow streets of the mediaeval towns. Each house had a frontage of sixteen to twenty feet; rows of them were set side by side with their gables towards the street. Each gable-end vied with its neighbour in architectural effect; the standard arrangement would be a doorway in the centre of the front with an attractive *bifora*, lighting the chamber, over it. In small town houses a ground-floor entrance would probably have been unavoidable, as the narrow frontage would not have provided enough space for a rising stair; this, moreover, would have arrived in the middle of the upper end wall of the chamber, a most unsuitable arrangement in a mediaeval house. It seems reasonable to suppose that access to the chambers of these narrow-fronted town houses would have been provided either by a ladder-like stair leaning against the back wall of the building, or, perhaps, by an inner stair leading to a trap-door in the solar floor. In the latter case, the floor would, of course, have been of wooden construction.

It is clear, however, that many early town houses had the usual vaulted basement, with the solar floor above supported on a pair of central pillars. The ground levels of our mediaeval towns having been steadily rising— as the result of the accumulation of centuries of rubbish in the streets— throughout the whole of the mediaeval period, most of these vaulted lower storeys are now well below the level of the ground, and appear to-day as cellars.

These so-called crypts still exist—in probably far greater numbers than has been so far recorded—beneath many of the post-mediaeval houses and shops which line the streets of our ancient towns. The chambers which they once supported, however, have all vanished long ago. It is doubtful whether a single example of the early mediaeval town house, narrow-fronted and with its gable-end to the street, remains anywhere to be seen at this day.

In the steep street which climbs up to Lincoln, however, on sites which may have offered small attraction to the average builder of later days, are the remains of some of the wider-fronted houses of late twelfth-century date, which have their long sides presented to the street (Plate 124). In this case there is a central doorway at street level; persons passed through this and across the basement storey to another doorway leading into the yard at the rear of the house, whence the usual timber stair led up to the first-floor entrance at the lower end of the chamber. The two 'Jews' Houses' at Lincoln have good façades, each with a pair of windows lighting the street front of the chamber; between them is a wall-fireplace

181

supported upon the slight porch formed by a heavy hood-mould covering the elaborately-ornamented entrance doorway. It is of interest to note that this utilisation of part of the ground storey of a house as a passage-way recalls the arrangement met with in the large monastic houses where the chapter house is reached through a vestibule constructed beneath the dormitory (Fig. 29).

A larger type of town house occurs in the same city, in the building known as 'St. Mary's Guild' (Plate 123). The difficulty which will always be encountered when erecting a house on a narrow urban frontage is that the building will necessarily obstruct access to any ground which might lie at the rear of the house. It is thus impossible to attain access to, for example, a stable yard, unless the entrance doorway should be enlarged to provide a wide entry passing through the middle of the ground storey. This large Lincoln house is a sole surviving example of its class in this country and only a fragment of it remains; it appears however that it could have been a courtyard house, perhaps of eastern European or even of Syrian origin, imported as a result of the Crusades.

Another house to which a Hebraic origin is ascribed may be seen at Bury St. Edmunds (Plate 94). Of late twelfth-century date, it is planned on exactly the same principle as the fortified tower-house of the early Norman castle, having a large hall and a smaller chamber set side by side, with a spacious vaulted storage basement beneath both. It is thus another late survivor of the Byzantine 'turriform' class of house.

The single-fronted town house with the chamber over the storage basement is the origin of the shop. Generally speaking, the owner of a town house would not require the whole of the ground floor in which to store his personal goods—which might include a stock of food—as would the owner of a rural house. In any case, part of the storage space was taken up by what was, in fact, an entrance porch containing the street door. As the owner of a town house was usually either a craftsman or a merchant, he would probably ply his trade in the basement of his house, achieving contact with his customers through its front door.

The transition from front door to shop window was not very difficult; it probably merely meant enlarging the opening. The arrangement of a mediaeval shop window may still be seen in some of the old towns and villages of this country (Plate 131). The opening, which does not reach down to the ground, is closed by shutters when not in use. The upper part has a pair of these which open in the normal fashion; the lower, however, is a long horizontal shutter, known as a 'stall-board', which drops out into the street and is supported there on two legs to form a counter.

In mediaeval days the finest town houses were those occupying double-frontage sites and thus had their long front walls lining the street instead of their upper ends as was the case with the single-frontage variety. Conditions in the towns were such that ground-floor entrances could be used; thus the lower storey was not wasted as a storeroom but used for living accommodation. In order to make this part of the house as comfortable as possible the 'front door' was moved from its central position to one end of the front; a screened-off passage from it to the 'back door' converted the ground floor into a sort of small hall, or 'parlour'.

The great advantage the 'double-fronted' house had over that having its gable to the street lay in the fact that a passage could be formed leading into the yard at the back in which the cooking of meals was done. In late-mediaeval days most of the better-class houses occupied double frontages where these could be acquired; a kitchen was eventually built out into the yard from the 'upper' end of the house. The ell-shaped type of house was the normal urban residence of the fifteenth century.

It is from this type of structure that the first inns were developed. Mediaeval hostelries were wide-fronted and had an archway leading into the yard at the rear. In the finest examples there was a great parlour, perhaps with a bay window, on one side of the entry, balancing the dining parlour with its kitchen at the rear. Above were the bedchambers. Such inns do not however appear until the wool boom of the fifteenth century (Plate 132).

No mention has been made of the probability that a great many mediaeval private houses, both rural and urban, must have been constructed of timber framing. Possibly both stories were so constructed, but most probably the particular function of the lower storey would render it highly desirable that this should be built of more thief-resisting materials. An upper storey constructed in timber was always, for reasons described earlier, built out over the wall-face in the form of a 'jetty'. In town houses the floor joists of single-fronted houses were supported, not across the building, but resting upon heavy beams or girders passing across the house from side to side. Where the floor joists rested upon the end walls of the house, they had to project in the form of jetties, which in this case overhung the street. The great mercantile boom of the fifteenth century, which brought such wealth to the towns connected with the wool trade, resulted in the erection of commodious houses; as there was no room to expand laterally, houses had to be built as 'skyscrapers', each storey of which had to project beyond the next lowest as a jetty. Thus were produced the remarkable street-frontages of our mediaeval towns.

Town-planning was unknown in mediaeval days, although as early as Henry II's reign the Crown was issuing bye-laws regulating such matters as party walls and the drainage from urban areas.[28]

The village grew up as a huddle of hovels in front of the entrance to the manor-house or the porch of the parish church; the long 'street' villages belong to late mediaeval days, having been the result of settlement by squatters along the roadside waste after the Tudor wool boom had ruined agriculture and thrown thousands of labourers out of work and their village homes.

The ruins of Roman towns, laid out as a grid of streets—the only form of town-planning known until recent days—were in many cases occupied by the Anglo-Saxons, when some attempt was often made to retain the principal thoroughfares. Their own *burhs*, however, having been but small, hurriedly set-out camps of refuge, were hardly suited to town-planning; so that little is left of their original lines except where, as at Wallingford, the earthworks have been used as a basis for the fortifications of a Norman castle.

Havens were probably among the earliest places to be occupied by the Anglo-Saxons. In a practically roadless country, it was the vital importance of inland water transport which supplied the reason for the foundation of the great river ports, set, as at Norwich or Exeter, in the heart of the countryside. It was at such places as these that the first important market towns arose; in them, the Conqueror established his bishops to found their cathedrals.

Small towns grew up outside the gates of important castles; still more flourishing ones—probably with markets—before the west fronts of the great monastic churches. The custom of a large monastic house was of far greater value than the patronage of an episcopal see.

Fords and bridges, which regulated communications, became the sites of towns, often with a castle or monastery to supervise the crossing and derive custom thereby. A cross-roads or a meeting-place of important routes would form a suitable site for a town, the buildings of which would extend—in the form known as ribbon development—along the entering ways.

In mediaeval days, when a house was added to the ribbon, its outer limit marked the line of a possible connecting route or short-cut between one main thoroughfare and the next. Many of these routes would probably have been used too frequently to be blocked, and thus would become consolidated as side alleys to the main thoroughfares.

The spaces before the gates of castles, abbeys or palaces, and the 'gore' or wedge of land between two roads meeting at an acute angle, would generally remain unbuilt-upon, and would thus remain always as open spaces: village greens or, in towns, market squares. The true market-square, laid out deliberately on rectangular lines, is a late development in town-planning which belongs to the Renaissance, rather than to the mediaeval, epoch.

Early in the twelfth century, some of the more public-spirited amongst the Norman barons were founding new towns at the gates of their great castles. These new sites were set out on the usual grid plan and surrounded by a rectangular frame of earthwork fortification. Part of the little town of Castle Acre in Norfolk still survives; not far away, however, only the ramparts remain to indicate the site of the town of Mileham. Ongar in Essex, and Ludgershall in Wiltshire are other examples of Anglo-Norman country towns. The finest example of all is the fortified city of Old Sarum.

It has always been difficult to persuade persons to live in places not of their own choice, even if protection should be offered to encourage prospective inhabitants. Winchelsea in Sussex was so frequently being assaulted by the French that Edward I refounded it on a new site, which he fortified with walls of stone. The new town was laid out on the usual grid, and was similar to the 'bastides' which Edward was also constructing in his French possessions. The new Winchelsea, however, never became popular, and now appears half-deserted, with its ruined walls threading the fields in which the town gates stand isolated.

FIG. 28. Plan showing a type of later-mediaeval house developed as a diminutive copy of the great house of the period.

CHAPTER X

Monastic Houses

Monasteries are of two kinds: those in which the monks live separately as recluses, and those in which they are organised as a community. It is the latter form of monasticism with which we are concerned in this country. Monastic houses have existed since the early days of the Byzantine Empire; Syria is covered with monasteries of cells built round courtyards and incorporating a small church.

Monasticism has existed in England, at any rate in its Celtic northern and western parts, ever since Christianity itself was introduced. Celtic monasteries, however, were merely collections of huts, each occupied by a monk, with a humble chapel; the whole being surrounded by a rough wall. This last was essential to a monastery; a cloister does not really mean an arcaded courtyard, but an area enclosed by a wall.

The earliest Monastic Order introduced into this country—which moreover remained, until the Dissolution, always the most powerful and popular—was the Benedictine. Monasteries of this Order began to be founded in the seventh century; they were at that time, however, probably merely humble little settlements on the Celtic pattern with, perhaps, a church of some pretensions. The first important Benedictine colonisation took place just after the middle of the tenth century, under the aegis of Archbishop Dunstan. With the Conquest there was a considerable increase in the numbers of the 'Black Monks'; in the course of the next fifty years or so, both they and the brethren of many other Orders covered the whole countryside with monastic houses, many of them large settlements attached to a vast church which in later years was to become a cathedral.

A reformed branch of this Order, known as the Cluniac, appeared in England soon after the Conquest; its head house in this country was at Lewes in Sussex, where a great church was built soon after 1077. This Order is supposed to have greatly influenced English architecture; it seems, however, that its influence was negligible compared with that exercised by the Benedictines as a whole, except in so far that the Cluniacs, who were very wealthy, became exceptionally extravagant in the ornamentation of their buildings.

Monks were laymen incorporated in a religious Order, and were not

186

themselves in Holy Orders. There were, however, Orders of Regular Canons; these, although priests, were, unlike the secular canons of cathedral churches, incorporated in an enclosed Religious Order. Chief of these Orders in this country was the Augustinian, known as the 'Black Canons'; they became rich and powerful, and built many fine monastic houses, the churches of some of which eventually became cathedrals.

The attempted reformation of the Benedictine Order undertaken by the Cluniacs was not along the lines of austerity; indeed, the Cluniacs rivalled the Benedictines in the magnificence of their houses. The first serious attempt to reject the pomp and magnificence which had come to surround monasticism was begun by the Order known as the Cistercians. These 'White Monks' avoided the towns in which the Benedictines had begun to found their houses, settling instead in remote rural districts, where they lived humbly as pastoral communities of sheep farmers. To help them with their farming they augmented their numbers with lay-brothers who acted as labourers. The Cistercian monasteries became very large; each house had extensive buildings, well but simply constructed without any ostentation other than the extent of the buildings themselves.

As the Augustinian canons were, in a sense, complementary to the Benedictine monks, so were the Premonstratensian or 'White' canons to the Cistercians.

The only English Order in which the monks lived in separate cells was the Carthusian.

There were, of course, a number of monasteries—some of them very large and wealthy—occupied by nuns; the Benedictine Order being the one chiefly popular amongst women.

England possessed the only Order which was shared by both sexes. This was the Gilbertine; the monasteries were double, with two cloisters but a common church, divided down the middle by a wall.

There were a number of Orders of Friars, the members of which travelled about the countryside preaching and begging. Their houses, therefore, were seldom large or magnificent; their churches were mainly designed for the purpose of preaching to the laity.

The life of a monastic house was concentrated around its church. This was always the first building to be constructed. The first monastic churches were isolated structures, either on the Romano-Celtic plan we have seen at Southelmham (Fig. 9) or, after the end of the ninth century, on the Byzantine 'turriform' plan introduced into western Europe by the Carolingians. Only during the ecclesiastical renaissance inaugurated by St. Dunstan during the third quarter of the tenth century did the extended Ottonian church appear in this country, to take its place soon after as the principal structure in a standard claustral plan.

Owing to its size, it was always necessary to build a great abbey church in sections. The first part to be erected would be the presbytery which contained the high altar; to be followed by the central part of the church containing the choir. This would be the most difficult part of the church to construct as it would contain the crossing with its lofty piers. In order to give support to these, and also to provide accommodation for the choir, it was usual to construct two bays or more of the nave at the same time. For the same reason, the central part of the transept would be constructed, although the actual ends might be left until a later stage. Such portions of the church as were originally erected might not be finished up to the full height; the clerestory and vaulting might be left for the time being, a temporary roof being erected instead. The construction of the long nave, and the final completion of the high vaults, towers and façade would probably be achieved many decades after the laying of the foundation stone.

The buildings forming the monastic house itself were laid out round a courtyard (Fig. 29), one side of which was formed by the nave of the church. Generally the church was on the north side of this cloister, in order not to take away the sunlight from this and at the same time to give protection from the north winds. It was vital, however, that the monastery should be so planned as to be provided with a stream, on the side farthest from the church, which could be employed for the water-disposal of sewage; thus it was occasionally necessary to vary the standard relationship between church and cloister.

In Gilbertine churches where provision had to be made for both sexes, the principal or nuns' church was provided with a kind of wide aisle, separated from it by a solid wall instead of an arcade, on the side farthest from the cloister. This aisle formed the church of the canons, who had, however, a cloister of their own, having a small church attached to it. The reason for including canons in the Gilbertine Order was in order to supply priests for conducting the services in the church of the nuns.

The peculiar constitution of the Carthusian Order and the austerity of its rule did not normally make for fine churches; Carthusian churches are therefore, for the most part, humble and undistinguished.

The churches of the Friars, also, were on a smaller scale than those of the monks and canons. By the Edwardian period, however, when parish churches were being provided with fine naves, many of the Friars' churches were being similarly expanded; it is not impossible that there may be some connection between the two, as the naves of parish churches are principally designed to facilitate preaching to congregations.

The primary difference between a parish church and a great church is that the latter belongs to a religious community and is designed especially to accommodate this. The portion of the church containing the seats occupied by the community is known as the choir; this contains opposing rows of stalls lining the side walls. At the west end of the choir, the stalls are 'returned' across the building, so that the more important officials of the monastery can have stalls which directly face the altar. The choir is entered by a doorway in the centre of the 'return stalls'; at the eastern end of the side stalls, lateral doorways provide access to the aisles, and thence to the ambulatory, should one exist, passing behind the high altar (Fig. 15).

The western end of the choir is shut off by the choir screen (Plate 185) with its central doorway, on either side of which are ranged the 'return stalls' facing east. West of this screen is the nave, containing the altar for the lay folk. It was not possible to site this directly against the pulpitum, owing to the presence of the central doorway; so a second screen was provided, one bay west of this, having the nave altar against this, flanked by two doorways. Between this 'rood screen' and the pulpitum was the 'retro-choir', in which old and infirm monks, who might not have been able to stand for long periods, listened, seated, to the services. Crowland (Plate 186) and St. Albans abbeys, amongst others, still possess their rood screens. In parish churches, the chancel screen, with its central doorway, is known as the rood screen; here there is, of course, no nave altar.

In the great churches of the latter part of the tenth century, the choir was usually sited in the crossing beneath the central tower. As it was customary, in building this part of the church, to include within the central portion some two bays of the nave in order to give support to the tower, the choir often extended westwards into these two bays. In very long naves, the choir is entirely accommodated in the eastern bays of this, leaving the crossing free; with short naves, however, the choir may not extend west of the crossing at all. From the end of the twelfth century, when the architectural presbyteries of the great churches began to be extended, the choir came to be moved eastwards so that it became accommodated entirely in the eastern arm of the church, thus leaving the crossing free. In the late-mediaeval period, therefore, the choir screen usually forms a feature occupying the east arch of the central tower; in which case the retro-choir and the rood screen were omitted. Choir stalls were generally provided with walls or screens at their backs; these completely enclosed the choir and were sometimes continued between the arcades for the whole length of the presbytery until they met the great screen or 'reredos' behind the high altar itself. There would always be lateral doorways provided through the choir screens, immediately east of the stalls.

In the majority of monastic churches the nave was intended to provide accommodation for the laity, who had their own altar against the rood screen. This does not mean to say, however, that the laity had any

189

rights in the nave of a monastic church; if there was no parish church already in existence, the monks would probably build one. It was nevertheless important for a great abbey to provide its church with an ample nave, in which sermons could be preached to large congregations, for the greater advertisement of the dignity of the house.

It was due to the affection which the parishioners of monastic towns often had for the great naves of their churches that these were sometimes saved from the general wreck of the monastery at the Dissolution. Some-

CLAUSTRAL PLAN OF A MONASTERY

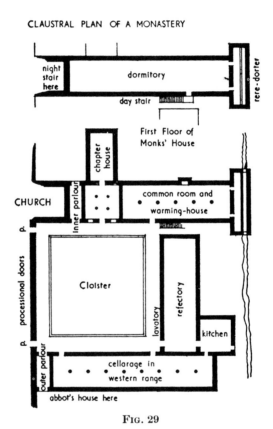

Fig. 29

times the whole nave with its aisles was retained. Occasionally only the nave itself or a few bays survived, as at Thorney Abbey in Cambs. At Little Dunmow in Essex, the south nave aisle is all that is left of a beautiful monastic church; it now serves as a church for the village.

The peculiarity of Cistercian monasteries is that these were all erected in remote districts where such congregations would not be procurable. The Cistercian Order, however, had provided itself with its own laity by attaching to the houses large numbers of lay-brothers who acted as farm servants and assisted the monks with the agricultural and pastoral occupations by which the monastery was supported. The nave of a Cistercian church, therefore, became the church of the lay-brothers.

From the tenth century onwards, the central tower of a monastic church indicated the site of the choir; the monks, seated in their stalls, could look upwards into the highest part of the building which they had created. Soon, however, towers had begun to serve another function, that of belfry. This is the purpose of the western tower, which later became, in most cases, a pair of towers. The monks said their offices at regular hours; the laity needed to be reminded of the times of services by means of the bells. Thus the bell-tower of a monastery was generally attached to the secular portion of the building; in some cases, notably at Evesham in Worcestershire, the bell-tower was a detached structure, standing in the graveyard.

After the church, the most important building in the monastery was the monks' house (Fig. 29). This was probably built at the same time, or very soon after, the eastern and central portions of the church. It was invariably a long two-storied building extending from the transept—generally the southern end of this—having the dormitory of the monks on the upper floor, immediately adjoining the transept wall. The dormitory was approached by two stairs; the main 'day stair' generally led up from the corner of the cloister farthest from the church, while the 'night stair' was contrived in the thickness of the transept wall which formed the 'upper' end of the dormitory, or in one of the angle turrets of the transept.

Although at first the monastic dormitories were merely long bare apartments having the monks' pallets arranged against the side walls—as in a modern barrack room—it was not long before it became the practice to erect timber partitions so as to provide each monk with his own cubicle.

At the end of the monks' house farthest from the church was a long narrow building, set at right-angles to the dormitory, containing the sanitary arrangements; a stream was led through the lower part of this 'reredorter' to provide water-carriage. The situation of this building in relation to the local watercourses was often the fundamental factor in the planning of a monastic site.

The dormitory floor was supported by the usual row of pillars passing down the centre of the building at bay intervals. The basement beneath, however, was not, as in the case of the ordinary private house, used merely for storage purposes. A number of special planning features had to be accommodated in the end nearest the church. At the further end, however, was often the monks' common room, an apartment also used, on occasion, for the instruction of the novices.

After the monks' house, the most important domestic building in the

191

monastery was its great hall, or 'refectory' (Plate 108). As most monasteries, from an early period, came to be planned round the quadrangle of
the cloister, this provided, unless the site presented exceptional difficulties, the opportunity for an orderly system of rectangular planning
such as might have been employed in the case of a house standing on a
clear site. It has been noted before that the customary method of asso-
ciating a house and a hall was to place them at right-angles to each other
(Fig. 30). The same scheme was adopted in planning a monastic house; the
refectory being set, at right-angles to the long two-storied eastern range,
along the side of the cloister opposite to the church.

The refectory, like its lay counterpart, had an upper and a lower end,
with a high table at the former, and the entrance at the lower end leading
direct from the cloister. Close to this doorway was the 'lavatory' where
the monks washed their hands before going in to their meals. The upper

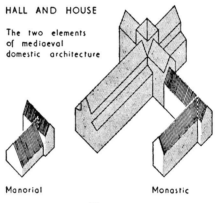

HALL AND HOUSE

The two elements
of mediaeval
domestic architecture

Manorial   Monastic

FIG. 30

end of the hall—except in Cistercian monasteries, where the refectory
was set at right-angles to the normal alignment—was towards the east.
Nearly all monastic refectories were built at ground level, but a few,
especially in Benedictine houses, were raised upon a vaulted basement;
there were various reasons, besides that of providing storage space, for
this arrangement.

The claustral plan of a Cistercian monastery differs from those of all
other Orders in that there were, in a Cistercian community, large numbers
of lay-brothers to provide for (Fig. 31). These were accommodated in a
long house erected on the west side of the cloister, parallel to the house
of the professed monks (Plate 127). The end of the ground floor farthest
from the church was generally the refectory of the lay-brothers; the
remainder of the storey being used—as in most monasteries—for storage
purposes (Plate 128).

The western range of the claustral buildings was the least important

138. Wall-towers protecting the early curtain walls of Ludlow castle in Shropshire

137. The small moated castle at Bodiam in Sussex

139. The 'grand front' of Harlech castle in Merionethshire with its huge gatehouse

140. The outer or 'mantlet' wall of Beaumaris castle in Anglesey

of the three; some monasteries dispensed with it altogether. When it existed, its ground floor was used almost entirely for storage; various apartments assigned to monastic officials were sometimes sited above. The subsequent conversion of part of it to form a private house for the abbot has already been discussed.

As in the case of any other great hall, the monastic refectory was properly equipped with a pantry and buttery. The latter being the servery for drinks, it was often accommodated in the adjoining western range, much of which was employed as the monastic ale-cellar.

The monks' kitchen was usually attached directly to the lower end of the side wall of the refectory opposite the cloister, service being through the 'back door' of the hall opposite the cloister entrance.

In Cistercian monasteries, the projection of the long western range which formed the house of the lay-brothers would have obstructed the

CISTERCIAN CLAUSTRAL PLAN

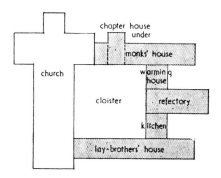

Fig. 31

lower end of a refectory planned in the normal fashion. Cistercian refectories, therefore, were built at right-angles to the cloister and had the entrance in the middle of the end wall. The kitchen was sited to the west of the refectory, between it and the western range; it could thus serve the lay-brothers' refectory in the ground floor of this (Fig. 31).

The cloister itself was, primarily, an enclosed space, entirely surrounded by the buildings occupied by the fraternity; all access to these was naturally obtained from the cloister, so that the house and its occupants were entirely cut off from the outside world. Two passages, however, led into the cloister from outside. These passages were known as 'parlours' from the fact that, in them, the rule of silence could be relaxed. The most important parlour was that which occupied the ground floor of the western range in the bay immediately adjoining the church; this, known as the 'outer parlour', was the main communication between the monastery and the outside world. The other parlour occupied exactly the same place in the eastern range as its counterpart in the western; the former passed under the monks' dormitory and beside the transept wall. Novices entering a monastic house passed through the western parlour; they left the cloister by the eastern parlour which led to the cemetery of the monks in the angle between the eastern range and the church.

The peculiarities of Cistercian planning extended to the eastern parlour, which, in their houses, was sited away from the church, the chapter house separating the two.

The cloister always had a paved walk passing around it; this was generally covered with a penthouse roof to protect persons passing along it from rainwater falling from the adjacent roofs. Intercommunication between apartments, however, formed a planning feature of no great consequence to the mediaeval designer. The very joining-together of a series of buildings to form a single architectural complex was a vast stride; even the planners of the early mediaeval royal palaces were very slow to discover how to achieve this result. Thus the arcaded monastic cloister as we know it was a rare feature until the Edwardian period, before which time most monasteries had but humble cloisters, with plain penthouse roofs supported by rows of timber posts; the whole quite lacking in architectural distinction. In the late twelfth century, however, a number of cloisters were being provided with attractive stone arcades with coupled colonnettes to support the penthouse roofs (Plate 129). At this time the new Cistercian cloisters were being set out with arcaded cloisters of this description. By the Edwardian period, cloister walks were becoming fine architectural features, covered with vaulting and with the arches filled with tracery similar to that found in the windows of the period (Plate 130).

The cloister garth began as the site around which the principal buildings of the monastery were set out. Its western side may or may not have been subsequently closed by the provision of a range on that side. The small houses founded by the thirteenth-century friars were, however, designed with a properly constructed cloister as a nucleus. The arcades were part of the structure of the buildings surrounding the cloister and its alleys were generally enclosed within their lower storey, the refectory generally being raised to the upper floor to allow for this. The church, however, was usually sited at a short distance from the north walk of the cloister in order that this might not obstruct the large south windows of the nave.

The cloister served two purposes. Functionally, it was a covered way between the doors of the various monastic buildings which surrounded it. These buildings were on three sides only, the fourth being taken up by the great church; this being, as has been noted before, almost invariably placed to the north of the cloister. The north walk, therefore, was used much less than the other three; it was, moreover, the sunniest and best sheltered of the four cloister alleys. This walk became a popular place for the monks to congregate and was sometimes provided with alcoves in which they could work at such occupations, for example, as the illumination of manuscripts. The elaborate cloisters at Gloucester show this idea at its highest achievement.

The most important doorways in the cloister were those which led from the ends of the east and west alleys into the church. Known as the east and west processional doorways, they were usually very elaborate architecturally (Fig. 29).

Every Sunday morning the whole convent left the choir by the doorway through the screenwork on the side opposite to the cloister, passing all round the eastern parts of the church until they came to the eastern processional doorway. All the principal buildings of the house were then inspected in a convenient order, after which the procession re-entered the church by the western processional doorway. Passing up the nave, the monks formed up into opposite lines in front of the nave altar; at the end of the inspection, they turned and filed through the two doorways of the rood screen and so re-entered their choir.

The Carthusian claustral plan was entirely different from those of other monasteries in that there was no communal house nor great hall, each monk having his own small cell. The cloister was surrounded by these cells, each entered directly from it.

Architecturally the most important building, after the church, was the hall in which the monks met to discuss the affairs of the house. The council of each monastery being known as its 'chapter'—from the fact that the reading of a chapter of some religious book preceded the business of the meeting—the building itself was known as the 'chapter house'. The chapter house was always situated as close as possible to the church, being separated from it—in all houses except the Cistercian—only by the eastern parlour.

The first chapter houses were long apartments, always on the ground floor, and set out on an east–west axis; rather like chapels in form, they were, however, rather low in section, owing to the fact that the dormitory passed above them. As this latter feature was inevitable, owing to the necessity for nocturnal communication between the dormitory and the church, it soon became the practice to move the chapter house eastwards of the whole range, its old site being then occupied by a vaulted vestibule passing under the dormitory.

Chapter house vestibules are often fine features of the claustral plan. They usually take up three bays of the ground storey of the monks' house; there is generally a façade to the cloister consisting of an elaborate central doorway flanked by two windows (Plate 126).

Freed from the compression of the dormitory above, the chapter house then became a fine structure, equal in architectural magnificence to the church itself. Some remained rectangular in plan, as in the case of the important late twelfth-century example at Bristol. In the western Benedictine region, however, a fashion for circular and polygonal chapter houses became established. When the cathedral chapters began to provide fine houses in which to meet, it was the polygonal plan which became generally adopted. The result was such magnificent creations as exist at Westminster, Southwell, Wells or Lincoln (Plate 111); these glorious structures, vaulted from a lofty central pillar of incredible slenderness, form some of the most beautiful examples of Gothic architecture to be found anywhere in the world (Plate 112).

The Cistercian chapter-house, however, remained in keeping with the traditional austerity of the Order. Generally maintaining its original position beneath the dormitory, the Cistercian chapter house frequently, however, expanded laterally into three alleys in order to conform with the bay-design of the main structure.

Monastic refectories, unlike the secular great halls, do not appear to have been heated, either from a central hearth, or by wall-fireplaces. Even the monks' dormitory had no fire. There was, however, one apartment in which a fire could be enjoyed by the community; the room in which this was situated being known as the 'warming house'. In most monasteries, the monks' common room at the end of their house farthest from the church was usually provided with the fireplace allowed by the Rule of the Order; this sensible arrangement allowed the dormitory above to receive some benefit from the fire (Fig. 29).

Cistercian practice, however, was to provide a special warming-house, with a central hearth, in the space between the monks' house and the refectory. The rural life which these monks led probably made it frequently desirable that there should be some place in which they could dry their clothes after a soaking day in the open. The common room, having the dormitory over, could not have a central hearth; its use as a novices' schoolroom would have probably also made it an unsuitable place in which to dry clothes. Openings were sometimes made in the wall between the Cistercian warming-house and the refectory in order that some of the heat might penetrate into the latter (Fig. 31).

It has been noted that a few Benedictine refectories were raised upon a low-vaulted basement. Although this was provided principally for the purpose of increasing storage space, it was sometimes found convenient to insert a fireplace in part of it, in order that the heat from the warming-house could be felt to some extent in the great hall above.

The manner in which the abbot of a monastery generally took advantage of the provision of a guest hall in the upper storey of the western range to make a private house for his own use in this part of the building

196

142. The effects of mining upon the tower-keep at Corfe castle in Dorset

141. The circular keep at Pembroke Castle

144. A twelfth century monastic gatehouse of a form imitating that of the contemporary castle. Bury St. Edmunds Abbey, Suffolk

143. The late mediaeval monastic gatehouse of Battle Abbey, Sussex

has already been described in a previous chapter. By the thirteenth century, many of these houses had been extended by the provision of a great chamber, in which even the king himself could be lodged when necessary. Such abbots' houses often became very fine architecturally; some survive the obliteration of the whole of the monastery itself, including the great church.

On the eastern side of the monastery, far away from the bustle of the outer parlour, was a building which played an important part in the social life of mediaeval England—the monastic hospital or 'infirmary'. This was a detached building in the form of a hall, generally aisled, and many bays in length. Such important monasteries as the cathedral priory of Canterbury (Plate 107) or the abbey of Peterborough had infirmary halls as fine as any church, the resemblance being heightened by the existence of the inevitable infirmary chapel, projecting from the east wall like a chancel. The aisles were partitioned-off into private wards; beds were also arranged in two rows on either side of the central portion. Each infirmary had its own kitchen attached to it; there was sometimes a small detached house for the accommodation of the monk in charge of the hospital. Near the infirmary was sited the monks' graveyard adjoining the east end of the church.

Monks whose state of health required that they should have better food than was provided by the standard refectory fare took their meals in a small apartment, known as a 'misericord', attached to the refectory.

As monasticism gained in popularity, and the power of the Orders increased throughout the country, the monks found their organisations becoming even more elaborate. A large monastery would have its own administrative heads in the abbot, the prior and the sub-prior; there would also be any number of officials with special tasks, such as the cellarer, the almoner, the infirmarer, and so on. As time went on and monastic austerity, especially amongst the higher ranks, began to lose popularity, many of these officials provided apartments for themselves, either in separate buildings, or in the western range.

A monastery was invariably surrounded by an area known as its precinct (Fig. 32). This was usually approximately square in shape, having the great church and the claustral buildings in the centre. The quarter of this area lying on the opposite side of the nave of the church to the cloister and including the forecourt at the west end of the church, were excluded from the purely monastic area and given up to the lay-folks' cemetery. The remaining three-quarters or so of the precinct was enclosed by a high wall, leaving the west front of the church at the angle next the cloister and passing westwards for a short distance before reaching the great gate-house of the monastery. After continuing round the whole of the monastic

197

buildings, the wall would return to the church, probably at the transept, on the opposite side to the cloister.

It has already been noted that the life of a monastic house centred round the cloister and that contact between this and the outer world was effected through the outer parlour which was sited near the west end of the church, and thus just inside the monastery wall; near the same spot would be the house of the abbot, who could thus survey from his chamber

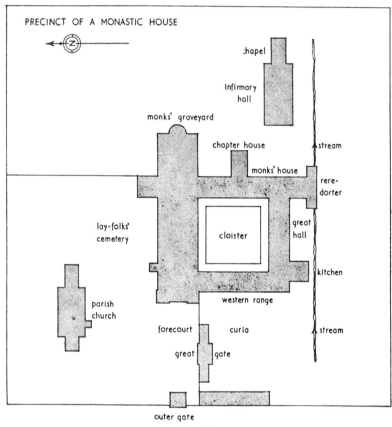

PRECINCT OF A MONASTIC HOUSE

chapel

Infirmary
hall

monks' graveyard

chapter house

monks' house

stream

rere-
dorter

lay-folks'
cemetery

cloister

great
hall

kitchen

parish
church

western range

forecourt

curia

stream

great

gate

outer gate

Fig. 32

the comings and goings below. The space immediately before the outer parlour was known as the 'curia'; in it the cellarer discussed matters of provision with local suppliers who would deliver their goods to the storage space in the nearby western or 'cellarer's' range.

The word 'curia' signifies much more than a mere yard. Even the modern form of the word 'court' does not create an adequate impression of the mediaeval curia, which was the space occupied by all the various buildings—domestic and official—connected with a great establishment of the Middle Ages. The king's palace is 'Curia Regis'.

The monastic curia soon became surrounded by buildings, the first of which would have probably been the thirteenth-century house of the abbot, built-out westwards from his hall in the cellarer's range. There would be bakehouses, brewhouses, dairies, and all the essential domestic offices.

Access to this busy court was provided by the inner gatehouse of the monastery. This was often flanked by offices—such as, for example, the almonry, where alms were dispensed to the poor—a range of which followed the line of the boundary wall and were entered, either from within the curia, or from outside in the space before the west front of the great church.

In this outer court, various semi-secular buildings would tend to collect. There might be hostelries for the accommodation of the traveller; in some cases there would be shops, in which products of the monastery—books, medicines, wine, farm produce, and so forth—might be sold. A wealthy and powerful monastery, founded upon a route or site much frequented by traders, might obtain from the Crown the necessary permission to hold a market in the open space before the west front of its church.

In the most important monasteries of all, however, such as Peterborough or the cathedral priories of Canterbury or Norwich, secular activities were excluded altogether from the outer court. It was then enclosed by its own wall, access to which was effected by means of one or more outer gatehouses, the finest of which would be that opposite the principal door of the church. Lodgings and guest houses, as well as offices and muniment rooms, were then sited in this court, which might also contain the private houses of ecclesiastical officials of various descriptions. It is these forecourts which in some places form the cathedral 'closes' which, with their modern swards of green turf, provide such lovely settings to the great buildings which they now enshrine.

Near to the inner gatehouse leading to the curia there was always a small chapel, provided for those persons who were for some reason debarred from entering the curia. These chapels were often very lovely little buildings; many of them yet remain within the cathedral closes.

At the east end of the church was the graveyard of the monks. That for lay-folks generally extended alongside the church on the flank of this opposite to the cloister; the precinct wall separated the two cemeteries. As many large monasteries, especially those of Benedictine foundation, eventually became the centre of considerable villages, the monks often had to build a parish church for the inhabitants. This was usually erected, beside the great church, in the midst of the lay-folks' burial ground. Often, as at Evesham, a bell-tower was built between the monastic and lay cemeteries.

Secular cathedrals such as Wells, Salisbury and Lichfield, were often completely surrounded by walls to form 'closes' in imitation of the monastic precinct. The close wall would be provided with gatehouses at suitable points and would include the bishop's palace and the houses of the dean and canons. The close at Lichfield was fortified with wall-towers, enabling it to stand a considerable siege during the Civil War.

The arrangement of the western part of the Cistercian precinct differs considerably from that of the more 'urbanised' monasteries. Although following the main lines of the standard monastic plan in their claustral lay-out, the Cistercians did not fence themselves in to the extent followed by most other Orders. There was no enclosed curia; the wall separating this from the forecourt of the church was omitted from the plan. With it went the great gatehouse; one of the entrances through the main precinct wall was provided with special architectural treatment to make up for its loss. The opening-up of the west side of the claustral complex focussed attention upon the long range, housing the lay-brothers, which extended southwards from the west front of the church (Plate 127).

This fact is of the greatest significance in the history of elevational design. For the first time during the mediaeval era the long front wall of an important two-storied building was being displayed as a façade—one moreover, which as it happened adjoined the only feature upon which elevational treatment had up to the present been attempted, the west front of a great church. Not only the spreading façades of the huge castle-like monasteries of Post-Reformation days in Europe, but even those of palaces and great houses, owe their origins to the twelfth-century architectural experiments of the Cistercians.

On the other side of the picture from this display of architectural magnificence is the practical problem of the water supply to these vast rookeries. Water was required for two purposes. On the one hand we find it needed for normal drinking and cooking purposes; most important of all, however, was the fact that it was absolutely essential for water-borne sewage from institutions which accommodated more individuals than any other class of mediaeval building complex.

The standard plan we have been considering was based upon the assumption that an artificial watercourse could be engineered which would first of all pass along the southern side of the claustral complex and moreover, if possible, take a course flowing from west to east so as to pass the refectory kitchen before it reached the sanitary block at the end of the monks' house. Thus most monastic sites will be found to have a slope from north-west to south-east.

It is for the most part due to site inadequacies in this respect that deviations from the standard plan occur. Thus a reverse slope may force the cloister to the north of the church. On very awkward sites a fall from east to west may transfer the monks' house to the west range.

It will be appreciated that, in addition to the great monastic houses which have formed the subject of this chapter, there were also a great number of very much smaller priories, accommodating perhaps only half-a-dozen monks or even less. Such houses would not possess a church of anything like the scale of that which would have formed the principal feature of one of the larger monasteries. Perhaps there would only be a small chapel; in a number of cases, however, there would be the usual form of monastic church with a choir and a nave. This last would in some cases actually form the parish church. The choir might subsequently be enlarged and extended; if the parochial population grew, the nave might be extended also.

Small monasteries would have nothing in the nature of a cloister garth; the claustral principle being maintained simply by enclosing the buildings with a wall. There would be none of the usual claustral buildings such as a great hall or a chapter-house. The monks' house would probably be very much like any other private house of the period; in very small houses, a tiny domestic chapel attached to this might take the place of a priory church.

An important mediaeval establishment was the monastic farm; this was called—after the barn which was its principal building—a 'grange'. During the late mediaeval period some of these granges came to be well-designed groups of buildings, often laid out round a rectangular court-yard surrounded by a wall or even a moat. The great barn itself—sometimes called, incorrectly, a 'tithe barn'—was by far the largest building; there would also be a small house and a chapel, in addition to other farm buildings.

Some granges had their houses expanded to form manor-houses of the normal mediaeval pattern. The fine grange at Tisbury in Wiltshire has a good gatehouse of the usual late mediaeval domestic type. Some granges were raised to the dignity of priories, one of the monks who were in charge of the establishment being called the 'prior'. Such priories would only have two or three monks on their establishment; none of the usual claustral buildings would be provided. The chapel might form a part—possibly the chancel—of the parish church.

The forlorn sites of hundreds of mediaeval monasteries scattered throughout the country represent the scene of the greatest architectural tragedy of this country, when the results of more than five centuries of skill and devotion were swept away in the space of days.

The chief material spoil of the monastic houses—apart from their lands and treasure—was the lead from the roofs.

This was stripped from the boarding and brought, rolled into bundles, into the choirs of the churches, there to be melted into pigs over fires made from the richly-wrought joinery of stalls and screenwork.

It was the eastern arms of the churches—the first portion of the monastery to have been erected—which suffered most; for this represented the very core of the monastic idea which was now to be stamped out. A common practice was to spring a mine under one of the crossing piers so that the fall of the great tower would bring most of the central part of the church into ruin.

Sometimes the local townspeople were allowed to buy the nave for their own use as a parish church. At St. Albans the whole church was rescued; by a curious chance the mine which had already been constructed under one of the great central piers was not properly filled in. Only during the last century the collapse of one of the timber props called attention to this state of affairs.

Although in nearly all cases the monastic church was completely erased by the destroyers, the claustral buildings were often allowed to remain as farm buildings attached to the estate of the new owner. If the abbot's house were a fine one, it might be preserved as the nucleus of a mansion. For the most part, however, the walls were all overthrown and the stone used as building-rubble.

The Cistercian houses, and others situated in remote districts, are for obvious reasons the best preserved to-day. Many of the immensely powerful Benedictine abbeys, however—such as Evesham, or Bury St. Edmunds—which, being situated in towns, formed useful quarries for its enlargement, have vanished as utterly as if they had never existed.

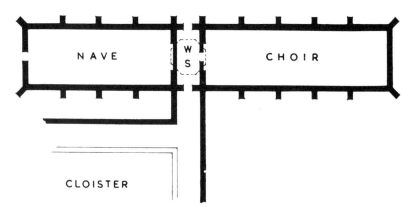

Fig. 33. Plan showing arrangement of Friars' church with 'Walking Space' separating nave and choir and giving access to cloister from outside. The Walking Space is usually lit by an octagonal lantern tower

CHAPTER XI

Castles

From the earliest times, man must have been used to selecting, when necessary, naturally defensible sites such as the tops of hills, the ends of promontaries, or the edges of cliffs. And in those prehistoric days, he had already discovered how to augment the potential military strength of such sites by means of fortification, or even to provide this where no natural defences at all were available.

The fundamental factor in prehistoric fortification is the ditch, into which an attacker has perforce to descend—placing himself, at that instant, at a disadvantage to the defender standing upon the opposite side. If the earth excavated from the ditch be placed upon the defender's side of this, the height of rampart so created greatly augments the defensive qualities of the earthworks.

Where very steep slopes are to be made more defensible, the excavated earth cannot be placed above the ditch as it would fall back into this. The method of 'scarping' will then be adopted; this consists in placing the excavated earth on the natural slope *below* the ditch, deepening this and providing it with a rampart at its outer edge. The Norman castle-builders made great use of this method.

The slope of a ditch which faces the attacker is known as its 'scarp'; the opposite slope, down which the enemy must slide, is the counterscarp. In the case of scarped defences to a steep hillside, the artificial slope reaching away from the bank at the outer edge of the ditch is the 'glacis'.

In the examination of earthwork plans, it is sometimes of interest to attempt to recover the settling-out line from which the digging was begun. This is the contour formed on the main scarp—or, in the case of scarped defences, on the counterscarp—by the natural line of the ground. It can be roughly ascertained, in the case of simple ditch-and-bank work, by setting-off the counterscarp on the main scarp opposite.

The principal rampart was, wherever possible, provided with palisades of timber planted firmly in the earth; sometimes these boarded stockades were known, in the Middle Ages, as 'bratticing'. No examples remain; the numerous illustrations which appear in the Bayeux Tapestry have so far not been satisfactorily elucidated. The builders of many of the early castles had to content themselves with hedges of thorn or briar in place of stockades; natural defences of this nature could doubtless have proved very unpleasant obstacles to a besieger attempting to pass them.

All fortified sites, whether the defences be of earth, timber or masonry, can be classified in accordance with the nature and extent of the natural defences. There is firstly, of course, the site which needs no artificial fortification at all, being entirely surrounded by natural defences. At the other end of the scale is the site entirely unprotected naturally, requiring a complete perimeter of fortification; a variety of this class, in which the site is somewhat elevated above its surroundings so that the lines can be set out to follow the contours, is known as a 'contour fortress'.

Between these two limits are various types of fortified sites which possess varying proportions of natural and artificial defences. There is the promontary site, in which only the neck of the promontary requires fortification. Another very common form is the lunate type of plan formed by making use of the edge of a cliff, or a river or marsh, as the chord of a semicircular sweep of artificial defences. Between these two is the quadrant-shaped fortification produced when a lateral ravine or watercourse has been utilised to reduce the amount of fortified perimeter. Sites which may be classified into one or another of these types may be met with when considering the military architecture of any period, whether prehistoric, Roman, Anglo-Saxon or Danish; all castle sites likewise fall into the same classification.

Prehistoric earthwork probably dates from neolithic times, when the pastoral nomad was settling down as an agriculturalist, acquiring wealth and feeling the need for fortification. Such could only be provided, however, through the concerted efforts of an organised community of a considerable size. The prehistoric earthworks which crown the hills of England are in reality the town walls of little tribal states.

The Romans employed the science of earthwork fortification with the same skill as in all other military matters. Their marching camps were all laid out in accordance with the drill book; permanent forts and barracks were designed along equally orderly lines. When it became necessary to fortify the new towns of Roman Britain, Roman military earthwork, later reinforced by the use of low walls and towers, was employed.

With the departure of the Romans the science of fortification lapsed throughout the country. It was not revived again until the beginning of the tenth century, when very small defensive perimeters known as *burhs* were laid out by the Saxons to protect the local population from the Danes. Later, the Danes themselves constructed similar perimeters.

It will be noted that all these fortifications have been provided by the efforts of a community for its protection. On the Continent, however, the new Frankish aristocracy was beginning to construct small editions of

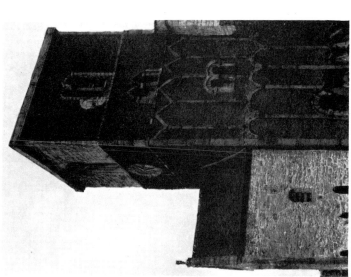

145. An eleventh-century bell-tower ornamented in imitation of timber bracing, Earls Barton, Northampton

146. Ancient 'turriform' church at Barton on Humber, Lincolnshire, raised during the twelfth century to form bell tower

147. The 'turriform' nave of Barnack church in Northamptonshire, later the west tower of an extended building

148. The Late Gothic west tower of Gresford church in Flintshire

149. East Anglian round tower of the twelfth century at Forncett St. Peter, Norfolk

150. A rare type of Early Gothic west tower at Middleton Stoney, Oxfordshire

these communal fortresses, each one surrounding the house of a feudal magnate. It was these small earthworks which were the original castles (Fig. 34), the Latin word *castellum* being a diminutive of *castrum*, the designation of a fortified town.

The sites for castles were selected in the same way as were those for the larger fortresses (Fig. 35). The castles of the Rhine provide examples of situations almost invulnerable naturally. The countryside of Flanders and northern France, however, provided no such ideal sites as these; thus the Frankish lords had to study the science of earthwork fortification. The Norman Conquest of England brought in its train a complete system of castrametation such as had not hitherto been seen in the country.

A word is needed upon the vexed subject of the reasons governing the siting of castles. One may hear a good deal of speculation concerning the possibility of a certain castle having been erected in order to 'command' some road, ford, or some other such feature.

Motte and Bailey Castle   Residential Castle with Barbican

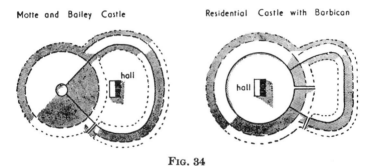

FIG. 34

From the time of the Conquest onwards, fortresses were always being founded and garrisoned by the Crown; either to overawe a powerful town, such as London, or to police an area, as at Conway, or an approach, as at Windsor. There were also ephemeral castles, mostly small, connected with some campaign. Such were the scores of 'adulterine' castles which were built, without licence, during the anarchy of Stephen's reign; also many siege-castles of all periods.

But by far the majority of our castles were built upon private estates by feudal lords, great and small, for the protection of their homes and property against neighbours, tenants, or any other potential aggressors. From the Conquest to the Wars of the Roses, anyone having upon any of his manors a site suitable for a castle might consider obtaining a licence for its erection; in later days he might build himself a toy 'castle' such as Hurstmonceux. Many mediaeval castles were probably built without licence but subsequently—perhaps for political reasons—allowed to remain.

England possesses few sites for entirely natural castles; Bamborough in Northumberland is, however, an outstanding example. 'Spur-castles', in which the neck of a promontary is fortified, were popular among the invaders, especially in those parts of England which resembled the Norman countryside of the Pays de Caux: chalky downlands provided excellent sites for scarped spur-castles, such as that of Bramber in Sussex.

For larger castles, however, the lunate plan was more popular. The first great castles of the Conqueror were laid out on the squared-up form

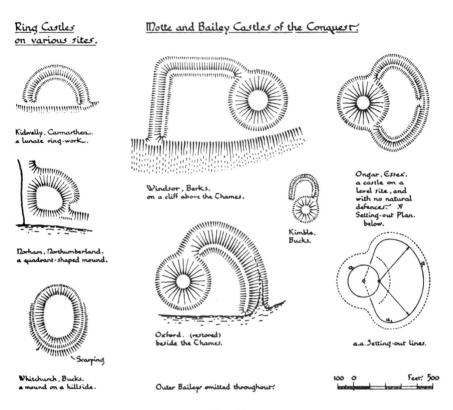

Ring Castles on various sites.

Motte and Bailey Castles of the Conquest.

Kidwelly. Carmarthen. a lunate ring-work.

Norham, Northumberland. a quadrant-shaped mound.

Whitchurch, Bucks. a mound on a hillside.

Windsor, Berks. on a cliff above the Thames.

Oxford. (restored) beside the Thames.

Outer Baileys omitted throughout.

Kimble. Bucks.

Ongar, Essex. a castle on a level site, and with no natural defences. Setting-out Plan below.

a.a. Setting-out lines.

FIG. 35

of this, as at Windsor (Fig. 35)—which has a great 'motte' forming part of the defences—or the castles constructed outside the Roman walls of the Anglo-Saxon towns. A good example of the more normal plan is Kidwelly (Fig. 35) in Carmarthenshire, or the great 'motte-and-bailey' at Oxford, laid out beside the Thames. 'Quadrant-castles' are also common; Ludlow in Shropshire is a notable example. Ringworks of all shapes are common throughout the plains; Framlingham in Suffolk is a large example (Fig.36).

The square angle was generally avoided in military earthwork. This was due, partly, to the difficulty of dispersing the soil from the ditch over the rampart at this point, and also to the problems connected with the horizontal members of the stockades. Even in square plans, therefore, the angles of a castle earthwork were generally well rounded-off.

The square form is, of course, the only really orderly type of layout. The twelfth-century castle-designers devised a variation of this especially suited to earthwork construction; the sides of the square were bowed out to ease still further the junction with the curved angles. This is the 'squaroid' plan, the most interesting achievement of the early castle-planners. Knockin in Shropshire is an example (Fig. 36).

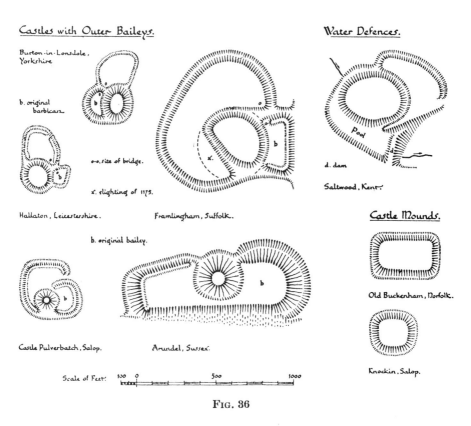

FIG. 36

The earthwork of a small castle differed from those of the larger fortresses in yet another important particular. This was that, in the case of earthwork of considerable scale, the excavated material, when piled up to form a rampart, was apt to take up far too much of the area within the defences. It was therefore frequently the practice to spread the material from the ditches all over the area within them, thus creating a broad low mound or 'motte'. It is these mottes which form the most striking feature of Norman military earthwork.

It will be appreciated that mottes could be formed, not only from

ringworks, but also where there was a small proportion of artificial defences in the perimeter. Many quadrant-castles, such as Barnard in Durham, or Norham in Northumberland (Fig. 35) have their defences arranged
to form a mound; the scarped and mounded spur-castle is a very common
type.

The entrance to a castle was situated at the point in its perimeter
most easily protected. In semi-artificial castles such as those sited along
the edges of cliffs, the entrance would be next the cliff. A re-entrant
angle in the defences, where two lines of works met, was a suitable
site for an entrance system through one of these where it could be
enfiladed from the other. Where two alternative positions existed, the
lowermost would be selected, so that the besiegers would have to advance
uphill.

The summits of ramparts, or the edges of mottes, were invariably
defended by a stockade or by hedge-work; the last was often used as a
'hedgehog' above the counterscarp of the ditch. It is unfortunate that so
far no satisfactory examinations of the crests of earthworks have been
made in order to find out something about the timber defences of mediaeval castles. As the mediaeval word for them, however, appears to have
been 'bratticing', it appears that they were formed of boards, probably
planted closely together in the earth and united at their tops by a strong
horizontal member.[29]

There would have to be some sort of entrance gate through these
stockades, access to which would need to be by a sloping bridge, supported on some form of trestle, crossing the ditch; illustrations of such
bridges appear in the Bayeux Tapestry (Plate 103).

As soon as the Normans had completed their conquest of south-
eastern England, they built roughly rectangular earthen mounds immediately outside the Roman walls of such cities as London, Winchester,
Rochester and Canterbury; from the summits of these mounts they could
attempt to overawe the Saxon population within.

A serious problem which always confronted the defenders of a stockaded castle was how to see what was going on beyond the stockades without leaving the protection of these. What was needed was something upon
which to stand in order to overlook the defences; the vantage point itself,
moreover, would require to be protected. The early castle-builders, having
discovered the military value of a mound, began to exploit further possibilities with regard to this. They discovered that, if they raised the mound
with material excavated from its surrounding ditch, the higher the
mound rose the smaller the amount of excavation was needed to supply
the necessary soil as the area at the summit of the mound grew less. Thus
they could quite easily erect, not merely a broad low plateau, but a
towering construction of conical form which it would prove a formidable

152. The central octagon of Ely

151. Late Gothic market cross at Chichester

153. Bayeux Tapestry illustration of Westminster abbey church at the time of the Conquest

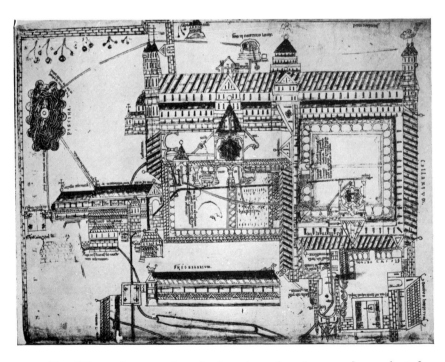

154. Twelfth-century engineer's drawing of water-supply project for Canterbury cathedral priory

task to assault. Thus we get the finest of all types of military earthwork in this country—the great 'mottes'.

These great structures did not stand alone, but were provided as citadels and watch-towers to the actual castle or 'bailey' below. Scores of them exist throughout the country; the best-known is that which, originally founded by the Conqueror, now supports the Round Tower at Windsor. The largest is the enormous motte at Thetford in Norfolk.

The original mediaeval castles were designed as fortified residences; the house being either surrounded by defences or sited on the summit of a plateau motte. Early mediaeval campaigns, however, produced a new kind of castle, employed for military purposes only. These castles incorporated in their defences the conical form of motte, for use as a citadel. Such castles are known as 'motte-and-bailey' castles. The simplest form of these is a ringwork with the centre of the motte on a point in the ring, thus leaving a kidney-shaped bailey (Fig. 34). Sometimes a convenient natural mound was scarped to form the motte. The favourite position for the motte was next to the entrance, so that it could overlook this point, which was always the weakest spot in the defences.[30]

A few small motte-and-bailey castles were constructed in this country in 1051 by the Norman friends of Edward the Confessor. The first great motte-and-bailey, however, was that built at Berkhampstead in the autumn of 1066 for the purpose of receiving the surrender of London. The bailey in this case is a hurriedly set-out oval. The later castles from which William policed the country have baileys designed on a more orderly rectangular plan; with, however, the usual rounded angles to facilitate the disposal of the excavated soil.

Sieges of early mediaeval castles were often of long duration, owing to the feeble nature of the assaulting devices. Thus the operations frequently degenerated into mere blockades, necessitating the construction of a 'siege-castle' a short distance away; such siege-castles being generally small motte-and-baileys.

It was probably some decades before the stone palisades of the Norman castle were replaced by stone walls. When this was done, the first part of the castle to be strengthened in this manner was the motte, which had its summit fortified with a low stone wall, to form what is known as a 'shell-keep' (Plate 133).

Whether or not the early castle possessed a conical motte, the weakest point in the perimeter was always the entrance. It was difficult to protect the gap in the earthen rampart, usually inadequately filled with some form of removable timber obstruction easily burnt by a besieger. Hence a number of castles were at an early period equipped with a stone tower over the gap in the rampart; arches at the outer and inner ends of the entrance passage framed properly hung gates, which could themselves be defended by the garrison from the upper part of the tower.

Castles having no lofty motte were at a serious disadvantage in respect of defences at their entrances. The weakness was generally remedied by extending a small enclosure beyond the foot of the timber bridge spanning the ditch. In the case of castles making use of natural defences, the 'barbican' was usually a small copy of the main lines and used the same principle in its layout; ringworks generally employed a shovel-shaped plan (Fig. 34). The outer entrance to a barbican was always at one end of its lines, either next the natural declivity or, when none existed, at the lowermost junction of the barbican rampart with the counterscarp of the main ditch.

The great fortresses built by William I and his powerful feudatories excepted, the areas enclosed within the defences of the early castles were necessarily restricted; the effort needed to excavate the deep ditches and raise the mounds and ramparts threw a considerable strain on the labour available in a sparsely-populated countryside which had, moreover, its agricultural economy to consider.

In the twelfth century, however, by which period castrametation had become an important feature of the English scene, castles were becoming greatly enlarged by the addition of 'outer wards'. These enclosures were generally set out so as to radiate from the original central feature—enclosure, 'plateau motte' or conical motte—without, however, interfering with any bailey or barbican which might be already in existence. The large motte-and-bailey castles generally had the second bailey laid out opposite the original enclosure; the central motte overlooked the whole castle, the plan of which then became—as at Windsor, or Arundel (Fig. 36) in Sussex—of an 'hour-glass' form. Ringwork castles on free sites often had their outer wards set out, as at Framlingham in Suffolk, concentrically with the original castle and serving as an outer line of defence to the weakest portion of the inner perimeter.

The principle involved in designing the entrance route to a castle was to site the barbican entrance next the central feature and skirt its ditch until the bridge-foot was reached. The attacker might have to pass an outer entrance, a barbican entrance, and then take the bridge itself, before he could attain the inner gate to the castle proper. Even the motteless residential castles must have been formidable structures to assault.

The great stone houses or 'hall-keeps', referred to in a previous chapter, were essentially features of the residential castles, which were normally unprotected by a motte. The house or keep itself took the place of the earthen citadel and for this reason was frequently placed next to the entrance.

Contemporary records often refer to the 'wooden towers' which were to be found on the mottes of early castles. This probably refers to the timber houses, illustrations of which may be seen in the Bayeux Tapestry. Such houses were probably built of post-and-sleeper construction, similar to that employed in the contemporary wooden churches. What the form of the house was, however, cannot now be ascertained; it would seem most probable, however, that its plan must have been something like that of the great stone house or keep by which it was superseded.[31]

By the eleventh century, Continental military engineers had already begun to appreciate the defensive value of the stone tower; wherever the necessary skill and materials were available, a keep is found incorporated with the defences. The lofty stone 'tower-keep' is found in England soon after the conquest, the first to be erected being probably that at Rochester in Kent, constructed early in the twelfth century.

This form of keep having been designed more as a military feature than a residence, its plan is simpler than that of the hall-keep; the latter is commodious, the former essentially lofty. If the span of a tower-keep should be very great, however, it may be necessary to introduce a cross-wall; in which case, however, this will usually be carried, at any rate on the principal floor of the tower, by an arcade as at Rochester, or a flying arch as at Scarborough. Both forms of keep are entered by means of a wide stone staircase leading to the first floor (Plate 177), the ground storey being always used for storage purposes only. One of the most attractive of the tower keeps is that at Hedingham in Essex (Plate 136).

Earthwork castles were assaulted by the most primitive means. Generally it was a matter of brute force, augmented perhaps—in the case of first-class sieges—by the employment of crude engines which threw stones and blazing material at the stockades.

When the castle was taken, it was often 'slighted'. This was effected by destroying the most exposed portion of the perimeter and returning the earth of the mound or rampart back again into the ditch below. Framlingham Castle in Suffolk was so slighted in 1174; the shape of its inner ward, as subsequently refortified, illustrates the result (Fig. 36).

The reply to the stone castle was the mine. Quarrymen and miners were available for the purpose; these were set to work, protected by the fire of the besiegers, to undermine the walls, supporting the masonry upon props as they proceeded. A fire subsequently lit amongst the props would consume these and bring the masonry above to ruin. Sometimes the besieged castellan was invited to inspect the mine as an inducement to surrender his fortress to avoid its destruction.

The weakest portions of masonry structures are their angles. It was common practice for besiegers to attempt to cut off the angle of a stone tower by means of a mine; the heavier and taller the structure, the easier it was to bring it to ruin by this method. An unfinished mine, which may be dated to the summer of 1174, may be still seen under the angle of the keep at Bungay in Suffolk; a long gallery cuts across the corner of the foundations, at right-angles to its diagonal, but the three cross-galleries have been abandoned in an incomplete condition.

In order to combat this menace of the mine, the military engineers of the late twelfth century began to abandon the use of square towers; replacing these with polygonal structures which had no projecting angles offering temptation to miners. The first of these polygonal tower-keeps to be erected in this country was probably that built by Henry II at Orford (Plate 135) in Suffolk about the year 1165.

Except on rocky sites where mining would have been out of the question, the ultimate form of all types of military tower was the circular (Plate 141).

In an ordinary residential castle, the house within the defences only differed from its unfortified counterpart in so far as the defensive works interfered with the freedom of the site within them. There would thus generally be a great hall; unless, however, a stone house had been already erected which would, in part, serve the same purpose. The purely military castle would be less likely to have a great hall of the spacious feudal nature usually represented by these structures; more likely there would be buildings of a less imposing character serving as lodgings for the garrison, with possibly a small house of stone or timber for the constable. Some early castles, although originally constructed solely for defensive purposes, later became important residences, sometimes even of a palatial nature.

There seems to be some popular misapprehension as to the size of the garrison of a mediaeval castle. Although the great castles of the hey-day of the Middle Ages were designed to contain a large force when necessary, the normal peacetime garrisons of even the largest castles were seldom more than twenty or so strong.

The chief engine employed by the besiegers was the old Byzantine catapult known as the 'mangon', which had a short wooden arm, the lower end of which was fixed in a twisted skein of animal sinew. The upper end of this arm had a spoon-shaped cup in which was placed the projectile; this end was hauled down by means of a tackle, and let go in order to fire the engine. Flaming material could be hurled at the wooden stockades or they could be battered down with heavy stones.

About 1174, however, a far more destructive engine reached this country—the 'trebuchet'. This was a huge affair of great timber baulks built up into a lofty trestle, at the summit of which was supported a long balanced beam. The shorter end of the beam was weighted with a large box of earth or stones. The longer end, which held the projectile, was hauled down in the same fashion as had been the case with the mangon;

when released, the weight revolved the beam and flung the projectile. Its velocity was generally increased by the attachment of a long leather sling to the end of the beam. These trebuchets could throw a projectile weighing perhaps half a ton, and ranges of a quarter of a mile are recorded.

The deadly feature of the trebuchet, however, was its high trajectory, which enabled it to hurl its projectiles over the top of any stockade, or even over the low stone ringwalls of mid-twelfth-century castles. Stone balls, arriving at considerable velocity and striking the insides of the walls or the sides of a masonry building, would shatter into a shower of death-dealing splinters. No castle was able to stand more than a few hours of such bombardment without surrendering.

As a result of the introduction of the trebuchet, therefore, the low ringwalls of the early mediaeval castles came to be replaced by the lofty 'curtain' walls which form such notable features of the castles of the later mediaeval era (Plate 130).

These lofty curtains rendered useless the great stone towers which had been the principal features of twelfth-century castles. The idea of providing a citadel began to give place to the principle of concentrating the whole effort upon the defence of the perimeter.

The disadvantage of the tall curtain walls lay in the amount of dead ground created at their foot, in which besiegers could engage in such activities as mining, out of sight of the defenders upon the wall-walks above. The development of the crenellated parapet, the temporary expedient of providing this with wooden 'hoards' as the height of the walls themselves increased, and the final device of machicolation, have all been described in an earlier chapter.

One method of protecting the bases of high walls, however, had been in existence from a very early period. The Assyrians had known how to enfilade their town walls by providing these with projecting bastions, from the flanks of which the defenders could cover the faces of the main walls with their fire. The great triple defences of Byzantium, built early in the fifth century, were the model for masonry fortifications of the mediaeval period from the Crusades onwards.

The first stone enceinte to be provided with wall-towers appears to be that at Framlingham in Suffolk, built soon after 1189. Here the towers are merely portions of the wall brought forward in square projections. By the thirteenth century, however, the wall-tower had come to present a semicircular face to the field in order to offer as much resistance as possible to the miner.

As soon as the semicircular wall-tower came to be adopted as a necessary adjunct to the curtain wall it was discovered that the best form of gatehouse was provided by siting two such towers close together with the entrance between them. This became the standard form of gatehouse—

used for both castles and walled towns—throughout the Edwardian period.

The first castles had all been sited upon high ground in order that the fullest use might be made of natural slopes in the defences. This scheme admirably suited the designers of the primitive stockaded earthworks; when these became replaced by masonry structures, however, their high sites offered temptation to miners.

There is one certain defence against the mine. If the castle can be surrounded by water, the miners cannot reach it, as their galleries will become flooded. By the thirteenth century, therefore, when the stone castle had entirely superseded the more primitive form, it became the practice to site new castles on low ground, where, if possible, water defences could be provided.

The moated castle is a familiar feature of the English countryside (Plate 137); its humbler counterpart, the moated manor-house, is even better known (Plate 179). It was important that the moat should be kept clean and free from silt which would reduce its efficiency; moated sites, therefore, are not found on marshy ground, but in places where the moats can be kept scoured, as well as filled, by a stream.

Some of the earlier castles could be converted to water defence by diverting streams into the land surrounding the site and impounding the water by means of a dam, in order to surround the castle with a lake. The most vital portion of the defences of a lake castle being the dam, this was often itself strongly fortified with walls and towers. The classic example of this is the great fortified dam at Caerphilly in Monmouthshire.

By the Edwardian period, when the stone castle and the walled town had become universal features of the European countryside, and campaigns involving the assault of these were the order of the day, the devices employed in siege warfare were becoming more and more elaborate and destructive.

There were movable towers of the same height as the wall to be stormed. There were battering rams to break up the outer face of the masonry of the wall, and similar engines, armed with a point instead of a ram, to peck out the dislodged stones in order that the miners could get to work upon the rubble core. Such devices as these were generally protected by movable penthouses of strong timber construction. These cumbersome engines were propelled laboriously on rollers to the foot of the high wall.

Such engines as these were, of course, rendered impotent by the existence of water defences. Where there were none, however, it was then necessary to devise some other scheme for keeping the engineers at bay. The method employed in the Edwardian period was to surround the castle with a 'list' or border, itself protected by a low stone wall called a 'mantlet' wall (Plate 140). Such walls were of no great strength, as they could be protected fairly easily from the summits of the great curtains beyond; their function was merely to offer obstruction to the advance of the siege engines. The mantlet wall had its own gatehouse, sometimes called a barbican (Plate 139).

Throughout the mediaeval period castles could always be divided into two principal classes—the primarily residential and the purely military fortresses. Residential castles themselves were of two types. One was developed from the improvement of an earlier, more primitive, stronghold; the other was the result of fortifying an existing manor house.

During the thirteenth century a considerable number of manor-houses came to be fortified under a 'licence to crenellate' from the Crown.

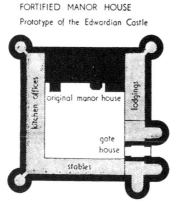

FORTIFIED MANOR HOUSE

Prototype of the Edwardian Castle

Fig. 37

The defences were arranged quite simply by enclosing the forecourt of the manor-house with a high wall having towers at each corner for its protection. Close to one angle—in which position it could most efficiently share in the defence of the curtain—a twin-towered gatehouse of the usual form was constructed (Plate 57). The offices, lodgings and stabling of the house was then reconstructed round the remaining three sides of the castle 'ward' (Fig. 37).

The Edwardian campaigns on the borders of Wales and Scotland produced an entirely new type of royal castle having a plan based on the above arrangement. These structures were laid out—wherever the site permitted—upon a strictly rectangular plan, the curtains being enfiladed by regularly sited wall-towers. In the centre of the entrance front was a gatehouse of a magnitude not hitherto conceived (Plate 139). Against the inner face of the curtain facing this feature was the principal range of buildings, containing the great hall and the chamber block. For convenience of construction these two buildings were sometimes set out end to end, instead of being on the normal mediaeval L-shaped plan.

By this period, attention had become so focused upon the defences of a curtain, that such features as a citadel or even a dwelling-house had come to take second place. The Edwardian military architects combined both of these functions within the gate-house, which thus became the principal feature in the castle—commodious as a residence, lofty as a citadel (Plate 139).

The ground floor of the Edwardian gatehouse was divided into three; the entrance passage being flanked by two guard chambers terminating externally in strong semicircular towers. The whole of the first floor was occupied by a large apartment representing the constable's hall; above was his sleeping accommodation. The internal angles of the gatehouse were provided with lofty turrets containing stairs.

It will be observed that the huge gatehouse-citadel forming the principal feature of the castle of about 1300 is a direct descendant of the hall-keep of two centuries earlier in that both form complete residences. Ordinary houses having small but lofty halls attached to two-storied chamber blocks of normal design were erected in other castles of the period, such as Chepstow in Monmouthshire. Houses of this type, however, only appear in military architecture; they appear to indicate the unwillingness of the constable of a castle to associate with his garrison in the great hall.

The rectangular castle of Edwardian days, with its orderly plan and symmetrical entrance front—the twin-towered gate-house flanked by the two terminal towers—was the first building in this country to be designed in an architectural manner, as opposed to the haphazard growth of the ordinary mediaeval building. In these stately buildings one can see the germ of the great house of the late Tudor period (Plates 163, 164).

It is interesting to note that the grand front of an Edwardian castle represents the first conscious attempt of the mediaeval architect to erect a façade. The west fronts of great churches had formed frontispieces which by the end of the twelfth century had become standardised and more or less symmetrically designed; yet these formed terminal features rather than true elevations. The huge Edwardian castles were designed by the leading architects of their day, the royal 'engineers' of the Crown; the spreading fronts of the noble structures present to the beholder an aspect monumental in design, as well as in mere scale, setting the fashion for the façades of great house and palace in ages yet to come.

During the fourteenth century, England came to be covered with small editions of the Edwardian castle in the form of fortified manor-houses, either newly built, or the result of surrounding an earlier house with fortifications. Most of these little castles were, of course, moated.

They were of but little defensive value. As time went on, their walls became thinner and lower, and their towers more slender. In the eastern parts of England in particular, bricks from Flanders were imported for use in their construction. Maxstoke in Warwickshire (Plate 169) is an example of this pseudo-fortification; its finest surviving product is lovely Hurstmonceux in Sussex.

The last stage of all is that of the Tudor mansion which retains in its general form the salient features of the Edwardian castle, reduced, however, to a scale when they are merely architectural features of no defensive value whatsoever (Plate 163).

The humblest form of fortification, the ditch, required no licence for its construction and was employed throughout the mediaeval period as a protection to manor houses. After the middle of the thirteenth century the water-filled moat took the place of the dry ditch as a simple type of defensive enceinte. The moating of houses was usually undertaken during periods of unrest or anarchy. Thus some moats may date from the period of the Barons' War; most, however, may possibly be assigned to the era of the Wars of the Roses.

Side by side with the protection of residences, the community defences of the mediaeval towns progressed also. Whereas the private castle, entirely an importation of the Normans, was probably at all periods a feature generally alien to the English countryside, urban defences had been known since prehistoric days, when the stockaded market towns had crowned the summits of the hills. A number of walled Roman towns, too, remain; some of them the nucleus of mediaeval cities, others long ago abandoned. In the tenth century, the children of Alfred the Great had been constructing small fortified enclosures of ditch and rampart to protect their people against the Danes; this example was later followed by the Danes themselves.

Many a Norman feudal lord, whose castle became the nucleus of a small town such as at Castle Acre in Norfolk, enclosed this with stockaded ramparts in the traditional manner. Most of these Anglo-Norman fortified towns were laid out on an orderly rectangular plan, and are for this reason often mistaken to-day for Roman camps.

It was in Edwardian days, however, that the great era of walled cities reached its zenith, when the burghers of many a rich wool town in England surrounded their homes with lofty curtains protected by wall-towers and pierced with entrances guarded by twin-towered gatehouses in the manner of the contemporary castle.

Even the advent of fire artillery in the middle of the first half of the fourteenth century failed to deter the builders of these fine fortifications. It was probably two or three generations at least before the bombards of the period could fire their projectiles with a power equal to that of the trebuchet; the principal feature of early cannon seems to have been the terrifying noise which they emitted. The only change noticeable in fifteenth-century mediaeval architecture is the provision of large embrasures through which the cannon of the defenders could be fired.

At the time of the European Renaissance, however, many of the most famous Italian architects and engineers of the day were considering the problem of designing artillery forts. By the end of the fifteenth century in this country, the dying architecture of the Middle Ages brought to an end the pride and magnificence of the mediaeval castle. Its lofty towers and curtains offered too large a target for the great guns, and the inherent lack of stability in tall structures made them a prey to the powerful blows of the new artillery.

The strictly military castles of the Tudor period, therefore, are low buildings, with walls of great thickness, capable of withstanding the impact of cannon-balls.

The civil war of the seventeenth century, which itself produced nothing in the way of military architecture except elaborately planned earthwork fortifications designed according to contemporary Continental practice, resulted at the same time in the utter destruction of a great number of the mediaeval castles of England. Under siege, such castles proved hopelessly vulnerable to cannon. Only the courage of the garrison and the inefficiency of the besiegers produced anything like a siege of useful duration.

Once taken, castles which had held out against the Parliament were systematically destroyed. The method employed was the mediaeval one of mining. The best example of this is at Corfe (Plate 142) in Dorset, where the angles of the keep have been cut off and the wall-towers tipped forward intact by mines sprung beneath them. Thus the same ancient device which had tumbled into ruin the tall towers of the proud abbots was employed a century later to destroy the grim donjons of their secular counterparts—the feudal nobles of mediaeval England.

CHAPTER XII

Towers

Whether it be constructed in stone or timber, the tower represents one of the most notable achievements of building skill. Possessing as it does in the first degree the monumental factor of height, the erection of a tower also tests the ability of its creators by forcing them to devise various methods of raising the building material to its summit.

No other architectural style produced such magnificent towers as did the mediaeval architecture which we call the Gothic. And of all Gothic towers, the finest may be found in this country.

The Romans used towers, mainly in the form of projecting bastions attached to walls of fortifications. The isolated tower was employed for special purposes, such as a lighthouse, or in its truly monumental capacity as a funerary monument.

The Byzantines were tower-builders. By the sixth century they had invented the campanile for carrying the bells of their churches. Their multi-storied private houses displayed a more pronounced vertical element than had been seen in the homes of any earlier civilisation. The Byzantine house was thus definitely tower-like in its mass. The whole spirit underlying Byzantine church design was the effort to raise a lofty nucleus having its vertical element elevated to a monumental degree.

The stone tower is not indigenous to England. Nor, in all probability, is the timber tower; the tall wooden churches of the Anglo-Saxon period were almost certainly importations from the Continent. Tower-houses of timber are first mentioned in western Europe during the twelfth century; they probably appeared in this country about the same time. These were in all probability wooden copies of the 'turriform' type of Byzantine house.

Towers may be divided into two main classes: military and secular. The great hall-keeps of Norman castles which, first introduced at the end of the eleventh century, continued in use well into the next, were probably the first secular structures of this height to be seen in England (Plate 134). Although always considered by the contemporary writers as towers, they were in reality fortified houses, comprising two main apartments—

219

hall and chamber—set side by side and surrounded by a very thick wall (Fig. 38). The principal floor, containing these two apartments, was raised above the ground on a basement, often vaulted, and used entirely for storage. The entrance at the lower end of the hall portion was reached by a wide stone stair (Plate 177) passing up the outside of the wall. The main entrance itself was generally protected by means of a small porch-tower which projected before it. This 'forebuilding', as it was called, provided, on its first floor, a porch to the entrance door; a second doorway in the flank of the forebuilding gave on to the staircase passing down the side of the keep to the ground. Some of these forebuildings were quite large structures, occasionally, as at Dover, incorporating a small chapel or oratory; the basement was generally used as a prison or 'oubliette', accessible only by means of a trap-door in the porch-floor above.

NORMAN HALL KEEP

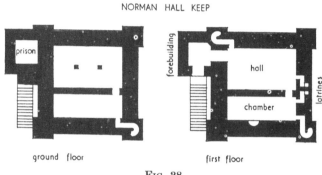

ground floor   first floor

Fig. 38

Near the hall-doorway was the stair turret giving access to the basement beneath this apartment. In large keeps, such as Norwich, there was sometimes a small kitchen provided at the lower end of the hall. At the upper end of the hall was the doorway to the chamber, near which were latrines concealed in the thickness of the wall. The chamber itself generally had a fireplace; at its lower end was a stair turret leading to the 'wardrobe' beneath. The two stairs also gave access to the roof of the tower and the wall-walks around its summit.

The great towers of London and Colchester had the principal apartments on the second floor; the first floor being used as an entrance storey. These were very elaborate houses, the former actually serving as the Conqueror's palace. They had fine chapels incorporated in the design. The hall-keep at Canterbury had three main apartments on its principal floor; it is a pity that the functions served by the various portions of these fine houses cannot be appreciated to-day.

It seems probable that the accommodation may be compared with that of the timber tower at Ardres discussed in Chapter IX of this work. It seems certain that the Norman hall-keep must represent a fortified copy of the timber residence. The masonry form is presumably a product of the Crusades, during which both the stone Byzantine houses and the fortified Moslem *kasr* or strong house must have been encountered by Englishmen. The flying arch spanning the main floor of a keep such as Scarborough is certainly an importation from Syria.

The hall-keeps must have been very expensive buildings to construct, and their place was soon taken by ordinary halls and houses, with possibly a tower-keep for the castellan, surrounded by the stone ring-walls of the defences. One of the most decorative of the later hall-keeps is the mid-twelfth-century example at Castle Rising (Plate 134) in Norfolk.

The lofty tower-keep which succeeded the large squat hall-keep was a structure which may be compared to the private house of the period. It was generally, however, of *three* stories in height, the lowermost of which was the inevitable storage basement. The first floor may have served as an entrance storey or may have been used as a hall; many tower-keeps, however, are found in castles which have the usual ground-floor hall in addition. The 'great chamber' was usually on the second floor of the tower.

Some tower-keeps were fine structures of considerable architectural merit. The largest is at Rochester in Kent; the most beautiful is the little example at Hedingham (Plate 136) in Essex.

By the third quarter of the twelfth century the square keep was giving way to one of a polygonal or circular form, except where the nature of the soil made mining impossible. The octagonal tower of Orford (Plate 135) has three subsidiary turrets; one forms the forebuilding, the others contain small apartments, an oratory, latrines, and so forth. Of the late twelfth-century circular keeps, the finest is the great tower of Pembroke (Plate 141).

With the development of the perimeter defences of the castle, the keep eventually disappeared entirely. The feature was revived, however, during the unsettled period which followed the Black Death and which resulted in the Wars of the Roses. At this time the remnants of the old feudal aristocracy were beginning to surround themselves with private armies of retainers, assembled under the scheme of 'livery and maintenance'. Denied the resources which would enable them to build great castles, they constructed instead large tower-houses which were at the same time both residences and strongholds. The example at Warkworth in Northumberland is one of the finest; the great brick-tower at Tattershall in Lincolnshire is also of this period, as are other smaller copies scattered throughout eastern England.

To approximately the same period belong the small 'pele' towers which are common features on both sides of the Scottish border; these, however, are designed purely as protection against local marauders.

Towers

During the latter half of the twelfth century, when the keep had become considerably reduced in efficiency as a military structure through being surrounded by high curtain walls, it became the practice to incorporate the great tower with these instead of leaving it isolated within them. The episcopal castles of Wolvesey and Bishops Waltham in Hampshire show towers of this description.

As wall-towers for the protection of the curtain appeared, the keep became, in effect, merely the largest of these; such structures as Marten's Tower in Chepstow Castle exhibit the thirteenth-century form of keep or 'Lord's Tower'. The principal tower was usually at an angle, and often attached to the chamber of the castellan.

Some unfortified manor houses were provided with a Lord's Tower. Attached to the chamber of the house at Longthorpe in Northamptonshire is a fine example.

Some of the earliest stone towers to be erected in this country were those which covered the entrances through the palisades of the Norman castles. These were square towers having large arches in their front and back walls, somewhat resembling the 'axial' towers of churches; there was one floor over, which may have served as a chamber for the castellan. That at Exeter may be of eleventh-century date; a fine mid-twelfth-century example may be seen at Newark-on-Trent.

With the development of the wall-tower it became the practice to flank the gate-tower with a pair of projecting towers, the side walls of which were carried back to provide two 'guard chambers' beside the entrance passage. These twin-tower gatehouses were the normal entrance features of the thirteenth-century castles; in Edwardian days they developed into large structures of several stories in height.

The timber bridge which crossed the ditch of the early mediaeval castle was probably so constructed that a section of its flooring could be removed during a siege. When the wooden bridge became replaced by a stone structure, this always ended in a gap left before the actual entrance. The twin-towered gatehouse usually had a stone-lined pit provided between the projecting towers; some kind of removable timber floor was devised to cover this 'bridge-pit'.

The first permanent bridges were balanced across the pit on a pivot crossing its middle, in such a fashion that a little extra pressure on the inner end of the bridge would raise the whole device to a vertical position; this was known as the 'turning bridge'. Later, the balanced form of bridge was replaced by one which was pivoted at the inner side of the pit so as to make full use of the length of this. At first the bridge was hauled up by means of a windlass situated in the chamber over the gate. In the thirteenth century, however, it became attached by its chains to the vertically-sliding gate known as the 'portcullis'; this, when released by the watchman in the chamber above the gate, dropped suddenly and with its weight pulled up the bridge. The final arrangment—which is still to be seen to-day in nineteenth-century forts—was to balance the bridge with a door pivoted above the entrance and having a pair of arms to which the bridge-chains were fastened. When the door was allowed to sink into position behind the gate, its arms pulled the bridge up before it.

The final achievement in gatehouse design was the great Edwardian gatehouse with its large twin-towers and its lofty staircase turrets at the rear (Plate 139). This type of gatehouse incorporated the house of the constable of the castle; the strongest structure in the whole castle, it also formed, in effect, its citadel.

Thus by Edwardian times the Norman keep, rendered militarily useless when the curtain walls rose around it and at all times an uncomfortable form of residence, had become replaced, in both these capacities, by the spaciously-planned gatehouse.

The complicated castle plans which included a mantlet wall surrounding the whole fortress, provided for a small barbican gatehouse through this; sometimes the main gatehouse was connected to the barbican by a fortified passage.

The gatehouse was not a structure used solely in military buildings. Even as early as the twelfth century, elaborate versions of the square gatehouse tower of the Norman castle were being constructed to mark the entrances into the precincts of the great abbeys and cathedrals; the beautiful tower at Bury St. Edmunds (Plate 144) is a notable example.

Structures of this type, however, like the early stone gate-towers of Norman castles, were hardly scientifically planned for defence, being merely towers with a passage through the ground storey. In monastic houses they were employed more for effect than security. The great gatehouse of the curia, however, was often an imposing structure, though it never attained the twin-towered form of the castle gatehouse. Architectural dignity, however, was often maintained by adding flanking stair turrets. A feature of monastic gatehouses is the small postern in the external wall alongside the main archway (Plate 143). The rear wall has only the one wide arch. The outer gatehouse was generally sited to face the principal door of the church, which, in small monastic houses, might be the north door to the nave.

The fifteenth-century tower-building craze found its way into domestic architecture when the hall-porches came to be raised to form towers; that of the Bishop's Palace at Exeter is an example. The first floor was often embellished with an oriel window, from which approaching visitors could be examined. By the Tudor period the first-floor oriel had become a standard feature of gatehouses as well as domestic porches; even monastic gatehouses generally had one. When the porch-tower came to be moved away from the house to the opposite side of the courtyard to form a gatehouse, the oriel window and stair turrets of the prototype were usually retained.

Towards the end of the mediaeval period the great gatehouse had become such an imposing architectural feature as to be universally adopted as the symbol of pomp in secular design. The magnificent Tudor buildings, which were generally confronted by some sort of enclosed courtyard, nearly always incorporated with the surrounding wall a tall turreted gatehouse (Plate 163), often constructed in the brickwork which at this period had begun to replace the masonry of the Middle Ages.

In Essex, particularly, the brick gatehouses of Tudor days form notable features of English monumental architecture. The multi-storied gatehouse of Layer Marney, erected during the first quarter of the sixteenth century, is perhaps the finest example in the world of this class of structure. Designed probably by an Italian architect, it incorporates Renaissance detail within its otherwise mediaeval forms.

Wall-towers as military features date from at least as early as the Assyrian Empire. The Romans, who relied on their strength in the field, and were poor designers of masonry fortifications, surrounded their low-walled enceintes with half-round bastions, solid in order to support their military engines. It was the great towered walls of Byzantium which really set the fashion in mediaeval European fortifications.

The first English wall-towers were merely portions of the curtain brought forward, on a square plan, with short side sections joining the front wall to the curtain itself. The 'gorge', where the tower joined the curtain, was open and the tower had no floor. When wall-towers became semicircular on plan, to preserve them against mining, they still often remained open at the gorge; later, however, when the accommodation value of the wall-tower began to be appreciated, the gorge of the tower was closed with a wall and floors inserted within the structure.

The angle towers, which protected the vulnerable salients of the fortifications, were sometimes polygonal, often square when the nature of the soil prohibited mining, but most frequently circular or 'drum' towers. The drum towers at the angles of the Edwardian castle are imposing structures; the towers of Conway and the still finer octagonal examples of Caernarvon are, of course, well-known.

Mediaeval castles frequently had an isolated tower projecting from the curtain well into the castle ditch, and connected with the castle itself by means of a thick wall containing passages. This was a sanitary tower accommodating latrines, the flues from which led downwards into the castle ditch.

After the acceptance by military engineers of fire artillery as a vital factor in the design of fortifications, lofty wall-towers, with their curtains,

155. The central tower of St. Albans Abbey: late-twelfth century belfry stage raised upon earlier lantern

156. The Rhenish 'helm' roof of the tower of Sompting church in Sussex

157. An East Anglian arcaded tower of the twelfth century at Great Tey, Essex

159. The Angel Tower of Canterbury

158. The remains of the west front of Ely

disappeared altogether. As the curtains gained in thickness proportionately to their loss in height, so the wall-towers became low bastions with walls of immense thickness, containing casemates for cannon. The castles built by Henry VIII in 1539 for the defence of the south-east coast have a squat tower rising in the midst of a ring of artillery bastions; Walmer and Camber are examples.

Although the stone tower was a late arrival to English architecture, Saxon builders had exploited the monumental factor of height to the full in designing their timber tower-churches. The score or more which remain of these structures in Essex (Plate 76) indicate the form; rather more elaborate, and possibly slightly later, examples may be seen in the stave-churches of Norway.

The square church which King Alfred the Great built at Athelney was probably a tower-like structure. Shorn of its nave, the eastern parts of the church at Breamore (Plate 71) in Hampshire might illustrate the 'winged-square' form of the Wessex churches of the tenth century with their stone walls and central timber structure. The isolated example presented by the remarkable stone tower at Barton-on-Humber (Plate 146) appears to be an East Mercian variation of the same turriform type of church.

Although the tall slender tower as an adjunct to a church was well-known in Syria during the sixth century, it does not appear to have reached western ecclesiastical architecture until the tenth century. It is probably not until the very end of the first millennium that the slender bell-tower appears in England, where it is attached to the west end of some of the Mercian churches.

It has hitherto been supposed that the origin of the western bell-tower is illustrated by the practice of raising the western porches of early Romano-Celtic churches, such as that of Monkwearmouth, to form slender campanile. In Chapter VII of this work, however, the origin of the western tower has been explained as having been developed through the practice of adding a long Ottonian church to the eastern side of an early turriform Carolingian building.[32]

Reference has been made elsewhere to timber tower-churches of the tenth and later centuries which have been preserved through having been retained as bell-towers at the west end of later stone naves. Some primitive stone tower-churches, also, such as that of Old Shoreham in Sussex, or the larger examples in eastern Mercia—Hough-on-the-Hill and Broughton in Lincolnshire, Barnack (Plate 147) in Northamptonshire—were similarly turned into bell-towers after a long nave had been added to the east. It is not a very long step from the converted nave at Barnack, with its additional storey indicating the new function of the structure, to the fine bell-tower at Earls Barton (Plate 145).

Towers

A feature of many eleventh-century western bell-towers is the first-floor chapel, inserted beneath the belfry storey itself and usually having an east window looking into the church. These elevated western chapels were common features of contemporary Teutonic architecture; the English examples were originally approached by external timber stairs, later replaced by circular turret-stairs of the normal Teutonic type employed in Flanders and the Rhineland.

The three-storied arrangement became the standard form for the English bell-tower and continued to be so throughout the mediaeval period. With the abolition of the Rhenish first-floor chapel, this storey became the stage for the ringers.

Except in the Anglian regions, the Conquest seems to have slowed down the building of the western bell-tower, although the central lantern, for practical reasons, continued to be popular.

The church towers of the post-Conquest period would appear to have been designed by the same engineers as those who were building the castle-keeps; one can detect the same broad, flat pilasters placed in the centre of each face, and also the thickened-out angles, one of which would perhaps contain a stair.

The two-bay form was maintained by the designers of most of the more important church towers during the whole of the mediaeval period. The medial pilaster, however, disappears from the ordinary western tower during the twelfth century to make way for a good west window and single lights in the lateral walls of the ground and ringing floors. Some of the very finest parochial towers adopted the three-bay system in their principal belfry stages.

The thickened-out angles of the early towers, whether western or lantern, were usually capped by turrets. With the decay of tower-building during the thirteenth century, the sturdy angles began to disappear and the turrets with them. (Plate 150). The development of buttressed angles, however, brought the corner feature once more into use, but in the form of a tall pinnacle, generally octagonal in plan instead of the square or circular turrets of earlier days.

Western towers are of two classes. The great Teutonic structures were built above the two western bays of the nave—as at the Rhenish cathedral of Soest—and formed an integral part of it. The tower of Bury Abbey was possibly of this type; it may have been that some of the other long Anglian naves were intended to be completed in this fashion. Our own great surviving example of this class, however, that at Ely (Plate 158) has had its lower stage altered so as to convert this into a 'crossing' out of which led the large western transepts.

There are a few good parochial west towers of twelfth-century date. On the whole, however, this form of structure seems to have been too big a venture for the provincial builders to attempt. The small towers of the 'axially-planned' churches, in which the base of the tower formed part of the church, was a more economical form of planning.

The thirteenth century saw very few parochial church towers erected. We have seen how the old-fashioned timber churches of Essex were retained, after the erection of stone-built successors, as western bell-towers to these. It is possible that in many other cases the old timber churches were retained, not in the Essex manner, but as isolated structures which would carry the bells until such time as a stone western tower could be achieved. There seems to be no other way of accounting for the noticeable scarcity of bell-towers of the thirteenth and fourteenth centuries.

Lateral bell-towers, often of late twelfth- or early thirteenth-century date, are occasionally met with in the south-eastern parts of the country where the small aisle-less 'pseudo-cruciform' church was popular. When the church came to be enlarged with a single aisle, which obliterated the 'wing' on the rear flank of the nave, the survivor was sometimes raised to form a humble bell-tower. Stoughton church in Sussex has a flanking bell-tower produced by raising the southern of its two wings, both of which, in this case, remain.

Except in the East Mercian stone-producing district, where masons were plentiful and material at hand, it was not until the beginning of the fifteenth century that the western tower became a general feature of the parish church. Thirteenth-century towers are usually simple unbuttressed structures, occasionally pleasantly ornamented with arcading and good windows, but otherwise exhibiting no great richness of design or execution (Plate 150). During the fourteenth century, there appears to have been even less enthusiasm for western towers; this period, however, was mainly occupied in enlarging the naves of churches.

It was the great wool boom of the fifteenth century which produced magnificent towers. There were two principal areas affected. One was Somersetshire, at the south-western end of the building-stone belt, which likewise possessed an ample supply of masons. The other was Yorkshire, Lincolnshire and East Anglia. The first two of these region had ample facilities for building; the latter had none.

It so happened that East Anglia, with its Continental connections, was the richest wool district of all England. Nowhere in the country are there such magnificent churches as in the small towns and villages of Norfolk and Suffolk. East Anglia had no masons, and building-stone was very hard to come by. The local builders, therefore, devised a technique entirely their own. The walling was built of flint rubble or anything available; in many cases Flemish brick was used. The whole of the outside of the building, including the lofty west tower, was covered with a panelling formed of applied stone strips like the tracery of windows. This panelling was filled up with what is known as 'flush-work', formed of flint nodules broken in half to produce two approximately smooth faces. These were then 'knapped' square so that they could be built-in to give an appearance of a wall constructed of squared flint blocks (Plate 11).

The wool towers, both eastern and western, were of the most elaborate design conceivable. Their angles were embellished with decorative buttresses, set sometimes diagonally, but more often in right-angled pairs. The summits of the towers were parapeted and pinnacled. An unusually plain East Anglian tower, of great size and magnificently proportioned, may be seen at Wymondham in Norfolk.

There were usually three stories. The lowermost formed part of the nave of the church, a wide lofty arch joining the two. In the west wall was a fine window above a doorway. The first floor of the tower was the ringing chamber, which would probably have good windows in each of the four walls. The upper, belfry, storey was the most elaborate of all, great play being made with the fine windows, which were often arranged in pairs on each face of the tower.

Some towers had, instead of buttresses, circular or polygonal turrets passing up each angle. A number of Devonshire towers have a single stair-turret passing up the centre of the north or south wall.

In some parishes where lack of means made it difficult to employ a more durable material the churches have been provided with complete western bell-towers, entirely constructed, from the the ground up, in the same half-timber style as that employed for contemporary domestic buildings. Sometimes, as at Warndon in Worcestershire, the framework is exposed; in many cases, however, it must have been protected by boarding, shingles, or some other form of waterproof sheathing. The tower of Perivale church in Middlesex is now covered with clap-boarding; this probably replaced the mediaeval covering.

The round flint towers of stone-less East Anglia (Plate 142) are, of course, well-known.

From contemporary descriptions it is clear that the Benedictine abbey churches of the late tenth century in England had central towers, supported on arches, rising above their choirs. From the contemporary example at Soignies in Flanders, it would appear that such were of little altitude, rising only high enough above the surrounding roofs in order that windows might be inserted to light the choir below, which, without the lantern, would have been situated in the darkest part of the building.

The early tenth-century turriform churches of Wessex, once they had been enlarged westwards by means of a rectangular nave, soon abandoned the original square nucleus by absorbing this into the new nave, of which it then formed the eastern end, marked by the lateral arches leading into the retained 'wings' or transepts. Even when the nave became aisled, the

162. Late Gothic stone spire. Weobley church, Shropshire

161. Mid Gothic stone spire. Bainton church, Northamptonshire

160. Early Gothic timber spire. Eynesford church, Kent

163. The turreted gatehouse leading into the courtyard of a Tudor great house at Cowdray, Midhurst, Sussex

164. The 'show front' of the great house itself

larger eastern arches still remained—as, for example, at Great Paxton in Hunts.—suggesting in embryo the later 'crossing' of the true cruciform church.

The pre-Conquest cathedral at Dorchester in Oxfordshire, which had an aisle-less nave, still retains the crude lofty lateral arches of its 'crossing'. There are also some remains of the western bell-tower of what must have been a typical Ottonian church of cathedral, though not monastic, rank.

A lantern tower above such a 'crossing' as this would be provided by throwing two arches, sprung from as high up as possible, across the nave from north to south to carry the east and west walls of the lantern, which, rising but little above the roof, would not represent a very great load. This is the typical central tower of the Anglo-Saxon great churches. In the west of England at any rate, the pseudo-crossing continued in use well into the twelfth century, where it appears in all the great cathedral and abbey churches.

Soon after the middle of the tenth century, however, the fully-developed crossing had appeared on the Continent; the Ottonian abbey church of Gernrode in Old Saxony (Plate 20), erected in 961, is an example. The finest English example is the magnificent crossing at St. Albans (Plate 3), dating from about 1080. The Anglo-Saxon pseudo-crossing, however, continued in use for long after the Conquest; it was not until the change in fashion, which introduced the cruciform pillar in place of the clumsy pier, took a hold on English architecture that the true crossing with its towering clustered pillars came back into the style. One of the earliest of these is at Wells (Plate 26); later conservators, however, recalling the collapse of crossing after crossing owing to insufficient top-loading, stiffened their piers with stone saltires copied from timber prototypes.

The central tower raised over the crossing of an aisle-less cruciform church is, in essence, of mid-tenth-century origin. In large parish churches, both cruciform and of 'axial' type, good central towers with belfry stages appear in some numbers during the twelfth century. Such towers as these, however, were probably never attempted in the case of the greater churches, with their dangerous height and the less secure support provided by the crossing piers, until at the earliest the latter half of this century.

The form of the Ottonian lantern tower—which continued until the end of the twelfth century—may be seen at St. Albans (Plate 155) and Tewkesbury (Plate 93), both of which, however, were raised half a century or so after their erection. The lantern walls rise only a short height above the ridges, on either side of each of these being a window of the same form as those in the nearby clerestories.

It is greatly to be deplored that no trace remains to-day of the elaborate timber features which originally crowned the low stone lantern-towers of the tenth-, eleventh- and twelfth-century great churches. The Bayeux Tapestry, however, provides an illustration of the central steeple of eleventh-century Westminster Abbey (Plate 153). These timber structures were clearly built in stages, each of which was probably framed-up —in much the same way as the ordinary wooden bell-frame—with a long sole-piece, a shorter head-piece, and two vertical posts stiffened by raking struts supported on the projecting ends of the sole-piece. Each stage would be narrower than the one below, so as to leave room for the supporting struts; hence the pagoda-like silhouette of the whole erection. The uppermost stage would presumably be the bell-frame; hence, perhaps, the form of this when transferred to the walls of a stone tower. The silhouette of the eleventh- or early twelfth-century wooden church (Plate 76) may enable one to form some slight impression of the appearance of these steeples.

The twelfth-century form of the timber steeple is illustrated by a contemporary drawing of Canterbury Cathedral (Plate 154). The upper stages have here become octagonal, echoing the oriental domes of the Crusader churches and indicating the origin of the exactly similar stone copies which crown most of the contemporary Rhenish great churches. The advantage of the octagonal form of steeple is that it enables the angle features of the lantern to be carried up as turrets.

All the available skill of the Anglo-Saxon wrights must have been lavished upon these elaborate timber steeples which indicated the choirs of the great churches of the day. With their sides and roofs covered with shingles, and ornamented with grotesque animal heads, each construction was surmounted by a weathercock. The whole lofty construction rose from amongst the four angle turrets of the lantern below.

With the refinement of the architecture of the supporting piers below, however, it was discovered that the superincumbent weight of these central features was insufficient to counterbalance the thrust of the arcades upon the tall crossing piers of the greater churches. It was this defect which eventually caused the collapse of most of the eleventh-century central towers with their wooden spires.

The only original towers which have survived are those of such great churches as, having no western towers, raised their central lanterns by adding a belfry storey. St. Albans (Plate 155), Tewkesbury (Plate 93) and Norwich are examples of this. (The two latter towers were built during the period at which wall-enrichment reaches its most elaborate form; the tower-transepts of Exeter also belong to the same era.)

Notwithstanding the early· date of these belfry stages, however, it is clear that the necessity for weighting the tall crossing piers of churches was not realised in this country until much later during the Gothic era.

This is perhaps due to the successful efforts of the French designers, whose immensely lofty bays and acutely pointed arches exerted much less lateral pressure; Westminster Abbey is an example of a great church which has stood perfectly well with nothing but a low lantern as its central feature.

But the English builders widened their bays without increasing the heights of these; nor was the pitch of the arches raised sufficiently to minimise lateral thrust. During the twelfth century and the early part of the next, a number of crossings collapsed, but still the engineers failed to appreciate the reason for these disasters. At Wells, the desperate builders of about 1338 strutted their crossing piers with heavy stone saltires; the same device was repeated at Salisbury. Also at Salisbury in 1220, the central lantern was unprovided with a belfry; the lateral arches gave trouble, having to be strutted during the fifteenth century.[33] Soon after 1239, however, in which year the combined thrusts of choir and transept arcades overturned the south-eastern crossing pier of Lincoln Cathedral, the rebuilt structure was provided with a belfry storey above its lantern (Plate 111).

The popular early twelfth-century parish-church plan consisting of a nave and chancel separated by a small lantern tower has already been discussed. These 'axial' towers were originally quite simple structures, having arches to east and west, and a lofty ground storey with windows high up in the side wall; towards the end of the twelfth century they were generally raised to provide a belfry floor lit by a *bifora* on each face.

Although the tower plays little part in the parish-church architecture of the thirteenth century, the same is not entirely true in respect of the greater churches. The possibilities of the lantern tower, in particular, appear to have seized the imagination of the designers of the period. Beautiful lanterns such as that at Pershore Abbey belong to this period. Unfortunately the interest taken in vaulting during the fifteenth century caused many of these lanterns to be mutilated when the crossing was thus ceiled.

The fourteenth century, however, saw the completion of what is perhaps the finest central feature of any mediaeval church—the great octagon of Ely (Plate 152). After the collapse of the four crossing piers these were not rebuilt; possibly the glorious structure which was devised to take the place of the fallen tower represents the last relic of the elaborate timber features which had crowned the churches of Ottonian and later days.

By the fourteenth century the race for altitude was beginning in earnest. With what appears to be the utmost recklessness, designers began piling stage after stage upon the crossing piers of such cathedrals

as Salisbury and Lincoln. The whole amazing series of achievements culminated in the Angel Tower at Canterbury (Plate 159), constructed just
after the turn of the century. It was possibly due to these fine structures
that the parochial tower-building craze of the fifteenth-century wool era
set in.

Notwithstanding the early essays in tower-raising encountered late
in the twelfth century, however, the glorious central towers of this country are all of late-mediaeval origin. The interesting principle (Fig. 16)
upon which the Ottonian church was developed out of the earlier turriform nucleus left the latter as an architectural feature of monumental
proportions indicating the principal entrance of the great nave. It is easy
to appreciate that the opportunity thus presented to the mediaeval architects was not ignored by them. Indeed it was at this stage that they first
began to experiment with elevational architecture in the creation of a
frontispiece to their most important class of building (Fig. 39).

After various modifications of the existing turriform nucleus the first
definite step towards a façade came when its western aisle was removed
so as to expose this face of the tower right down to the ground. With the
lateral expansion of the transept on either side a magnificent façade was
produced which can still be admired in a truncated form at Ely (Plate
158) and in utter ruin at Bury St. Edmunds.

But such vast late-twelfth-century undertakings as these could not
survive their era and we find the great west towers vanishing from the
English scene. The next stage, encountered at Peterborough and Lincoln
(Plate 102), is to raise a pair of humbler towers over the end bays of the
aisles. The breadth of effect is retained by the projection of small narrow
transepts from the flanks of the towers; the whole façade is completed by
facing it with a kind of monumental narthex consisting of three gigantic
arches reproducing the cross-section of the structure within.

The final stage in the design of the west front is to absorb the flanks
of the design within a pair of large towers supporting the main gable of
the nave.

By the end of the twelfth century English architectural practice seems
to have become agreed upon the pair of western towers (Plate 214)
notwithstanding the strong national tendency towards the Rhenish
school, which favoured twin-towers at the other end of the building,
flanking the presbytery, as at Hereford. Durham Cathedral appears
to have had all four towers, the western pair being, however, the
larger. Fine transeptal towers remain at Exeter; similar ones probably
also formed part of the original cathedral at Old Sarum.

In the twelfth century, the principal Flemish church was the great
cathedral at Tournai. This had a central lantern-tower and twin towers at
the ends of the aisles of each of the transepts. Winchester Cathedral—

which has a twelfth-century font of Tournai marble—also attempted to construct similar towers above the end of its transept aisles.

An early advantage of having a central tower was that this provided a lofty apartment in which to site the choir. During the Middle Ages, choirs were apt to shift their position, first westwards into the east end of the long nave, then eastwards into the extended presbytery. At Wymondham in Norfolk, where the choir was situated west of the original crossing, a second and much loftier tower was constructed above the choir

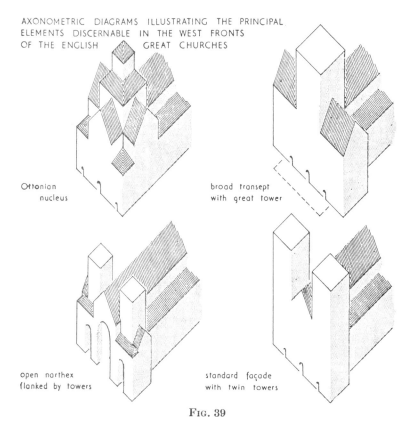

AXONOMETRIC DIAGRAMS ILLUSTRATING THE PRINCIPAL
ELEMENTS DISCERNABLE IN THE WEST FRONTS
OF THE ENGLISH   GREAT CHURCHES

Ottonian
nucleus

broad transept
with great tower

open narthex
flanked by towers

standard façade
with twin towers

FIG. 39

stalls during the fourteenth century. This seems to have set a fashion amongst the friars' churches in the East Anglian region; several of these, as at Lynn, erected towers within their otherwise towerless churches to separate the nave from the choir. This feature of the inserted 'central' tower is met with in other small monastic churches throughout the country.

Some of the early western towers in this country, as in the case of the Lincolnshire examples at Broughton and Hough-on-the-Hill, have circular staircases provided for access to the first-floor chapel. These turrets are universal features of the Ottonian churches of the late tenth century, and appear in Flanders, as for example at the fine church of Celles, in the early eleventh century; the English examples probably date from the middle of this century.

The earliest stair-turrets were placed in the centre of the west wall. Later, as in the cathedral at North Elmham, they are moved towards one angle, eventually taking up a position enclosing the angle itself. At the time of the Conquest the circular stair-turret was in common use, not only for the ascent of towers, as at the White Tower in London, but also for access to the galleries of the great churches; a fine example remains attached to the transept of the priory church of Christchurch in Hampshire.

By the twelfth century the stair-turret had become an ubiquitous feature in architectural design, being employed, in particular, to flank the gable ends of important buildings. Lofty circular stair-turrets, elaborately arcaded, may be seen, for example, in the west transept at Ely (Plate 158). Soon, however, the practice of thickening-out the angles of tall buildings and siting stairs in the space so provided, led to the adoption of the square stair-turret as the universal form of this feature: to continue thus throughout the whole of the early mediaeval period. The finest square turrets in this country are the elaborate examples attached to the west walls of the eastern transept at Canterbury Cathedral. Such prodigal ornamentation as this, however, had ceased by the end of the twelfth century; later turrets are arcaded only in their upper stages.

The development of the buttress, and the introduction of pairs of these at the angles of buildings, produced another form of stair-turret, in which a splayed face was introduced between the buttresses, to give room for the stair and provide sites for its windows. By the Edwardian period, however, the pair of angle buttresses had been superseded by the single diagonal one, which provided no space within it for a stair. The angle turret then came back again, but in an octagonal form which lasted until the end of the mediaeval era.

Except in rural districts, very few of the older church towers in this country retain their original appearance, owing to the introduction of lead roofs, flat in pitch, and requiring the provision of parapets to conceal the lead box-gutters which replaced the earlier eaves.

Until perhaps the Edwardian period the normal form of tower roof was a pyramidal cap matching in pitch that of the roofs covering the rest of the building and overhanging the wall-faces with eaves. During the eleventh century, the Rhenish form of tower roof consisting of four gables with their ridges inclined upwards to form a cap with its faces passing down to the corners of the tower—called a 'helm' roof—was sometimes employed; Sompting (Plate 156) in Sussex is the only remaining example in this country.

The high-pitched roofs of the Norman keeps, including those built on a circular plan, were always concealed by raising the surrounding walls to the height of the ridge; this was, of course, to protect the roofs from destruction by siege artillery. The circular tower-keep of Conisborough in Yorkshire has a small central turret specially provided for this purpose.

The timber structures which crowned the crossings of Anglo-Saxon cathedrals have already been referred to. These features diminished in size until the uppermost storey was quite small on plan, forming a small square or octagonal turret. The culminating feature of a timber roof appears to have frequently been a slender spirelet known as a 'broach'—the Saxon word for a spit—such as may still be seen to-day perched upon many a tower-roof (Plate 76). The roofs of ordinary square towers were also finished off with the broaches (Plate 160), an echo of which remains in the fifteenth-century 'Hertfordshire spikes' which are familiar features of the churches of that region.

The form of stone roof which we call a spire is undoubtedly of French origin. In the twelfth century, the Continental designers were experimenting with various forms of stone translations of the timber features which crowned the towers of the period; before the century was out, they had produced the octagonal stone spire, flanked by tall stone dormers and with the transition between square and octagon masked with four sturdy angle-pinnacles or turrets. Such spires were clearly nothing more than acutely-pitched stone roofs, rising direct from the wall-face as had their timber predecessors.

There are few examples of this type of spire in this country; that of Oxford Cathedral is perhaps the earliest. A classical French spire is, however, the magnificent mid-fourteenth-century example which rises above Salisbury Cathedral (Plate 92).

The English spire—or 'broach' as it was called throughout the Middle Ages—was developed along independent lines. The timber broaches of early days gradually expanded until their base became of equal width to the tower itself. The broach had then absorbed the whole of the tower roof—whether cap or helm—until nothing remained of this except at the angles. During the last century, confusion over nomenclature caused these vestiges of the roof to become termed 'broaches'; it is, however, the spire itself which is the broach or 'spit'. Most of the thirteenth-century stone spires which began to appear in the stone districts of the East Midlands were developed from the broach superimposed on the cap roof (Plate 161). Some, however, as at Etton, Northants, and Bythorn (Hunts.), are based on the helm roof.

The reduction in the pitch of roofs brought about by the use of lead, and the consequent disappearance of eaves in favour of the lead box-gutter concealed behind a parapet, caused these latter features to become the universal method of capping the walls of all buildings, including towers. As the old form of roof disappeared, so did the primitive form of stone spire become obsolete, being replaced by simple octagonal spires which rose from behind the parapet. These 'parapet spires', which were the ultimate form of this feature, crowned many of the great towers of the wool period, especially in the eastern building-stone district. They began to associate themselves with the angle pinnacles of the towers from which they rose in a multitude of varied and delightful arrangements (Plate 162). The spires themselves were frequently embellished with miniature dormer windows taken from the domestic architecture of the period. In the stoneless counties, slender timber spires, covered with lead, rise behind the parapets of their towers; Harrow in Middlesex and Hemel Hempstead in Herts are notable examples.

Bell-towers were not always attached to buildings. It was sometimes found easier, instead of opening-up the west wall of a nave and building a tower against it, to erect the whole structure on a separate site. Perhaps the most remarkable of all the detached towers of English churches is the curious timber structure at Brookland in Kent. Within its comparatively modern octagonal skin is a four-poster framework of huge timbers rising from sleepers; these, however, are not laid parallel, as in the Essex churches, but in a square, as in the mast-churches of Norway. The structure may thus indicate a twelfth-century nucleus, and may be the original church, but the four posts lean slightly inward, instead of being vertical, as in the normal four-poster church.[34]

If this undoubtedly very ancient structure is indeed the remains of a church, its 'battering' shape may account for the curious inward-sloping jambs of some eleventh-century doorways, such as that in the Deerhurst chapel. If, on the other hand, it has always been a tower, a careful examination may give a clue or two which will assist in the elucidation of the principal architectural mystery of the period surrounding the Conquest—the true nature of those elaborate wooden towers and steeples so entrancingly depicted on the Bayeux Tapestry.

166. The late mediaeval dining hall of St. Cross
Hospital, Winchester, Hampshire

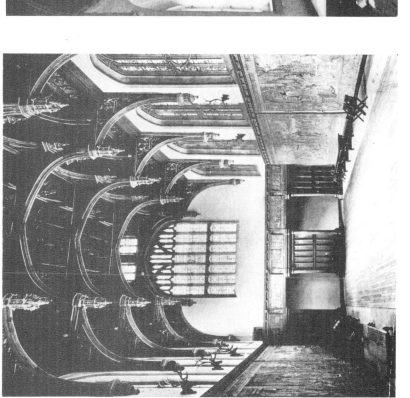

165. The banqueting hall of a Tudor palace. Hampton
Court, Middlesex

167. A stone bay window has been added to this fifteenth century hall of Gainsborough Old Hall, Lincolnshire

168. A large yeoman's house of the end of the mediaeval era at Brewer Street, Bletchingley, Surrey

CHAPTER XIII

Great Houses

Throughout the mediaeval period the poor man lived in a hut or hovel the squalor of which is probably quite unimaginable to-day. There was an insignificant middle class of merchants and a few well-to-do craftsmen who, together with the lesser aristocracy, were able to afford small private houses.

Important landowners, having a crowd of feudal tenantry or a garrison of soldiers to accommodate, usually had to provide a hall for these; this might similarly be either unfortified, or protected by the defences of a castle.

The early-mediaeval private house was the residence of an upper-class family, or even of a middle-class household such as that of a merchant. The heads of most feudal communities must have provided themselves from an early period with private houses in which they and their family could live. This necessary association of such a house with the feudal hall brought about, towards the close of the twelfth century, the conjunction of these to form one building, which we may call the great house (Fig. 30).

In its simplest form the great house consisted of these two parts: a spacious—possibly barn-like—hall at ground level with, attached to one end, a small two-storied building representing the house portion. The axes of the two portions would normally be at right angles to one another.

It would appear that the whole germ of the English farmhouse plan (and the first great houses were certainly nothing more than farmhouses) lies in this principle of providing a large barn-like building having the residence of the farmer at one end of it. It was probably so in Anglo-Saxon days. Even in the eighteenth century, farmhouses of this type were still being built throughout the countryside. Often a single roof covers the whole, so that only the window arrangement indicates the internal division; occasionally, however, the house portion boasts a transverse roof of its own with a gable to the front.

The entrance to the hall would be at the end of its long side wall farthest from the house, the gable end of which would probably project as a feature on the same front, and would exhibit, on its chamber floor, an

237

attractive window indicating the actual abode of the Lord of the Manor himself. Thus we get, in embryo, the makings of a 'front' to the manor-house, that is to say, the face which it would present to the visitor and, thus, that by which it would advertise its dignity. At the beginning of the thirteenth century, these small manor-houses seem to have been fairly common throughout the country. That of Longthorpe in Northamptonshire and the abbot's house at Tavistock in Devon are examples.

Within, the ground floor of the house portion would be a vaulted cellar, remaining inaccessible from ground level until well into the Middle Ages. By the Edwardian period, however, when the entrance to the chamber began to be by a stair leading up from the interior of the upper end of the hall, the door to the storage basement might be placed near the foot of this.

It has been noted that by the middle of the twelfth century a number of great halls, especially those of the royal and episcopal palaces, were provided with a small block of storerooms attached to the lower end of the main structure (Fig. 28). By the end of the century many of these additions had been raised in height by the addition of a solar floor so as to provide a chamber over. The effect of this was to produce a house at the lower end of the hall instead of the upper. The episcopal palaces of Lincoln and Wells show this arrangement; the archiepiscopal palace at Mayfield, of Edwardian date, is planned as an entity with the hall porch combined with the gable-wall of the 'lower-end' house (Plate 115). In these later manor-houses the lower floor of the house-part forms the normal storage basement; Crowhurst, also in Sussex, shows this arrangement.

It would be obvious that such a useful apartment might be better employed as accommodation, especially when the old-fashioned 'stone solars' gave place to an ordinary timber floor, requiring no obstructive pillars to support it. In the early mediaeval period, it was customary for the master of the house and his family to take their meals at the high table in the hall. With the decline of feudalism, we find the erstwhile storage space below the great chamber being converted into a 'parlour'; a sort of private hall in which he could converse with his friends (Fig. 40).

The parlour—a French designation which in English was rendered 'bower', a *burh* or stronghold of privacy for the householder—was probably adopted from the urban residence which from the beginning had been provided with a ground-floor apartment of this nature. After the end of the early-mediaeval era the storage basements were all converted into parlours; the storerooms at the lower end of the hall were also knocked into one to provide a dining-parlour convenient to the servery in the screens passage.

While the logical arrangement of the great house was for the house-

⊃art with the great chamber to be sited at the upper end of the hall convenient to the dais, some manor-houses were from the beginning planned
with the house at the opposite end, even though this had not expanded
'rom a twelfth-century range of storerooms. The reason for this is prob-
bly the desire for a dining-parlour close to the servery; the food for the

DEVELOPMENT OF THE MANOR HOUSE

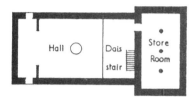

HALL WITH TWO-STORIED HOUSE AT UPPER END
GREAT CHAMBER OVER STORE ROOM

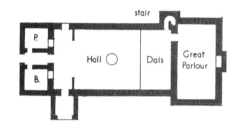

PANTRY AND BUTTERY ADDED
STORE ROOM BECOMES GREAT PARLOUR

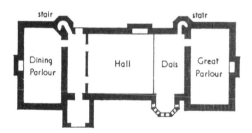

DINING PARLOUR AT LOWER END OF HALL

Fig. 40

igh table must have already reached it cold and the journey from the
creens to a 'great parlour' behind the dais would have been even longer.

The period of 'livery and maintenance' which coincided with the Wars
f the Roses produced a kind of semi-feudal organisation within the great
ouse, owing to the presence of the mercenaries which the great lords
·ere incorporating within their households. Such persons, however, bore
n entirely different relationship to the master of the house from the early

mediaeval tenantry; it may have been this fact which was the cause of the introduction of the private parlour into the great houses. Thus we find, for the first time in mediaeval domestic planning, properly paved ground-floor apartments suitable for the accommodation of upper-class people. Such parlours often had fine ceilings—the first appearance of this architectural feature—formed by enriching the floor-beams over.

It was about this period that the system of screens came to be developed which formed a passage connecting the principal entrance of the hall with the door opposite to it. This secondary door became the kitchen entrance, in place of that in the centre of the end wall of the hall which now led to the dining-parlour. The new apartment could be conveniently served from the screens passage at the same time as the company in the hall.

The hall might now have a small transverse building at its upper end balanced, on plan at any rate, by a similar adjunct at its lower end. It will be realised that it was an obvious course to make both of these two stories high, so as to provide a second chamber.

It is interesting to note that the tripartite arrangement which appears to have been employed in the small private houses of the twelfth century is now seen repeated in the plan of the great house of two centuries later the living-space in the centre of the chamber floor having been replaced by the great hall with its hearth. The whole of the great chamber being now reserved to the proprietor, one wonders whether the new chamber at the lower end of the hall could have formed the 'nursery'. It may, however have been the guest-chamber.

The great house began thus to present an appearance comparable with present-day standards of house design. Although the centre of the front was still occupied by the lofty mediaeval hall with its entrance at one end and the bay-window at the other, at each end of this nucleus was a comparatively narrow-fronted gable-end, two stories in height. The plan of such a house would resemble an H, having two short thin legs and a long wide cross-bar.

The addition of the dining-parlour at the lower end of the hall necessitated a complete revision of the cooking arrangements. Previously the kitchen had been at the end of the hall, separated from it by the short passage between the pantry and the buttery. The kitchen entrance had now become that at the rear end of the screens passage. As the space before the principal entrance of the manor-house attained something of the nature of a forecourt, so did the corresponding area at the rear of the house become the kitchen court.

Thus the plans of important manor-houses of the late mediaeval period usually exhibit two approximately square courtyards, separate

169. The pseudo-military gatehouse of a late mediaeval fortified manor
house. Maxstoke Castle, Warwickshire

170. The chapel and gatehouse tower of Magdalen College at Oxford

171. A mediaeval bridge crossing the Tamar at Lostwithiel, Cornwall

172. The ribbed barrel vaults of a mediaeval bridge at Eamont,
Penrith, Cumberland

by the great hall—nucleus of the whole complex. In front of the hall-porch extended the 'court of honour'.

Reaching round the kitchen court from the back door of the hall were the kitchen, pantry, buttery, scullery, dairy, and all the various offices connected with the feeding of a large household; kitchen servants, too, would be accommodated in small lodgings around this court.

With the expansion of Tudor magnificence, the great chamber, originally a bedchamber, became endowed with a pomp and circumstance far in excess of this ordinary domestic status. It may have been the council chambers of the bishops' palaces which set the fashion for the great 'audience chambers' which came to be constructed, especially at the time of the Dissolution of the Monasteries, at the upper ends of the great halls of secular palaces and mansions. Some of these chambers are halls in themselves; they may even have screens at their lower ends. The

LATER DEVELOPMENT OF THE GREAT HOUSE
Medioeval Manor House indicated in solid block.

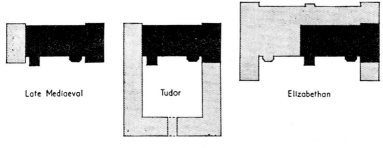

Lote Medioeval   Tudor   Elizobethon

FIG. 41

bedchamber then becomes a separate apartment, projecting from the upper end of the great chamber. It may eventually form the nucleus of a range of 'lodgings', entered one from another, ranged as a wing flanking the upper side of the great forecourt.

The lesser chamber at the lower end of the hall also came to be provided with a similar range of apartments; thus, from the development of the embryo wings of the H-plan, the Tudor architects arrived at the forecourt flanked, and eventually completely enclosed, by ranges of buildings (Fig. 41).

Tudor pomp and magnificence brought with it much dispensation of hospitality; it was for this purpose, and not for the housing of feudal tenantry, that the great halls of the period were constructed (Plate 165). Guests were accommodated in lodgings provided in the two ever-extending lateral wings as these crept along the flanks of the forecourt and turned towards each other and the great gatehouse which gave access to it (Plate 163).

The complete Tudor plan had, in effect, two show-fronts. The outermost was the range containing the gatehouse; it was usually of symmetrical design, probably terminating in a turret of some sort at either end, in pseudo-castellated fashion. Passing through the gatehouse and into the courtyard, however, the visitor was then confronted by the front of the house itself (Plate 164) with its entrance porch at one end, only partly balanced by the great bay-window at the other. It was upon these asymmetrical show-fronts that the Renaissance architects eventually began to turn their attention.

The central hearth was an important feature of the mediaeval great hall. Wall fireplaces had existed in the keep-towers of the eleventh century, and most twelfth-century private houses had one on the chamber floor. It was presumably realised that the wall fireplace was really unsuitable for heating an apartment as large as the mediaeval great hall; at any rate it is not until the end of the Middle Ages that it arrives there.

Its appearance made a striking difference to the character of the hall. Whereas this had hitherto been a barn-like building, open to the roof in order to allow the smoke from the fire to escape through this, it was now possible to ceil the hall throughout. Moreover, there was no need to have such an excessively lofty apartment in order to keep the hanging smoke-clouds well above the heads of the occupants. Thus the hall becomes reduced in height; in fact, except in point of size, like any other apartment.

This important alteration in the character of the mediaeval hall removes what had been the chief obstruction to the orderly design of a manor-house. Whereas this had hitherto been cut up vertically—its two ends inaccessible one from the other by reason of the intervening hall—it was now possible to complete the whole upper storey of the building above its ceiling. Great houses and palaces of the Tudor era retained the lofty hall as an architectural feature; the smaller manor-houses of the period were able to dispense with it entirely, improving the accommodation of their chamber floor by doing so.

When considering the private houses of the mediaeval period, most of which are to-day, of course, in ruins, it must be remembered that in those primitive days good use would almost certainly have been made of attics within roofs. Whereas the upper parts of more monumental structures such as churches or great halls would be given the utmost effect of height by the use of elaborate open roofs, the chamber floors of private houses would possibly often be floored over at the level of the wall-plate. The garret bedrooms thus provided would probably not have been despised by the mediaeval house-servant; in at least one great Continental house of the twelfth century we know that the owner's elder children slept there.

Great Houses

By the Tudor period the garret floor was being made full use of. Windows to it were being provided in the gables at the ends of the wings; the flanks of these were frequently broken by a multiplicity of lateral gables specially provided for the same purpose. The Continental type of dormer was never really popular in England; the gablet rising direct from the wall-face took its place.

Thus in Tudor days we get the complete three-storied house. Mediaeval planning made no provision for access between apartments, except in the case of the orderly monastic plans in which the various buildings were entered from the covered way surrounding the cloister. The assortment of houses which filled the 'curia' of the twelfth-century palace were connected with the great hall, if desired, by means of covered ways. Internal passages or corridors were unknown until the period of the Renaissance. Three-storied Tudor houses, however, sometimes had one long apartment passing down the centre of the uppermost floor from which some of the adjacent rooms were reached; this was the 'Long Gallery' which provided the occupants with an indoor promenade when the weather was bad, and which sometimes served as a picture gallery.

With the increased privacy obtained in the house through the abolishing of the semi-public hall much more attention began to be paid to its interior decoration. Craftsmen in wood, stone and plaster were imported from the Continent to try their skill in the embellishment of such features as fireplaces, the hall screens, the great staircase, and the ceilings of the more important apartments.

At the close of the Tudor period, the obsolescent mediaeval courtyards began to be abandoned as relics of the days when it had been necessary to shut oneself in behind the safety of high walls. Freed from this restriction, the central mass of the house was able to display itself; the skill of Renaissance architects enabled them to order its plan, and drag towards an all-important symmetry of elevation the haphazard features of its various show-fronts (Fig. 41).

Throughout the whole course of the Middle Ages, the 'wrights' who worked in timber were never lacking behind the masons who wrought in stone. For every building, large or small, raised by the latter there may have been a score of similar structures erected in the national building style. The fifteenth century was producing magnificent timber manorhouses (Plate 167); two centuries later the western carpenters were excelling themselves in the erection of great houses rivalling those of the masons.

The collapse of the old feudalism during the anarchy of the Wars of the Roses brought the English middle class to the forefront. Enriching themselves in the wool boom, rural farmers and urban merchants began building houses in imitation of their betters. The development of the manor-house with its two parlours is probably due to the desire of these people to maintain the nucleus of the feudal plan whilst modifying it to suit their more homely tastes. The Dissolution of the Monasteries produced further recruits to the middle class when the monastic estates were divided up into farms; the farm-houses needed were similar in form to those already being established by the yeomen wool-farmers.

It appears to have been the great ecclesiastics who gave the lead in matters of middle-class housing; one of the most important examples of the complete small house being that erected by the abbot of Glastonbury for his fishing holidays at Meare in Somerset (Plate 117). This perfect little structure possesses, enclosed within its four walls and covered by one roof, all the accommodation required. There is a tiny hall with a large wall-fireplace, a parlour at its upper end and a pantry and buttery at its lower. Above, entered by an outside stair, is a large chamber with a private bed-chamber adjoining it; a little latrine tower has now been removed. This

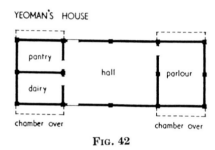

FIG. 42

little building gives at once the clue to the housing tastes of the fifteenth century.

The wool boom brought wealth to a part of England which had no building-stone nor masons to work it. This was the south-east, from East Anglia to the New Forest. In this region the new farmhouses had to be constructed by the village wrights. When they first began to appear, in the middle of the fifteenth century, these 'yeomen's houses' were set out with a central hall and a two-storied house at one end; better houses had living quarters at either end, in imitation of the manor-houses (Fig. 42).

As has already been explained, two-storied mediaeval houses entirely constructed of timber had to have their upper floors projecting in the form of 'jetties'; the yeomen's houses had, therefore, jettied-out chambers at one or both ends, while the central hall remained a single-storey structure (Plate 168).

With the introduction of wall-fireplaces, however, the yeoman's house achieved the same development as its stone counterpart, by lowering its hall and carrying the chamber floor right over this. At this stage, therefore, the house becomes jettied throughout (Plate 8).

Great Houses

In order to keep the plan simple, the whole house usually formed a rectangle, with only the jettied-out chamber gables to indicate the internal layout. With the advent of the complete two-storied house, however, these disappeared and the whole building came under one roof.

These yeomen's houses, originally country farmhouses, were speedily imitated by the rich merchants living in the growing 'wool-towns' of the eastern counties. By the end of the fifteenth century, the single-storey hall was already common in town-houses; an important step in house design which was followed more slowly by rural builders lacking facilities for constructing wall-fireplaces.

Yeomen's houses may still be met with in hundreds throughout the south-east of England. Some of them occupy isolated sites on their own farms; most, however, line the streets of the small towns and villages (Plate 7). Sometimes one of the parlours of such a house was designed, at the time of its erection, as a shop (Plate 131); two or three wide openings, once filled with stall-boards, in the wall towards the street, may still indicate this. Most of these village houses are to-day cut up into cottages or modern shops; the original form of each, however, can be appreciated by an examination of the roof.

The Elizabethan period was the era of chimneys. The population was wealthy and comfort-loving; the hardships of mediaeval life were being overcome. Thus the hall of the yeoman's house was well-heated by a large chimney—in which, moreover, the family cooking was done, for the yeoman's hall was also his wife's kitchen.

The great wall-fireplace was as much a feature of the exterior of a Tudor building as it was of the apartment within. Maintaining, with its terminal chimneys, that feeling of verticality which remains to the last the primary factor of mediaeval architectural effect, the massive chimney-stack is never concealed within the building as in Renaissance days. Elizabethan writers comment on the multiplicity of chimneys which had become the most prominent feature of the houses of the period.

The craze for building—mostly in speedily-erected timberwork—which swept over England during the Elizabethan period resulted in serious disafforestation. Laws were enacted to control building, and economy in construction was urged.

As more attention began to be given to this matter, improved methods of timber-building began to appear. The two-storied house being now the accepted form of structure, it became the practice to frame-up the building with posts passing up both stories, with the beams carrying the first-floor joists framed between these. This obviated the need for the mediaeval 'jetty'; owing to the fire-risk, Jacobean legislation was introduced to prohibit its use entirely in the narrow streets of mediaeval towns. This

245

improvement in timber-framing made it possible to construct internal chimneys, impossible in the case of jettied buildings as the floor-joists supported the upper storey and thus could not be cut.

The late Elizabethan yeoman's house generally had a single great stack; arranged at the end of his hall, it accommodated both the hall fireplace and that of the best parlour behind. The mutilated houses in the village streets of to-day usually exhibit an array of chimneys of all descriptions; amongst these, however, can usually be discovered the original large chimney of the yeoman's house.

In eastern England, especially, where Flemish brick was available, the wool boom produced a great crop of houses with fine brick chimneys, each advertising the comfort which might be enjoyed within.

Although the date of erection of these middle-class houses places them chronologically after the end of the mediaeval period, their planning arrangement of hall-kitchen with parlour and chamber at one end is essentially mediaeval. The isolated examples, standing upon their farms or straggling along village streets, present their long side as a front. In towns, however, where frontages were valuable, such houses had often to stand end-on to the street. It was then the upper gable-end of the house which became the show-front, with its parlour window, and above this the window of the principal chamber, serving as features upon which architectural skill could be displayed.

In this fashion rose the multi-storied town houses with the jettied façades so well-known to us; the inner ends of the joists carrying the jetties were bedded into the thick walling of the great stack which separated parlour and kitchen. Such houses were often entered from a side alley or 'fennel' passing along the flank of the house and giving access to the yard at its rear. The fifteenth-century type of 'double-fronted' house, having the entrance passage at the lower end of the parlour, was discussed in Chapter IX of this work. This and the primitive single-fronted type having the gable-end to the street are the true urban houses; the long yeomen's houses are really rural farmhouses, even though they be ranged along the streets of a country town.

The necessary economy in the use of timber caused the Elizabethan period to see a change in the arrangement of the framing of the wooden walls. Whereas during the mediaeval period it had been customary to set the vertical 'studs' close together and fill in the interstices with a minimum of wattle-and-daub (Plate 8), it now became necessary to frame-up the spaces between the main timbers in large panels which would use less wood. Brick 'nogging' became employed—generally set herringbone-fashion—to fill the panels (Plate 7).

The use of less timber reduced the rigidity of the structure, necessitating the introduction of diagonal bracing members. For some time past, the roof-builders of the West had been paying special attention to the bracing of the wide-span open roofs of their churches and halls (Plate 36). These braces were generally of more elaborate form than those in the south and east; Gothic decorative forms were employed to transform what were constructional necessities into fine architectural features.

The late mediaeval timber-building craze gave the western carpenters their chance to expose the results of their achievements on the external face of the structure. Hence that remarkable timber style—known as 'magpie'—which obtains in Herefordshire, Cheshire and the neighbouring districts. The use of short and curved pieces of wood enabled timber economy to be practised to the full.

Rural life in this country must have lost much of its neighbourliness when the mediaeval custom of building houses in timber gave place to the more formal brickwork of the 'contractor'. Timber houses were cut out and framed-up in the yard of the village wright, then taken down and carried to the site of erection. When all the joints had been inspected for the numerical symbols—still visible to-day—which indicated their proper order, the two gables would be assembled and pegged together ready for 'raising'. In true neighbourly spirit the villagers and their plough-oxen would combine to effect this operation. And if a man offended against his neighbours these might equally well combine to pull his house down again, bidding him take it elsewhere for re-erection.

All this was changed when bricks became the general building material. From the thirteenth century, bricks had been well-known in East Anglia; during the wool boom of the fifteenth century the walls of great churches had been built of this material, after which they were often concealed behind a facing of flint 'flush-work'.

Brick first appears in domestic building—apart from a few East Anglian houses probably erected by Flemish builders—as a material by the means of which it was possible to enlarge the ground floors of jettied buildings by building brick walls beneath the ends of the jetties and thus supporting the timber-framed upper storey independently of the floor-joists which had previously carried this. A great many Tudor houses have been transformed by this process.

By the Stuart period, common brick was fast becoming the universal building material, even for churches. The Renaissance architects were freed from the restrictive influences of mediaeval posts and studs; the small lumps of burnt clay—so easily made, transported and laid—proved a material aesthetically elastic enough for them to develop their skill to the full. But the fading-away of the great forests of England, and the village wrights who had for so many centuries been delving into them for building material, must have made great changes to the rural economy of this country.

Great Houses

Having considered the progress of domestic architecture in this country throughout the mediaeval period, some notice must now be given to public buildings. In the Middle Ages, administration was a far more intimate matter than it is to-day. The Crown ruled the nation, and the towns and villages governed their respective communities, in a manner which called for no government offices, certainly not outside the capital. The Crown and the great lay lords provided fortifications; the provincial communities saw to the upkeep of communications.

The lay and spiritual hierarchy dispensed hospitality in their fine houses to travellers of their own class; the poorer vagrant, if he could not chance upon some lodging in the outbuildings, had to fend for himself. As a feature of their constitution, the monastic houses took care of the local sick; such little education as was available also emanated from the monks. There were certain specialised organisations, mostly urban, connected with mercantile and professional communities; some of these, towards the end of the mediaeval period, provided themselves with buildings in which to meet.

The 'guildhalls' of the mercantile and craft guilds mostly date from the Edwardian era which was the hey-day of the mediaeval towns before the cataclysmic shock of the Black Death depopulated them. The buildings are similar in design to any other great feudal hall of the period, but appear to lack the domestic offices which invariably accompany private halls; there is generally no bay-window and the entrance is usually at the end, as in a great church. Guildhall in London, and the fine timber-arcaded hall at York, also destroyed by the Germans, were notable examples of the assembly hall of the Middle Ages.

In a Christian country, the care of sick and indigent persons is an important public duty. From the beginning of the mediaeval era until the sixteenth century, this duty devolved upon the Monastic Orders; thus all monastic houses of any size possessed a hall in which to accommodate sick persons. Such halls were usually aisled like the nave of a church; timber partitions divided the aisles into small rooms, later provided with fireplaces, and beds were ranged on either side of the central portion. The building was entered at its west end; at the other, approached through a large archway, was the chapel in which the sick could hear Mass.

There were occasionally hospitals founded by secular authority. That at Chichester—which, having a cathedral served by secular canons, had no great monastic house attached to it—is a good example of the ordinary mediaeval type of hospital, detached from contact with monastery buildings. Such hospital halls as survived the Dissolution were later divided up into small rooms; more in the style of an almshouse than the mediaeval —and modern—hospital ward.

The almshouse for the care of poor old men dates from the spacious days of the twelfth century. The best-known example is that near Winchester, known as the Hospital of St. Cross. In its original form it had a fine church, like a small edition of that of a monastic house, to the south transept of which was attached the two-storied house in which lived the thirteen inmates. This building, which has now vanished, was presumably of the same form as the ordinary monastic dormitory; it may be assumed that the old men ate their meals in an apartment on its ground floor.

The late mediaeval almshouse, however, was a quadrangular building enclosing a courtyard, around which the inmates had their own apartments; eating communally in a great hall having attached to it all the usual domestic offices, like that of a private house—or, perhaps, a university college of the period. The late-mediaeval living accommodation of the example at Winchester referred to above was replanned as two ranges of lodgings; its hall (Plate 166) is still in use.

The most convenient plan for a building designed to accommodate a mediaeval community was the monastic arrangement, with all rooms entered from the courtyard. This was the plan followed, therefore, in the construction of a university college. The peculiar feature of college planning is that, while the students could eat their meals together, like any other community, in a great hall, the communal house represented by the monastic dormitory was unsuitable for the purposes of study. It was thus necessary to provide separate rooms— as in a Carthusian monastery —for the accommodation of the students of a college. These rooms were arranged in the normal late-mediaeval fashion round the sides of a large courtyard to which access was attained through a lofty gatehouse tower (Plate 170).

Although the students' chapel was—as might have been expected at a period when most of the education was in the hands of the clergy—one of the finest of the college buildings, pride of place was given to the great hall in which the community gathered at meal times. It is not clear whether there was anything in the nature of a standard arrangement for college buildings; any suggestion of a monastic plan is limited to the claustral layout. The great hall, however, is usually placed, in early colleges, in approximately the position occupied by the refectory of a monastic house; it is generally kept as near as possible to the entrance gate for convenience of access. Later, however, with the development of the courtyard as a feature employed in domestic planning, the hall comes to be sited in its secular position at the far side of the court from the entrance; its principal elevation—with possibly a fine entrance porch— could then be seen to advantage from the gatehouse.

The late mediaeval almshouse often followed the college plan, though, of course, on a somewhat smaller scale. As in all mediaeval houses, the great hall was the principal apartment, while the usual emphasis was given to the monumental feature provided by the entrance gatehouse.

The first appearance of the inn is at the very end of the mediaeval period, when the European Renaissance was resulting in increased travelling, better roads, and the provision of suitable conveyances for the transport of human beings from place to place. The Elizabethan court-yard inns, with their galleried chamber-floors, are well-known; the plays of Shakespeare owe not a little to the invention of this very important type of building, which is merely a development, for public uses, of the communal type of house first employed in the plans of mediaeval monasteries. The galleries are simply the covered alleys of a cloister garth made two-storied in order that access might be attained to the upper floor of a building which was still unprovided with internal corridors.

One of the most important feature of mediaeval English life was the market. This had usually to take place in the open air or under temporary shacks of poles covered with a rough thatching of some handy material; the permanent market-buildings of contemporary oriental civilisations being unknown to mediaeval England.

Even before the days of parish churches, however, village life had tended to centre round the crosses erected by early missionaries as advertisement of the Faith and as a place at which to meet and pray. The village cross thus played an important part in the life of the community. As a place of meeting, it was thus an obvious place for barter. Hence the mediaeval structure known as the market-cross, which, first mounted upon a stepped platform upon which goods could be displayed, was later provided with a permanent roof over these. At first the shelters were simple wooden constructions supported upon poles; later, elaborate masonry compositions replaced these. The market-cross at Chichester is perhaps the best-known (Plate 151); there are also a number of fine timber examples, such as that at Wymondham in Norfolk.

Of the various buildings connected with agriculture, the most important was the storehouse for produce. The mediaeval barn would have, in most places, been of timber construction, with an entrance at one or both ends; large openings suitable for the passage of farm-wains could not have been constructed in the low side walls. The fine barns of late mediaeval date, however, are generally cruciform in plan, with the entrances at either end of a central 'transept'. A number of mediaeval barns in stone and timber, some of them very large, yet remain. Some of these were probably originally halls; the old hall-doorway may some-times be discovered in its normal position near the end of one of the long walls.

The nearest approach to an industrial building known to the Middle

Ages was the mill for grinding corn. At first this was a humble structure covering a primitive mechanism formed by a single revolving shaft carrying at its upper extremity the revolving stone; at the lower end a system of inclined paddles was turned by the weight of water leaving the artificially-constructed mill-dam. By the last decade of the twelfth century, however, the discovery of how to construct wooden cog-wheels and thus convert a horizontal rotation into a vertical enabled the wind to be employed as the motive power. The first recorded windmill, built in 1191 at Harberden in Suffolk, was destroyed by the Abbot of Bury, who feared that the new invention would take away trade from the water-mills which, as in most monasteries, were a source of revenue to his house.

Mediaeval windmills were small wooden houses perched upon a sturdy post, about which the whole structure containing the stones, shafts and cog-wheels revolved. The post was mounted upon two sleepers crossing each other and also carrying four strong timber struts to keep the whole structure vertical. There were four arms carrying canvas sails, reefed when necessary like those of a ship. These early mills have all vanished long ago, but the slight mounds covering their ruins still remain on many a hill-top; they are often mistaken to-day for tumuli.

Even before the Norman Conquest, one of the 'three necessities' which comprised the basic duties of an Englishman towards the government of his country was the maintenance of internal communications. The roads of the day were few and unmetalled, but they had to be kept free from obstructions due to falls of earth or encroaching undergrowth. The water-crossings, in particular, had to be supervised, or the traffic of goods might be seriously impeded, and the economy of the country thereby affected.

Bridges were important structures in mediaeval days. In addition to being employed for the crossing of waterways, every castle had to be provided with at least one, for access to the entrance across ditch or moat. The first bridges were constructed entirely of timber, their beams supported upon sturdy trestles; several illustrations appear in the Bayeux Tapestry. In later days, however, they became replaced, like most classes of mediaeval buildings, by masonry structures (Plate 171).

The people of mediaeval England were notable engineers in earthwork. Besides their fortifications, they were forced to construct the pounds and dams without which there could be no water-power with which to grind their corn.

From Roman days tracks had been carried over streams by means of causeways of stone or earth, having small-span culverts provided in them to carry the water through. These culverts were apt to get blocked, in which event the causeway would act as a dam; when the water reached the summit of this it would not be long before the whole structure would be carried away. Thus the clearing of culverts, as well as the maintenance of the trestles of timber bridges, was an important duty of the local authority of the day. The decay of the Roman road system was due to the failure of its river-crossings.

The first stone bridges were simple arches, each one a barrel vault. Later, as ribbed vaulting came in to assist in economy of wooden centering, the arches of bridges came to be constructed of a series of parallel ribs carrying an infilling of stone slabs (Plate 172). The piers of late mediaeval river-bridges were often provided with triangular projections on the upstream side so as to divert a strong current which might dislodge the stones of a masonry which, laid in lime mortar, was not such a sound engineering construction as could be produced to-day.

Mediaeval bridges are all quite narrow; seven or eight feet overall is the maximum width. Hence any parapets, if provided, were usually, to save space, of wood. These bridges are often called 'pack-horse bridges', as if they had been constructed especially for these animals. But there was hardly any wheeled traffic during the Middle Ages; even persons of quality travelled on horseback or in litters. For moving farm produce, sledges were used. Thus all long-distance transport had to be effected by means of pack-animals; a very narrow bridge, therefore, was all that was needed in mediaeval days.

CHAPTER XIV

Architectural Details

Windows, both by reason of the opportunities presented by varying their arrangement and also by virtue of the enormous possibilities suggested by the use of tracery, form a very important part of the architectural treatment of mediaeval buildings. The same cannot be said, however, of doorways; these are usually placed just exactly where they are needed. English doorways seldom attain the magnificence of contemporary Continental portals.

The most important structural factor in a doorway is the form adopted in providing it with a head which will carry the walling above. The simplest method of doing this is, of course, to span the opening with a lintel; the doorways of many ancient churches in this country exhibit this feature. The problem with a lintel, however, is that, unless this is very deep, it is liable to crack in the middle. A device sometimes employed in early eleventh-century doorways is to employ a series of lintels, one above the other, each one set back so that the whole series supports the full thickness of the wall; this may be seen in the tower of the church at Hough-on-the-Hill.

During the Edwardian period, the lintel returned to use in small doorways, especially in domestic architecture. Its span, however, was in this case reduced by introducing a pair of corbels to increase the bearing; this feature is known as the 'Edwardian arch'. Another form of door-head employed in the tenth and eleventh centuries is that formed by inclining two lintels, one against the other, so as to form what is known as a 'triangular arch'. Properly speaking, both these so-called arches are, in reality, merely varieties of lintel construction. The true arch is invariably formed of a series of small wedge-shaped stones known as 'voussoirs'; early arches are invariably of semicircular form, but in the latter half of the twelfth century become pointed.

The most primitive doorways are perfectly plain; yet from perhaps as early as the eighth century they begin to develop a characteristic ornament in the form of a frame. The lintel of a classical building is generally embellished with a moulding known as an 'architrave'; this being, in actual fact, another name for the lintel itself. The architrave moulding

253

always follows the same general lines; it is divided into two main areas, the larger of which is flat and only relieved by very slight breaks in the face. The upper part of the architrave, which, although the smaller, is much more prominent, has two separate members; the lower of these being of a protuberant section which, in its turn, supports the plain square fillet which completes the whole architrave (Fig. 43).

Architrave mouldings of this nature were employed in Byzantine architecture to surround doorway openings. By the end of the first millennium some knowledge of the feature appears to have penetrated to this country, so that a rough imitation of its main lines began to be introduced into church doorways. The plainer part of the architrave is sometimes represented by a slight setting-back of the face of the wall adjoining the opening. The more prominent portion of the moulding appears, subdivided into its two members, in the form of two ribs, separated from each other, the outermost being square in section, and the innermost round (Plate 81). These two primitive mouldings continue through various modifications throughout the early mediaeval period; the inner round member becoming a sturdy roll-moulding passing round the edge of the opening, whilst the outermost is retained, above the arch only, as a 'hood-mould'. It is in this last feature that, at about the time of the Conquest, the two portions of the moulding eventually reunite once more.

Another device employed in the design of Byzantine doorways consisted in the indication of the level of the springing of the arch by means of a horizontal moulding—of approximately the same form as the 'architrave moulding'—known as an 'impost moulding'. The Anglo-Saxon masons made great play with this feature, which they represented in a multitude of barbaric forms either with or without the mouldings surrounding the opening itself.

By the eleventh century, when the outermost square moulding had become the hood-mould over the arch, the inner roll had combined with a simplified form of impost, below which the vertical portion of this moulding had been given a cap and a base to form a small colonnette worked up the angle. Combined with a setting-back of the wall-face round the opening, windows surrounded by a frame formed of such colonnettes, continuing as a roll-moulding round the containing arch, and finished with a hood-mould, were universally popular features for a century after the Conquest. In a more refined form, with separate shafts, it continues into the thirteenth century.

A common form of Byzantine door-head, particularly popular in Syria, where earthquakes are not uncommon, was provided by combining the arch with the lintel; the former, by relieving the latter of its load, prevented it from breaking. The semicircular spandrel, known as a 'tympanum', was a popular site for sculpture; this country possesses a fine ries of twelfth-century sculptured tympana (Plate 173). As doorways ecame wider, lintels were abandoned; English architects were willing to ispense with the tympanum rather than follow the continental practice f supporting a long lintel with a central pillar. Relieving arches still ppear in the masonry above door and window openings.

The principle of economising in timber centering when turning arches ι thick walls by constructing the arch in receding 'orders' has already een explained. By keeping the inner face of the arch flat and arranging ll the orders on the outside of the building, a deeply recessed doorway as thereby created. Each order was often embellished with one of the ιany forms of sculpture ornament peculiar to the twelfth century; below he impost, ranges of colonnettes added to the richness of the feature.

In the west of England particularly, the walls at entrance doorways ere sometimes deliberately thickened so as to provide room for elab- rate portals of this nature; some almost attain the depth of embryo orches (Plate 83). The same feature may occasionally be seen on a mall scale in the doorways of twelfth-century town houses, as at Lincoln Plate 124).

The hood-mould over the doorway continued throughout the medi- eval period (Plate 174). Sometimes ending in small portions of itself set orizontally to suggest the relics of imposts, it more frequently termin- tes, however, in finials carved in floral form or as human masks. With he lowering of the arch form, the hood-mould follows the same shape until he fifteenth century; then, in conformity with the general rectangularity f wall decoration, it, too, becomes rectangular, with a horizontal portion nd two vertical ends dropping to finials at the level of the springing of he arch. The spandrels left between hood-mould and arch often provide paces for heraldic ornament (Plate 175).

Among special types of mediaeval openings must not be forgotten the ervice hatches which opened out of the pantry and buttery into the wer end of the great hall. Another feature, which has never been satis- actorily explained, is the small 'low-side' window frequently to be met ith in the walls of the chancels of parish churches. The broad low arch rovided at the base of the wall within a church to provide space for an terment is a feature which dates from the very beginning of the Chris- an era.

From a fair number of contemporary descriptions it is quite certain hat many of the more important timber buildings of the Anglo-Saxon ra were surrounded by porticoes of the same material; the arcaded lower tages of the walling of later stone buildings strongly suggest a survival f the architectural treatment of such features.

The timber technique which is so well illustrated by the arched braces f the twelfth-century wooden churches of Essex, continues to be used, throughout the mediaeval period, for the outer doorways of the wooden porches which are a feature of the south-east of England and the other timber region in the West Midlands.

The churches founded by St. Augustine in Kent at the end of the sixth century were also surrounded, except for the apse, by wooden porticoes. The eastern ends of the lateral porticoes were walled-up to form *parabemata* (Fig. 8). In front of the western doorway a section of the portico was flanked by walls to form an entrance porch; occasionally, lateral porches of similar form were subsequently provided. The stone-built churches erected by St. Wilfred in the North had small western porches.

It was some centuries, however, before the porch again appeared in English architecture. There are a few attached to great churches of the twelfth and thirteenth centuries; but it is not until the Edwardian period, when the naves of parish churches begin to be reconstructed, that the porch becomes a universal feature. The same applies to domestic build ings; some of the more important halls of the thirteenth century were provided with porches, but it is not until the fully-developed Edwardian manor-house plan has been achieved that the hall porch becomes a univer-sal feature (Plate 113).

The ordinary church porch is one of the most familiar objects of the English village. Usually on the south side, it provides architectural em-phasis to the principal entrance of the building. Often there is a chamber on the first floor, reached by a spiral staircase accommodated in a turret (Plate 84).

Some porches are very large and magnificent; that at Cirencester in Gloucestershire is a notable example.

Very large western porches, almost of the nature of a separate church, and sometimes two stories in height, such as are found on the Continent, do not appear in this country. Their place is taken, to some extent, by the elaborate constructions erected above the west ends of the naves of early great churches; these features, however, disappear before the Gothic era. The remarkable western chapel at Durham Cathedral, which is, in fact, its Lady Chapel, is an unique feature.

From contemporary descriptions, it appears that the Byzantine feat-ure of the enclosed forecourt before the west door of a great church may have existed in the century before the Conquest; no remains, however, are discoverable to-day. The narthex is represented by the huge arched porches of Lincoln, Peterborough, and Bury.

Mediaeval stairs may be classed under two headings: the stone newel stair, probably of Byzantine origin, and the straight stair, the ordinary form of which is simply a ladder-like arrangement ending in the 'oriel', a timber platform supported out from the face of a wall upon 'gallows

175. A Late Gothic doorway at Appledore church, Kent

174. An Early Gothic doorway at Canons Ashby church, Northamptonshire

173. An elaborate doorway of the twelfth century at Kilpeck church, Herefordshire

177. The 'grand stair' leading to the entrance of the

176. An elaborately-designed newel stair having the

brackets'. The more permanent form of this had treads carried at their outer ends by a 'spandrel wall' of masonry, the treads themselves being either baulks of wood or, in rare cases where suitable material could be found, of stone.

There is also the 'grand stair' of masonry upon a solid core of rubble, as in the day-stairs of the early monasteries or leading to the entrances of Norman tower-houses (Plate 177). A highly architectural example is that leading to the guest hall of the cathedral priory at Canterbury which is protected by a roof supported upon graceful arcading. Such stairs as these can only rise from the ground level to that of the *piano nobile*; it had to be left to the Renaissance architects to devise a grand stair which could be carried up through higher stories.

The circular spiral staircase of stone, recorded as having been in use at the end of the seventh century in this country, is certainly represented by a number of examples attached to western towers of the beginning of the eleventh century. Such features would probably have existed in the Benedictine churches of the end of the previous century, in order to attain access to their galleries and upper chambers. The pre-Conquest staircases are generally enclosed within circular turrets; for the next two centuries, however, space was generally provided for them in the purposely thickened-out angles of the higher parts of a building—especially, of course, in towers (Plate 176). From the Edwardian period onwards, the octagonal staircase turret is a universal feature of buildings of all types.

Elizabethan houses frequently had spiral staircases made of wood, mounting around a central pole; such staircases were usually built in a square shaft. Wooden stairs of the 'dog-leg' variety—or, as they were originally designated, a 'pair of stairs'—do not appear to have come into use until the Renaissance period.

The hearth in the centre of the hall is probably a feature as old as the habitation itself. In the mediaeval hall the smoke rose at will into the roof, to escape eventually through a wooden turret provided for the purpose. Some chamber floors on 'stone solars' also had open hearths.

The wall-fireplace, however, was known in this country at least as early as the first few years of the Norman occupation; it appears in the White Tower of London, which has wooden upper floors. Early wall-fireplaces were merely arched recesses (Plate 178) and had no chimneys, the smoke escaped straight out through the wall immediately above the arch. The fireplace was sited immediately in front of one of the pilasters running up the outside of the wall; the smoke-vents were on either side of this, so as to provide opportunities for adjusting the draught of the fireplace to the wind by blocking up the opening on the weather side. In the 'Jews' Houses' at Lincoln (Plate 124), the fireplace pilasters are supported on the hood-moulds of the entrance doors below. Chimneyless fireplaces continued to be employed until well into the thirteenth century.

Although the central hearth was the normal site for the domestic fire, in many rooms—such as, for example, the great chamber—there would doubtless be insufficient space for such a feature. The fire was then built against a wall of the building, the structure being protected by a flat slab, stood on end and known as a 'reredos'. Our twelfth-century ancestors were hardy enough to restrict the lighting of the chamber fire to certain periods—'the early dawn, or the evening, or during sickness, or at time of blood-letting, or for warming maids and weaned children'.

It was an easy enough matter to construct cavernous fireplaces in the thick walls of early keep-towers. In the case of private houses, however, it was usually found necessary to build-out some kind of a hood over the hearth of a wall-fireplace in order to catch a certain amount of the smoke which persisted in drifting into the room. The first hoods were of wattle-and-daub on a timber framework; towards the end of the twelfth century, however, they came to be permanently constructed in stone, supported on corbels of the same material (Plate 179).

By the end of the Edwardian period, when properly constructed chimney flues, supported on external 'stacks', had become the universal method of conveying smoke from the fireplace, these hoods began to disappear and the fireplace became once more an arched opening in the wall-face (Plate 180). The fifteenth century saw the development of the fireplace as an architectural feature; by the Tudor era it had become one of the most imposing objects within the house.[35]

A number of mediaeval chimneys still remain. Some are sturdy square flues, as at Abingdon Abbey (Plate 181); others, notably the beautiful example at Grosmont Castle in Monmouthshire, are very graceful architectural features, upon which much skill and attention has obviously been lavished (Plate 182). The openings are lateral; the open-top chimney of to-day dates from Tudor times.

Anything in the nature of a pinnacle or turret, which emphasised the vertical lines of a building, was invariably an object of interest to the mediaeval mason. One such feature was the bell-turret which might be set upon one or the other of the gables to the nave of a parish church. Something of the sort was invariably necessary when the parishioners could not afford the labour and expense of constructing a bell-tower—which might, in actual fact, cost as much as the rest of the church put together. In many of the timber districts, the parishioners were content with a small wooden bell-turret—either perched on the roof-timbers or supported on a framework rising from the floor—at the west end of the nave.

In the building-stone region of the East Midlands, however, and in

those districts which were being developed by the western Benedictine
monasteries, the stone bell-cote on the west gable appears at the end of
the twelfth century. It is usually an upward prolongation of the apex of
the gable to form a small feature consisting of two arched openings with
a gablet above. Bell-cotes of this description remain popular throughout
the rest of the mediaeval era (Plate 184); sometimes a slightly smaller
variety is provided on the east gable of the nave to carry the sanctus bell.
Towards the end of the mediaeval period bell-cotes sometimes swell out
on either side of the gable wall until they attain the form of low turrets
containing the bells.

Balconies, except in the wooden 'oriel' form employed in early houses
as an upper landing for the entrance stair, are not a feature of English
mediaeval architecture, although the stone oriel window is perhaps in a
sense an enclosed balcony. Late castles, however, sometimes have curious
features, projecting externally from the faces of their walling, which are,
in effect, balconies without floors. Such features, of which Compton Castle
(Plate 56) in Devonshire displays a remarkable series, are known as
'drop-boxes', and are used for the same purpose as the machicolations of
a parapet: that is, to drop offensive material upon individuals engaged in
hostile operations at the base of the wall below. Originally employed by
the sixth-century Byzantines, they probably reached England via the
Crusades. They provided a useful means of overlooking the base of a military structure erected on a soil too rocky to be excavated to form a moat.

In the interior of a church the most important item of its furniture is
the altar; in a great church there will be several of these. The number of
mediaeval altars remaining nowadays is comparatively small; as, having
been of stone, they were mostly replaced at the Reformation by wooden
tables more in conformity with Protestant tastes.

The most interesting ancient feature remaining in a church to-day
will probably be its font. Although, in early days of Christianity, baptism
was performed by means of total immersion in a tank provided in the
floor of the building, there are still plenty of examples remaining of the
ancient primitive 'tub' fonts of Saxon days. Some of these are very plain
and crude; others are embellished with primitive ornament. These tub
fonts, even if perched upon a step or two, were still inconveniently low
for the priest administering baptism, thus it was desirable to mount the
bowl upon a stem of some description. During the twelfth century, when
so much was becoming standardised, a common form of font had its bowl
hewn out of a solid rectangular block of stone, frequently ornamented on
its faces with arcading. This slab was supported on a squat pillar, sometimes surrounded by four more slender shafts which propped up the overhanging angles of the slab. In the thirteenth century various less massive
and more graceful varieties of this design appeared.

Architectural Details

By the Edwardian period, at which time so many naves of parish churches were being rebuilt, these were at the same time provided with new fonts. Such were usually of octagonal form, having a sturdy shaft supporting the upper portion which contained the bowl. Although consisting of only these two simply-shaped portions, late mediaeval fonts are usually very finely sculptured, often being, moreover, mounted upon a stepped base which gave height and dignity to this important feature of church furniture (Plate 86).

Pulpits are a rare feature of mediaeval architecture. There were, however, pulpit-like balconies provided in the monastic refectories for the use of the monk who read to the brethren during meals (Plate 109); such features were often of extreme elaboration, swelling-out from the wall-face like oriel windows, and approached by arcaded galleries and stairs constructed in the thickness of the wall.

The wayside cross is a well-known feature of certain parts of England, especially in the regions once within the sphere of the Celtic church. Most of these crosses were probably erected by early missionaries to denote meeting-places for worship; some, however, possibly marked the burial places of saints or martyrs. The practice of indicating the site of a burial by some form of head-stone was certainly followed in this country during the twelfth century; the churchyard of the vanished cathedral at Old Sarum still shows examples. Another method of indicating the site of the interment of an important personage was to cover the grave with a stone slab, originally intended to prevent animals from digging up the body. Out-of-doors, such slabs were often ridged like a roof, so as to throw off the rain; within buildings, however, where gravestones would form part of the floor, they were, of course, flat. From earliest times, it was customary to mark the site of an intra-mural interment by means of a gravestone, the surface of which would generally be incised with a portrait of the deceased, surrounded by an inscription. Some early twelfth-century gravestones are very fine; that of Walter de Gant, founder of Bridlington Priory in Yorkshire, is a great slab of Flemish marble depicting, in addition to the deceased, the church which he founded.

The practice of offering up prayers at the tombs of saints may have been the origin of the altar tomb, in which a rectangular mass of masonry is raised above the floor of the church to carry the gravestone. By the thirteenth century the altar tomb had become a popular form of memorial; its form made it possible for an actual effigy of the deceased to be placed on it. The spaces beneath the main arches of a great church provided good sites for rows of such tombs, all adding to the interest of the building. Later they became surrounded by screens, and, by the end of the mediaeval period, surmounted by stone canopies displaying a wealth of pinnacled tracery.

178. Twelfth-century fireplaces are merely recesses in the walling. Rochester Castle, Kent

179. The normal mediaeval fireplace has a hood over it to keep smoke out of the room. Boothby Pagnell Manor House, Lincolnshire

180. After the improvement of chimney design the fireplace of the fifteenth century dispenses with the hood. Tattershall Castle, Lincolnshire

181. Early Gothic chimney

182. Late mediaeval chimney

183. Crocketed pinnacle
with niche for statue

184. Double bell-cote above the west gable of a
parish church

192. Byzantine 'cushion' capital

194. 'Coniferous' capital

191. The Doric capital

193. 'Cubiform' capital

195. The Corinthian capital

196. Twelfth-century 'Corinthianesque' capital

197. Early Gothic 'Stiff-leaf' capital

198. Mid-Gothic 'Naturalistic' capital

199. The 'Attic' base

200. Pre-Gothic version of Attic base

201. Early Gothic 'waterholding' base

202. Mid-Gothic 'triple roll'

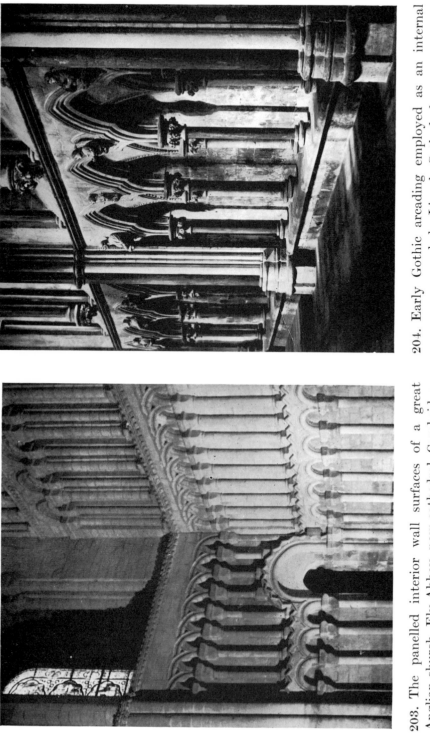

203. The panelled interior wall surfaces of a great Anglian church. Ely Abbey, now cathedral, Cambridgeshire

204. Early Gothic arcading employed as an internal dado. Lincoln Cathedral

triple and the whole feature is composed of a mass of small vertical rolls separated by deeply undercut hollows. As time went on, however, the subdivisions became fewer and the undercutting more restrained.

By the Mid-Gothic period the members of all mouldings were becoming fewer, larger and more coarse. The broad ogee moulding sometimes became, in pillars, a triple curve or 'wave' moulding. The simplification and coarsening of moulding members becomes very noticeable in the fifteenth century; it is interesting to note, however, that, while this is true of masonry, the contemporary wood-carvers, working as they were on a smaller scale, appear to be no less lacking in refinement than their predecessors.

Throughout the mediaeval period it seems to have been the intention of all skilled designers in masonry to reduce the amount of solid in their constructions; although this was probably partly due to desire for economy, the resulting lightness of effect was also much to be admired. The development of the design of arcades has been, broadly speaking, to increase the span of the arch and decrease the width of the support. By the fifteenth century this reduction in width had reached such a state that the pillars were no longer visibly cruciform; for, although they were still of the width of the wall above, their dimension in the opposite direction was actually less than this. Thus a transverse type of pillar is a common feature of Late Gothic churches.

The design of window tracery called for special skill; ready-made windows were frequently bought by the mason direct from the quarry, which often had a staff of specialists attached to it. Apart from the artistic talent needed to design the pattern incorporated in the window-head —which in itself involved much knowledge of geometry—the stonework of the window itself had to be arranged in a series of orders. The larger the window, and the more complicated its subdivisions, the more orders there had to be. As the tracery-bars of each order had to grow out of the side of the one above it, the moulding of each order had to be carefully designed to make this possible; the ultimate order, which had to incorporate the sum of all the window mouldings, was the actual arch of the window itself and was carried down its jambs.

The innermost order of the window was formed by the 'cusps' which separated the foliations. At first these were simply flat pieces of stone projecting from the socket and known as 'soffit cusps'. Later, the cusps were moulded, and, growing out of the side of the tracery bars, were known as 'chamfer cusps'; these elaborate little features generally had a triangular space, known as an 'eye', at their roots. A special type of window tracery found in Kent has each cusp doubled by being split down the centre, suggesting a wooden origin for this feature. The curved braces of some of the twelfth-century Essex timber churches are foliated.

The shallow external arcades of large arches indicating the bay

Ornament

designs of the Ottonian churches can also be seen in such of the Mercian polygonal apses which remain. Some of the great post-Conquest churches, such as Romsey Abbey, also employ this form of decoration; Hanslope church in Buckinghamshire exhibits an elaborate version.

The small wall-arcade which is so frequently met with at the base of the main walls of important buildings of the eleventh and twelfth centuries probably echoes the loggias with which the timber buildings of Anglo-Saxon days were in all probability surrounded. At first two to the bay—which possibly recalls the timber arrangement—the arches become narrower and more numerous until the whole building is surrounded by a kind of arcaded dado.

As was noticed in an earlier chapter, much of the design of window tracery probably developed from the wooden trellises which helped to brace the upper part of the early timber buildings. Another form of bracing met with in these structures is the saltire formed by two curved braces crossing each other so as to leave beneath them the shape of a pointed arch (Fig. 3). If we assume that the supports of the loggias which it is known existed round the fine timber buildings of the period of the Conquest were arranged in this fashion, the origin of the interlacing arcades which form such a common feature of the twelfth-century stone buildings in this country immediately becomes obvious. This interlacing arcading is largely limited to this country and must almost certainly have originated here.

The most striking feature of the external elevations of pre-Gothic churches is undoubtedly the wall-arcade. A purely ornamental feature, its origin may be due to the existence in the Rhineland of a fine monument of Roman architecture, the Black Gate of Trier, which is entirely covered with this form of wall-ornament.

Under the aegis of the Anglian architects, the wall-arcade became the principal feature of twelfth-century decoration. The bands of arcading soon spread to gallery level, indicating this externally; lines of eaves were carried across gable ends by the same aesthetic device (Plate 52). The stages of towers, and their angle turrets, were also marked by ranges of arcading, seeming to become ever more elaborate as the summit was reached. On screen-like west fronts such as that of Lincoln, the arcading becomes a sort of panelling (Plate 102). This type of frontispiece was later developed into a series of niches deepened to contain statuary (Plate 214). Employed as a dado, the internal wall-arcade remained a popular feature throughout the mediaeval period (Plate 204). With the abolition of galleries and the abandoning of the upper arcade, this feature was often replaced by a strip of arcading. In some of the great Anglian abbey churches the panelling motif is carried over a large expanse of the interior wall-faces (Plate 203).

Ornament

Perhaps the most fascinating form of architectural decoration to be met with in this country is that exhibited by the many forms of ornamentation found sculptured on the orders of arches of the twelfth century (Plate 83). It seems probable that the principle of this form of decoration is of English origin, as the multiple-order arch was essentially an invention of our architects. The French never really took to the system; the Teutonic world for the most part ignored it altogether.

The forms adopted by this form of ornamentation are legion. They can, however, be roughly classified. Firstly come the crude 'chip-carving' forms: the various types of 'billet' ornament—obviously derived from wood prototypes—employed, sometimes lavishly, along horizontal members such as string-courses. The most important of these is the zig-zag, which, developing through a multitude of variations, becomes the principal architectural ornament of the twelfth century (Plate 205), appearing frequently on vaulting-ribs. Some of the motifs employed by early sculptors suggest Scandinavian origins; this is particularly true of the curious 'beak-head' or dragon type of mask. The dragon-heads which crown the gables of the buildings illustrated in the Bayeux Tapestry support this theory.

Early in the century the many-ordered lavishly ornamented doorway had penetrated to those Continental regions which became the Angevin Empire; Poitou, especially, has a number of examples rivalling our own. The French influence appears to have resulted in the introduction of Classical forms in the paterae with which the voussoirs were sculptured.

It will be noted that these forms of enrichment are all designed to be applied to the face of an order, to its angle, or—as in the case of cable-mouldings—to the angle-roll. One form of billet-moulding, applied to a chamfered angle, consisted in a series of small pyramids resembling the heads of large nails (Plate 31). This 'nail-head' ornament came to be applied to the enrichment of the hollow moulding which began to appear in the latter part of the century. By the end of this, the pyramids had acquired four little chips cut in their faces, producing a group of four little leaves or petals, said to represent the dog-tooth violet (Plate 206); various forms of this ornament were popular during the first half of the thirteenth century. In the Mid-Gothic period this form of repetitive treatment of hollow members gave place to a series of small balls, crudely carved to represent the buds of flowers (Plate 207).

Apart from the 'Corinthianesque' form of capital, free carving does not appear much in English architecture until the thirteenth century, when the 'stiff-leaf' foliage begins to spread over capitals, corbels and other projecting features, especially the bosses (Plate 210) which mask the junctions of vaulting-ribs.

The hey-day of the stone-carver in this country was during the

Edwardian period immediately preceding the Black Death. Such lovely buildings as the choir of Selby Abbey or the chapter house of Southwell Minster give some idea of the skill and devotion of the carvers, who took their designs from nature and made such great play with fruit, foliage (Plate 211) and even animals. Statuary and the art of caricature are also much in evidence.

The subject of foliage-sculpture is somewhat outside the province of the student of architecture. For rough dating purposes it is, however, interesting to notice how the Corinthian volute—possibly the first notable sculptural feature—becomes the 'stiff-leaf' clover or trefoil of the Early Gothic and expands to cover the bell of its capital or corbel, perhaps in imitation of the open acanthus ferns covering its classical prototype.

The next stage is the naturalistic foliage of the Mid-Gothic period with the vine-leaf and its tendrils forming prominent features in the design. Most interesting of all is the way in which sculptural art collapses after the Black Death and a form of architectural vine-leaf is standardised for use in any position. Such leaves are set out as squares and turned out 'by the yard' with drill and chisel; in order to give them a little more value the three separate portions of each leaf are waved to resemble the characteristic English oak-leaf (Plate 212).

The application of the volute or 'crocket' to the upper edges of hood-moulds and the arrises of pinnacles resulted in the development of this feature along the same lines as other carved ornament; from the stiff-leaf form the later mediaeval crocket descends to the architectural vine-leaf apparently curled up in death. To the same era belong the curious vegetables known as 'poppy-heads' employed as finials (Plate 212).

In addition to the pseudo-architectural wall treatment provided by the various systems of arcading and panelling there are a number of forms which are purely ornamental. One which owes its origin to structural devices is the reeded motif, imitating the convexities of the bratticed walls of timber churches, which appears round the ruined apse of the eleventh-century 'cathedral' of North Elmham in Norfolk. But for the most part, wall-decoration takes the form of some kind of repetitive ornament, generally in the nature of diaper. Starting with primitive patterns rough-hewn with the axe, the diapers became more elaborate until by the latter part of the twelfth century they have come under the attention of the carvers' chisels. At this period it is reasonable to suppose that a certain amount of inspiration may have come from the Moslem carvers who were specialists in this non-representational type of ornament.

Besides the products of the skilled carver, however, the buildings of the twelfth century display a considerable amount of large-scale repetitive wall-decoration which may well have been turned out by the ord

205. 'Chevron' ornament of the twelfth century at Durham Cathedral

206. Early Gothic 'dog-tooth' ornament

207. Mid-Gothic 'ball-flower' flanking Late Gothic 'square-leaf'

209. Stone 'parclose' screen enclosing a chantry chapel at Christchurch Priory in Hampshire

208. Late Gothic stallwork in the choir of Lincoln Cathedral

212. Late Gothic 'poppy-head' and 'square-leaf' carving. Lincoln Cathedral

211. Corbel covered with 'naturalistic' carving. Exeter Cathedral

210. Vaulting boss showing 'stiff-leaf' carving. Lincoln Cathedral

213. The ruin of a fine twelfth-century facade at Castleacre Priory in Norfolk

214. The west front of Wells Cathedral is perhaps the loveliest Gothic facade in the world

nary hewers in their lodges. The principal artists in this case would appear to have belonged to the Anglian school; the centre of their operations having apparently been Norwich.

Many of the forms used in this type of decoration may have been derived from the employment of a sort of chip-carving technique; imitations of shingling may often be seen. A form of reticulated roll-ornament is particularly popular; it is richest at Norwich and Lincoln, but feebler attempts may also be seen at York and Canterbury. Similar ornament is also found in some of the continental areas within the Angevin Empire, which suggests that the contemporary repetitive ornamentation seen in the ordered doorways may also have an Anglian origin.

Another pre-Gothic decorative device is the incising of spiral grooves round stone pillars. First appearing in a rope-like form in the crypt at Repton (Plate 97), it is met with in a number of great churches in the eastern counties, and also in Durham Plate 23). The most elaborate example may be seen on the stumps of the great pillars which remain within the crypt of York Minster; the feeble reticulated ornament of the later work makes a poor showing in comparison. The spiral decoration of the great English churches did not spread to the Continent.

The most common type of wall-decoration was in the form of a diaper of small square stones, each carved with the same device. It can be seen in a crude form at Chichester Cathedral. A later example is that employed in Henry III's new east end at Westminster Abbey.

During the twelfth century the most usual situation for rich wall-decoration was the triangular upper portion of a gable; it is possible that this was a deliberate aesthetic device intended to lead the eye upward, and that the diaper decoration of 'triforium' spandrels may have been provided with the same end in view.

By the Mid-Gothic period, however, wall-decoration seems to have been abandoned; except in respect of such situations as the spandrels of the principal internal arcades, where panelled forms similar to those of the window tracery, or even carving, might still be employed to carry the eye upward. Externally, however, there were now many other opportunities for enrichment; besides the elaboration of the fenestration, there were now the foliations of pierced parapets and their crowning pinnacles. At the end of the mediaeval period, external ornamentation is always kept as high up as possible; parapets, especially, being selected as features for enrichment.

The development of the art of screenwork which characterises the wool era of the fifteenth century completely transformed wall-decoration to fit in with the designs resulting from the framing-together of the joinery. Some form or another of panelled treatment pervades everything (Plate 132), including the tracery in the fenestration. A form of panelling peculiar to East Anglia is the type of decoration known as 'flush-work', in which a rubble wall is covered with a panelling of stone strips, the spaces between these being filled with a facing of knapped flint (Plate 11).

One of the most important items in the decoration of a mediaeval building was the opportunities presented for a display of heraldry. Corbels, bosses, the spandrels of arches and many other features could be found as positions for shields, either isolated or incorporated with carved ornament. Badges, such as the Rose or Portcullis, were also popular ornamental devices, especially suited to repetitive treatment. Another variation of this type of ornament was the rebus or punning badge, recalling to the illiterate the name of some benefactor.

While the subject of statuary is scarcely within the scope of an architectural work, reference must be made to the frequent use of caricature in the form of masks attached to capitals, corbels, and the water-spouts or gargoyles leading the water from gutters through the parapets in front of these.

The walls of mediaeval buildings, if formed of other than properly-dressed freestone, would never have been left with rough rubble masonry showing—either inside or out—except in the case of the humblest structures.

Externally, the plaster rendering would often have been maintained in an imposing condition by being always kept white and glowing through constant applications of limewash. The White Tower of London—the Conqueror's palace—was doubtless so called for this reason. The first stone church at Durham was called the 'White Church'.

Internally, also, the rubble walls of church, hall or house would have been properly plastered. Many of the finer buildings had their plastered walls and their wooden ceilings or plastered vaults painted with patterns or pictures in bright colours. Some of the sculptured decoration also would have been painted to make it more lifelike.

Painted glass was known in this country from the beginning of the Christian epoch, but was little used until the end of the twelfth century. By the end of the mediaeval period, however, even the parish churches had magnificent windows illustrating religious subjects to their congregations.

To the poor peasant of the Middle Ages, these great buildings were his picture-books.

They can be ours to-day.

Glossary

---

abacus: uppermost member of a capital.

aisle: *ala*, originally a projection from the side wall of a building (see 'wing'), now a lateral addition separated from the main portion of a structure by an arcade or a row of posts.

almonry: monastic building from which alms were distributed.

almshouse: lodging for the indigent poor.

apse: semicircular or polygonal end to a building.

arcade: row of arches.

ashlaring: timber studs (q.v.) forming a wall or partition, esp. the vertical framing forming the side walls of an attic storey.

attic: space within a roof.

bailey: castle yard.

banker: stone bench upon which the mason works.

barbican: defensive work situated outside the entrance through a fortified perimeter.

barrel vault: stone arched roof like that of a tunnel.

bastion: solid tower or earthen mound designed to carry military engines.

batter: wall-face inclined from the vertical.

battlement: parapet broken by crenels (q.v.).

bay: transverse division of a building.

bay window: one which projects beyond the wall-face and rises from the ground (cf. 'oriel').

bifora: two-light window, esp. one having the two separated by a small shaft.

bolster: also 'boaster', the mason's tool, not to be confused with chisel used by carver.

bond: method of arranging vertical joints in masonry so that no two appear immediately above each other.

box gutter: lead gutter provided behind parapet to collect water falling upon roof.

brace: diagonal stiffener in woodwork.

brattice: boarded partition.

bressummer: timber beam carrying wall over opening, chimney beam.

bridge-pit: stone-lined pit before gatehouse covered by drawbridge when this is 'down'.

broach: cooking spit, the mediaeval term for a spire.

buttress: masonry support against overturning pressure upon a wall.

buttery: day-to-day storage for wine and ale.

burh: borough, fortified Anglo-Saxon town.

cap roof: low-pitched pyramidal roof.

cat-beam: timber passing longitudinally beneath the collars of a late-mediaeval roof and carried by the king-posts (q.v.).

centering: temporary wooden framing upon which an arch is turned.

chamber: room on upper floor, principal sleeping room of house-owner.

chancel: the easternmost or priest's portion of a parish church.

chevet: the elaborate eastern termination of a great church.

choir: portion of a great church in which those serving it sing the offices.

claw: bolster (q.v.) with a serrated edge used for smoothing axed stonework before tooling.

clerestory: portion of building raised above surrounding structures in order to provide sites for windows to light its interior.

cloister: originally the area enclosed by wall of monastic precinct, later the garth surrounded by principal buildings, eventually the covered walks enclosing this.

close: enclosed precinct of a cathedral church.

collar: short horizontal timber tying pair or 'couple' of rafters near the apex.

column: stone support either monolithic or, more usually, built in 'drums' (q.v.).

comb: see 'drag'.

coniferous capital: capital having its 'echinus' (q.v.) ornamented by a ring of cones set point downwards.

corbel: bracket, a small capital built into a wall and lacking a shaft.

corbel-table: feature at eaves level consisting of a miniature arcade carried by corbels.

core: hollow interior of a masonry wall filled with 'spalls' (q.v.) and mortar as the work proceeds.

cornice: projecting eaves feature in Classical architecture.

couple: pair of rafters pegged together at the apex of the roof.

course: layer of stones in masonry.

crenel: opening in military parapet through which defenders fire their weapons.

crossing: area beneath the central tower of a church.

cross-vault: intersecting barrel-vaults.

cross-wall: stone partition.

cruciform: church in which all four arms are of the same span as the crossing.

cruck: pair of heavy inclined beams supporting longitudinal roof-timbers.

crypt: properly a space beneath the main floor of a church, a vaulted lower storey.

crypto-cruciform: church having a central tower flanked by narrower wings or transepts.

cubiform capital: cushion capital with angles cut off and turned sideways to reduce projection of abacus (q.v.).

curia: area occupied by principal buildings of palace, outer court of monastic house.

curtain: wall of fortification.

cushion capital: Byzantine version of Doric capital having echinus (q.v.) square on plan.

cusp: point separating foliations (q.v.).

dais: raised area at upper end of hall.

drag: serrated scraper used for obliterating tool marks on masonry.

drop-box: projecting feature in military architecture through floor of which offensive materials could be dropped upon a besieger.

drum: masonry course, in pillar or column, formed by a single stone.

duplex bay: bay of great church having a pillar or column set between two piers.

eaves: projecting part of a roof.

echinus: portion of a capital joining abacus (q.v.) to the shaft of column or pillar.

enceinte: fortified perimeter.

embrasure: 'reveal' (q.v.) through thick wall of military structure.

fan vault: late-mediaeval vault in which ribs and web are combined to form a style of ornament resembling open fans.

flushwork: wall-decoration formed by stone panelling filled with knapped flintwork.

flying arch: one spanning a building, as in the case of the transverse rib of a vault, or carrying longitudinal floor or roof timbers.

flying buttress: a flying arch, or a system of these, carrying the thrust of a roof or vault towards an isolated buttress.

foliated: silhouette divided by 'cusps' (q.v.) into foils each of which is a segment of a circle.

forebuilding: small tower covering the first-floor entrance to a keep or house.

form: see 'template'.

four-poster: Byzantine or Byzantinesque church having a central feature carried upon four supports and surrounded by equal projections on all four sides. (Sometimes called 'cross-in-square'.)

frame: timber frame upon which later mediaeval buildings were constructed.

freestone: stone capable of being worked by a mason.

gable: wall filling the end of a mediaeval roof.

gallows-bracket: timber bracket of three members like a 'hammerbeam' (q.v.) but without any spandrel-piece.

garderobe: incorrect designation for a privy.

gargoyle: stone spout carrying water from a box gutter through the parapet.

garth: cloister yard.

garret: rooms in a roof.

gatehouse: tower covering the entrance through a wall of enceinte.

girder: beam tying opposite walls of frame structure.

groin: line of intersection between two portions of a cross-vault.

groined vault: cross-vault having no vaulting ribs.

hammer-beam: short length of tie-beam supported upon a wooden spandrel rising from a corbel or another hammer-beam.

head: upper horizontal member of opening or frame (see 'sill').

hoards: timber constructions built out from the parapet of a military structure to enable the base of the wall to be overlooked.

hoodmould: moulding provided above an arch to prevent water streaming down the wall-face from dropping upon those passing under the arch.

impost: springing line of an arch.

impost moulding: moulding indicating impost.

jamb: side of opening.

jetty: overhanging portion of floor-joists.

joist: small beam carrying floor.

keep: fortified residence within castle.

king-post: short post set upon tie-beam and carrying cat-beam (q.v.).

lantern: portion of central tower raised above roof to provide sites for windows to light crossing.

lavatory: a washing-place.

lierne: short length of vaulting-rib.

lights: principal divisions of a window.

lintel: timber or stone beam spanning an opening.

lists: space between main curtain of castle and mantlet wall (q.v.).

lodge: a small annexe to a building having a lean-to roof, the temporary structure in which a mason works (see also pent-house.)

loop: small unglazed window, often exhibiting an arrangement of slits to improve vision without exposing interior of apartment.

machicolation: parapet carried upon corbels, esp. in military structures, to facilitate inspection of foot of wall from top of this.

magpie: black-and-white style of timber architecture mostly found in north-west Midlands.

mantlet wall: outer wall of late-mediaeval castle between main curtain and moat.

masonry: dressed stonework laid in courses.

Mercian apse: three-sided apse.

merlon: portion of battlemented parapet separated by crenels (q.v.).

model: experimental device to investigate finished appearance of design, mediaeval word for template' (q.v.).

mortar: matrix in which masonry is set.

motte: castle mound.

nave: laymen's portion of a church, central portion of a secular structure flanked by aisles.

newel: post or shaft around which a stair turns.

ogee: double curve.

Order: Classical style of architecture.

order: single ring of voussoirs (q.v.) forming part of a complete arch.

oriel: projecting window supported upon a corbel

oubliette: prison entered only by an opening in its vault.

pan: principal beam carried upon posts.

pantry: bread-store.

parabemeta: sacristies flanking the sanctuary of a Byzantine church.

parapet: light protective wall.

parclose: screen enclosing chapel within church.

parlour: private living room, lobby joining monastic curia and cloister.

parvise: (paradise) space before west door of great church, council chamber of episcopal palace, room above church porch.

penthouse: *appentice*, lodge or subsidiary structure having a lean-to roof.

piano nobile: first floor of a mediaeval house containing the principal apartments.

pier: support formed in masonry and resembling portion of walling retained to carry arch or beam.

pilaster: vertical strip often fashioned to imitate a column.

pillar: slender masonry support.

pinnacle: masonry employed as weight at summit of buttress or in decorative form as finial.

piscina: stone basin provided in walling next altar for washing holy vessels.

pitch: inclination of a roof from the horizontal.

plaster: mortar employed to cover walls or ceilings.

plate: horizontal timber set upon wall-top to carry feet of rafters.

plinth: base of a masonry structure.

ploughshare: lateral portions of a sexpartite vault.

pole: mediaeval unit of measurement about sixteen feet in length.

porch: structure covering an external door.

portico: open porch or loggia passing along wall.

portcullis: vertically-sliding wooden grille found at entrances to military structures.

presbytery: eastern arm of a great church.

pseudo-cruciform: church with wings or transepts but no central tower.

pulpitum: elaborate structure forming screen at entrance to choir of late-mediaeval great church.

purlin: longitudinal timber passing between trusses (q.v.) and helping to support rafters.

quadrant castle: site formed by constructing line of defences between principal natural obstacle and secondary obstacle such as tributary or lateral ravine.

quadripartite vault: vault supported by pair of diagonal ribs only.

quarry: small diamond-shaped pane used in mediaeval glazing.

quoin: corner-stone.

rafter: timber carrying roof-covering.

relieving arch: one turned in walling above arch or lintel so as to relieve pressure upon this.

rere-arch: arched head to a reveal (q.v.).

rere dorter: monastic sanitary block

reredos: architectural background to altar.

respond: half-pillar terminating an arcade.

reticulated: like the meshes of a net.

reveal: masonry lining to door or window opening.

rib: light skeleton arch carrying vaulting.

ridge: spine or summit of a pitched roof, longitudinal timber beneath this.

ring-wall: primitive rubble wall replacing timber stockades of early castle.

rood-beam: beam supporting partition filling upper portion of chancel arch and forming background to a calvary or rood.

rood-loft: projecting gallery provided before rood to enable the lamps lighting it to be serviced.

rood-screen: chancel screen or that behind nave altar in great church.

rood-stair: stair to rood-loft.

rubble: unwrought stone.

saddle-bar: horizontal bar stiffening lead glazing.

saltire: figure formed by the diagonals of a rectangle.

sanctuary: area within the chancel rails.

scarping: increasing the angle of slope in natural soil by excavating and throwing the material downwards.

scoinson: quoin on inner side of reveal (q.v.).

scoinson arch: inner arch of reveal.

sedilia: stone seats formed in wall of sanctuary.

severy: portion of vault-web (q.v.) enclosed between a series of ribs.

sexpartite vault: one having an additional transverse rib crossing each bay.

shaft: slender column.

shell-keep: ring-wall at the summit of conical motte.

sill: lower horizontal member of opening or frame (see 'head').

six-poster: four-poster (q.v.) having intermediate posts on north and south sides.

sleeper: beam resting on ground and carrying posts.

soffit: underside of arch or lintel.

solar: *soller*, an upper floor.

sole-piece: short length of timber joining foot of ashlaring (q.v.) to wall plate.

spall: flake knocked off stone.

span: width of building or opening.

spandrel: approximately triangular area in elevation.

spandrel wall: supports the outer edge of a stairway passing up the face of a wall.

spur: short screen provided inside outer door to protect occupants of apartment from draught.

spur castle: site formed by isolating end of natural spur by constructing line of defences across it.

squaroid: plan-form comprising a square with its sides bowed outwards. (Sometimes called 'cushion'.)

squinch: arch constructed across an internal angle.

stanchion: vertical bar in a window light.

steeple: staged construction surmounting tower.

string-course: horizontal moulding used for punctuation.

strut: timber performing a buttressing function.

studs: secondary vertical timbers in a framed construction.

summer: large beam supporting floor joists.

tail: in masonry the portion of the stone concealed within the wall.

teazle-post: post formed of a tree set butt-end uppermost and left thick so as to provide good seating for end of beam.

template: full-size of a moulding used by mason in cutting stones.

tie-beam: beam used for tying across a building wall-plates threatening to spread outwards under pressure from roof, later the principal member of a roof truss (q.v.).

tracery: pattern of stone bars at the head of a window, also employed for ornamenting wall-surfaces, etc.

transept: transverse arm of a cruciform church.

triforium: cleaning passage to clerestory of large church; to-day improperly applied to gallery over aisle.

truss: timber construction set across building to provide intermediate support to longitudinal timbers of roof.

tympanum: semicircular space between lintel and its relieving arch.

vault: stone ceiling, sometimes supporting a floor; today improperly applied to a vaulted room.

volute: angle feature of a Corinthian capital.

voussoir: arch stone.

wainscot: boarding employed to ceil an open roof, later for partitions.

wall tower: tower provided to enfilade a section of curtain.

ward: division of a fortified area such as that within a castle.

warming house: common room of a monastery.

wattling: screen or partition formed by weaving willow wands as a foundation for plaster.

web: stone filling of vault between ribs.

wind-bracing: ornamental bracing seen beneath the purlins of some roofs.

wing: lateral projection from main wall of building.

Appendix

(1) Some of the richer Romano-British cities may have had some buildings of monumental scale. The size of Corinthian capitals found at Cirencester indicates that the Orders to which they belonged were of a considerable height.

(2) This is perhaps too sweeping a statement, although true of many free-stones; some limestones appear to stand up to the weather after re-tooling. The present shortage of new stone for restoration work is all too often forcing architects to use second-hand stones, so far without serious trouble.

(3) So far there has been no confirmation that sleeper foundations were in use in this country prior to the twelfth century, and then it was only in important buildings such as churches. The timber towers of contemporary castles had the feet of their posts buried in the ground which must surely have doomed them to a brief existence.

(4) This comment refers to *structural* timber architecture, not to ornamental joinery such as open roofs or framed ceilings.

(5) When Salisbury cathedral was building in 1220, the buttresses were not bonded into the aisle walling but were added afterwards, notwithstanding the fact that vaulting was being raised over the aisles.

(6) The use of a diminutive copy of a structural feature for ornamental purposes seems to have been a survival of the charming Classical device of the *aedicule*.

(7) The window formed by piercing a solid slab of stone continues in use, in the stone-producing areas, well after the end of the mediaeval period, being frequently found lighting the spiral stairs of small houses.

(8) The badly-robbed foundations of the Old Minster of Winchester, recently excavated by Mr. Martin Biddle, indicate that its central nucleus was flanked by apses instead of the more usual rectangular wings.

(9) The west tower at the end of the later nave at North Elmham had a stair which probably gave access to a chapel on its upper floor.

(10) The timber tower-churches had aisles completely surrounding them on all four sides. If a stone nave should be added subsequently on the eastern side, it would probably be built up against the eastern aisle but might later be

Appendix

extended westwards to absorb this. A curious feature of such naves is the half-bay at the western end of each arcade, apparently representing the absorbed eastern aisle of the timber 'tower'.

(11) The stave-churches of Norway have elaborately-constructed chancels projecting from the turriform nave. It is however possible that the chancels of English timber churches may have been elevated portions of the eastern aisle having no eastward projection from this.

(12) Mr. C. A. Hewett reported in vol. cxix of the *Archaeological Journal* that the results of 'Carbon-14' tests on the timbers of Navestock church in Essex gave a medial date of 1193, with a possible error of sixty years each way.

(13) The timber four-poster church is not limited to Essex but may be found as far west as Wiltshire.

(14) In churches with wings, the doorways are set in the gable walls near the west end of the wall. See drawing of plan of North Elmham church on page 108.

(15) The parish churches of Tavistock and Tiverton are examples of the spacious Western church of the later Middle Ages.

(16) The line drawings on page 108 show the plan, in which the position of the original west wall is conjectural, and a restoration of the south elevation. The later nave and west tower have of course been omitted from the drawing. A belfry of some sort would have been required by the original church, and therefore a timber structure of the simplest form has been indicated astride the main roof.

(17) The long nave added to extend the original short western appendage of the cruciform church at North Elmham is an example.

(18) The 'crypto-cruciform' type of crossing could not have long survived the widening of the crossing arches to their later form, as their abutments would have become dangerously reduced and the transept walling would have provided no assistance.

(19) Western towers which were once central can be seen at Netheravon in Wiltshire and Hemyock in Devon.

(20) For example the tower at North Elmham.

(21) A plan showing the arrangement of Friars' churches is shown on page 202. Note the 'Walking Space' separating public nave from monastic choir, giving direct access to the east walk of the cloister from outside. The small octagonal lantern tower, smaller than the normal monastic central feature, provided to light the Walking Space, usually forms the principal architectural feature of a Friary; that at Kings Lynn is a well-known example. The plan shown is of an early form of church; later churches, especially those

Appendix

in towns, developed spacious aisled naves as auditoria for preachers.

(22) The west end added to the cathedral at Old Sarum by the great Bishop Roger comprised a transept-flanked west tower.

(23) Salisbury cathedral was built up to and including the aisle vaulting in one operation; the buttresses, however, were added subsequently. Centering was struck and a pause elapsed before the work continued; during this lull the decision was made to vault the main spans. The aesthetic ordinance of the interior was modified for the new work but the innovations were abandoned before the clerestory was reached.

(24) Mr. Rahtz's discoveries at the Saxon palace of Cheddar, reported in vols. vi and vii of *Mediaeval Archaeology*, are of interest in connection with the discovery of a multi-bay hall spanned by a series of crucks.

(25) But see Mr. J. T. Smith's paper on 'Cruck Construction' printed in vol. viii of *Mediaeval Archaeology*.

(26) Although the development of the episcopal palaces varies little from current secular practice, mention must be made of the remarkable little houses built in the fourth decade of the twelfth century by Bishop Roger of Sarum— perhaps the greatest builder of this prolific era—at his castles of Sherborne and Old Sarum. These houses are planned with enclosed courts after a fashion which could only have been copied from the Levant.

(27) A type of late-mediaeval small house is shown on page 185. See also Mr. W. A. Pantin's copiously-illustrated papers on priests' houses in vols. i and iii of *Mediaeval Archaeology*.

(28) A few new towns were founded during the thirteenth century but none show any signs of town-planning. Fortified 'bastides' such as Winchelsea in Sussex were simply a grid of streets surrounded by town walls.

(29) It is of interest to note that partitions in mine shafts are still known as 'brattices'.

(30) Although a stockaded ringwork would hardly be defensible without the protection of a tower or an earthen motte from which the defenders could control the dead ground beyond the stockade, recent excavation has shown that not all mottes are contemporary with, or precede, their baileys. In some cases the bailey ringwork was constructed first, and the motte raised on its perimeter, the motte ditch subsequently seriously curtailing the space within the bailey. Siege castles seem to be of this type; the more permanent castle was more carefully planned so as not to obstruct the bailey with the motte.

(31) Excavation upon the tops of conical mottes has exposed the sites of wooden towers. It would thus appear that the motte was raised to provide a high point upon which to site a control tower. The fresh earth of a motte would not have carried a stone structure. The timber towers had their posts carried

down through the top of the motte to ground consolidated to some extent by the weight of soil.

(32) While the origin of the western tower seems to have been due to eastward extension from a cruciform nucleus, after its acceptance as a campanile one finds it added as the western feature of a nave added to the west side of an earlier nucleus.

(33) The progress of the building of Salisbury Cathedral is dramatically illustrated by the distortions suffered by its crossing piers. While these remained unweighted, the drift of all arcades towards them is clearly seen in the manner in which they lean inwards. When the crossing arches are turned a reverse drift into the clerestories takes place and the upper portions of the crossing piers are thrust outwards so that each appears as a bent bow.

(34) The posts of Navestock church lean inwards in the same fashion.

(35) While it may be regarded as a general rule that all mediaeval chimney stacks are built to project externally, towards the end of the period one finds stacks formed in thick gable walls and projecting internally.

Index

Index

Index

Index

Index

Crosses, wayside, 260
Cross wall, 171
Crucks, 60–1, 81, 83, 158
Crypts, 147–8, 181
Curia, the, 198–9, 223, 243
Cusps, 273

Dais, 162, 165, 169, 239
Domes, 31–4, 74 *et passim*
Doors, 104, 261, 62
Doorways, 137, 161, 181, 195, 253 *ff*., 262, 275. *Plates 173–5*
of churches, 125–6, 153
Doric style, 27, 267–9. *Plate 191*
Drop-boxes, 259
Dunstan, St., 43, 134, 186

Earthworks, 44, 184, 203–9, 214, 251–2
East Anglia, 50, 56, 66, 83–5, 130, 227–8
Enceintes, 213, 217, 224
Engineers, 32, 38, 47, 68, 143, 311–12, 226, 231
Engines, 54, 58, 68, 211–15
Exaeron, 29

Farmhouses, 63, 237, 244, 246
Fireplaces, 164, 166, 175, 181–2, 196, 242, 244–5, 257–8. *Plates 178–80. See also* Hearths
Flint, knapped, 66–7, 228. *Plate 11*
Floors, 62, 85–6, 171, 173–5, 181, 219, 221, 238, 242–3, 257
condition of mediaeval, 161–2
timber, 62, 85
upper, 85–6, 172
solar, 85–6, 172, 174–5, 181, 238
Foliage-sculpture, 276. *Plates 197, 198, 210–12*
Foliations, 105–6
Font-covers, 263
Fonts, 259–60
Fortifications, 35, 65, 179–80, 185, 203 *ff*.
France, architecture in, 77, 79, 87, 94–5, 97
Freestone, 63–5
Friars, the 48, 187, 194
churches of, 149, 188, 194, 233

Galleries, 32–3, 74–5, 166, 234, 250 *et passim*
Gatehouses, 199, 200–1, 215, 217, 223–4, 241–2
military, 213–16, 222–3
Gilbertines, 187–8
Granges, 201
Graves and gravestones, 260
Graveyards, 197, 199
Guildhalls, 248

Halls, 41, 67, 72, 155 *ff*., 179, 237, 239 *ff*., 242–4, 246, 256
Anglo-Saxon, 156

banqueting, 160–1
great, 161, 168, 179, 212, 238, 240–1, 249–50
early Persian, 31
timber, 155, 157–9
Halls at:
Clarendon, 159
Exeter, 159, 161
Farnham, 79, 157
Gainsborough. *Plate 167*
Hampton Court. *Plate 165*
Hereford, 71, 79, 157
Kenilworth, 165
Leicester, 79
Lincoln, 159
Mayfield, 81, 238
Northborough, 164. *Plate 182*
Norwich, 161
Oakham, 159. *Plate 105*
Penshurst. *Plate 110*
St. Cross, Winchester, 249. *Plate 166*
Salisbury, 179
Stokesay, 167. *Plate 106*
Wells, 159
Westminster, 158. *Plate 104*
Winchester, 159
Hammer-beams, 83. *Plate 39*
Hearths, 162, 165–6, 174–5, 242, 257–8. *See also* Fireplaces
Henry II, 47–8, 58
Henry III, 48, 58
Henry VIII, 52, 225
Heraldry, 278
Hood-moulds, 79, 182, 254–5, 258, 276
Hospitals, 163, 248–9. *See also* Monasteries: infirmaries
Houses, 131, 174, 216 *et passim*
abbots', 179, 197–9, 202, 238, 244
bishops', 167, 173, 176
Byzantine, 85, 171–3, 182, 219
Continental, 171
fortified, 162
great, 237 *ff*., 287 *ff. Plates 110, 113*
Jews', 181–2
Long Gallery in, 243
private, 167–9, 172 *ff*., 221, 237
privy of, 264
Roman, 170
sanitary block of, 177–8
stone, 47, 98, 167–8, 170 *ff*., 181
three-storied, 243
timber, 23, 62, 162, 170–2, 247
tower-, 171–2, 219, 221
town, 47, 181 *ff*., 246, 255
twelfth-century, 173, 181–2, 255
two-storied, 85, 167–9, 172 *ff*., 244–5
wings of, 241
Houses at :
Ardres, 171–2, 220
Bletchingley. *Plate 168*
Boothby Pagnell, 177. *Plates 68, 118, 179*

294

Index

Index